GROSSE POINTE PIMP

PIMP

Mark Steel

ISBN 0-9745806-0-0

Riveting Publishing
marksteelbooks.com

Cover design by Bruce Worden

Printed in the United States of America

I would like to gratefully acknowledge my editors: SUSAN, CHRIS, SANDY, PAT and JIM. Without your patience this book would have never existed.

"That which does not kill us makes us stronger."
—*Friedrich Nietzsche*

1

DAMN, IT WAS dark tonight! But the blackness was my ally. Wearing black jeans, black tennis shoes, and a dark coat and cap, I was as innocuous as possible in my seedy surroundings. If my victim were to glance away from the TV set and out the window, or to peer out of a lit bathroom during a middle-of-the-night pit stop, I might be less discernible in this inky gloom (and less of a target). Heavy clouds, no visible moon and an eerie, windless quiet calmed the usual thumping in my chest. I crept nearer to the dilapidated houses with the heavy hook attached to yards of rubber-coated, nearly-noiseless chain. Across the street and two houses away, my wrecker sat in a vacant lot. It was still running, but completely silent. I had installed extra mufflers and insulation many months ago, and tonight I found the truck's quiet presence reassuring.

A dark, devil-like head hung out of the passenger window of the wrecker, lolling tongue and white teeth forming a female Doberman's version of an adoring smile. Her worshipful eyes fixated on my every move, watching for any sign that I, her beloved, might be in danger. Unseen in the cab was the male Doberman, huge, strong, and dumb as a post. *His* adoring eyes were fixated on the female, ever watchful for her safety. One last look sideways, and I dropped down to the cool, hard concrete near the back bumper of the first car. I shimmied under the car on my back, hook in hand, reaching out for the rear axle. If someone approached me now, I knew that Sheba, the female, and Zorro, her paramour, would leap out of the wrecker and descend on them like the dogs of hell. There's an old adage among junkyard owners: the female protects the property while the male protects the pussy.

My objective, a small Honda, sat between two houses in a poorer neighborhood in Detroit. The single-lane driveway that it rested on led to a gate near the rear of the house with a dilapidated garage out back. Even if the Honda had been in the garage tonight, my visit would not necessarily have ended yet. I'd found that the garage doors often wouldn't lock (or even close properly) due to heaving or sinking concrete floors. Since a quick police response time to an attempted car theft in Detroit in the early 1980s was about a half-hour or so, I was unconcerned about a homeowner's outgoing phone call if I was spotted. Of course, I was also prepared with a folder of paperwork should a patrol unit ever blunder upon one of my repossession operations in progress. Legally, I was supposed to call the precinct and inform them of my intentions, but police apathy was legendary and I'd stopped doing that many repos ago. The down side of this shortcut policy was that I wasn't about to get any back-up either when irate deadbeats or homeowners started pulling out guns.

Nestled in my pant pocket was the spare ignition key for the Honda that had previously been taped to the folder in the wrecker. But tonight, the key wasn't useful for two reasons. The first…I couldn't drive both the Honda and the wrecker at the same time (and the last time I checked neither Doberman had a driver's license). In addition, while scoping out the downtrodden area, I hadn't found a single decent drop area to leave the wrecker in while I hoofed it back to the house on foot. The other reason the key was useless was obvious. A 4,500-pound rusty Ford LTD was parked directly in back of the Honda, effectively blocking it in. It was that car that I found myself under that night, my small semi-automatic handgun poking me in the thigh from my other pant pocket. I quietly placed the hook around the greasy rear axle. The plan, which I'd executed at least a dozen times before, was quite simple.

I intended to drag the LTD's corroded ass out into the front yard with the four-wheel drive wrecker so I could get at the Honda. I preferred these kinds of illegalities to occur in total darkness. (If there was a glow from a nearby all-night porch light that interfered...well then that's why God invented BB-guns, wasn't it?)

2

Grosse Pointe, Michigan, is much more than just an enclave of old money mansions sitting east of Detroit along Lake St. Clair. Its 48,000 residents are actually divided into five distinct sections. At the far south end is Grosse Pointe Park with its many architecturally intriguing homes, some dating back to the turn of the century. They range in size from 2,000 to 20,000-square feet, but averaging in the 3000 to 5000 square foot range, the Parks homes have no lack of imported brick, handcut stone, prominent gables, oak floors, radiator heat and multiple fireplaces. Even the immaculate, tree-lined streets with the lawn crew trucks parked bumper-to-bumper in the warm months project the air of "old money." Residents talk and point out former or current mafia homes and their secret "getaway tunnels." Whispers about some of the old money originating from prohibition days are bandied about during slow gossip weeks. The small downtown area of The Park consists of coffee shops and a gallery or two…speckled with insurance agents and financial planners. Any restaurants of note change hands every decade or so, the new owner injecting fresh excitement with an innovative menu or a startling and exciting new way to present fish. The eastern border is Lake St. Clair, but the owners of these properties are more prone to keep a boat or yacht at a local marina or at the Grosse Pointe Yacht Club than dock in front of the residence. The entire southern and western border of The Park is Detroit, with the southern being as sudden a transition from the "haves" to the "have-nots" as exists anywhere. When one crosses the southern border into Detroit traveling on Jefferson Avenue, there is an initial effort at a strip mall or two on the east side, but within blocks the housing and commercial endeavors deteriorate rapidly. Bars appear on the few storefront windows, the ethnicity of the pedestrians changes dramatically and seedy party stores actually start to look inviting in the event of a flat tire. After driving just a mile, burned-out or boarded-up becomes the rule. Late at night, limos from the Pointes shuttle residents down Jefferson Avenue towards events in downtown Detroit. The stark contrast between the two cities is overwhelming, and yet the passengers are apparently oblivious to it. While Sinatra or an oldies station blares in the back and multi-millionaires sip wine and laugh, the driver carefully threads his way past potholes and street people. He tries not to get sideswiped by listing, rusty cars with burned out taillights and mufflers and tailpipes that drop off into the road every few miles (as though the driver planned to use them as waypoint markers to find his way back home). Never do passengers in the limos yell out to the driver to stop at one of the storefront check-cashing establishments that seem to be the only industry.

To the north of The Park is the tiny city of Grosse Pointe and its 5,000 inhabitants. To the north of this city is Grosse Pointe Farms, quiet streets with incredible old stone and brick homes. Even the relatively newer ranch homes have each builder's own architectural stamp throughout. In spite of the name, I never noticed a single farming operation in The Farms and suspect that somewhere lies an 800-page ordinance book with several chapters specifically dedicated to outlawing any animal larger than a poodle. While the *older* money seems to be nearer the lake, there is no set rule, as even crossing the western demarcation line of Mack Avenue leads to a dramatic downturn in real estate values.

To the north of Grosse Pointe Farms is Grosse Pointe Woods, a veritable preserve of $300,000 bungalows and fashionable little colonials. The most populous (and the youngest) of the Pointes has 17,000 inhabitants, and residents of The Woods seem fixated with keeping up with the Joneses. If you are ever in a situation where you know that the home you're visiting is in the Pointes but you're not sure which enclave it is, go to the back of the house. If the house has an addition built onto the back, you are most assuredly in Grosse Pointe Woods. It seems that every Woods resident one meets aspires to live in the Farms. The additions they've added are merely a place to keep the new furniture they've purchased for their dream home in the Farms. After they identify the home, they check on it monthly or even weekly, waiting for a "For Sale" sign to be erected.

While it would be unfair to say that every resident of The Woods is a Farms resident wannabe, it would be very safe to say that most inhabitants of the Pointes have a fascination, to one degree or another, with Lakeshore Drive and the often stunning mansions alongside it. Impressive aerial views of this thoroughfare are in opening scenes of the movie "Grosse Pointe Blank" (remember that one...with John Cusak?). Lakeshore Drive, as it crawls though the Farms and into the smaller, sparsely populated (just 2800) and incredibly wealthy Grosse Pointe Shores, is an impressive mix of old and new money mansions on the west side. Freighters, yachts and lesser boats adorn the lake on the east side, blotted from view only by parks for the local residents and the occasional private marina.

As one approaches the Shores, the tall spire of the Grosse Pointe Yacht Club's clock tower pierces the horizon, soaring over the 294 boat wells nestled underneath its watchful presence. The tall masts of million dollar sailing yachts catch the eye first, but then one is drawn to the radar discs atop the bridges of the motor yachts. The experienced eye can spot the top of a 118 foot long Mangusta, a 10 million dollar Italian yacht belonging to the "Trailer Park King" of Michigan and named after his long time wife.

3

IN THE EARLY '80s a proliferation of buy-here, pay-here used car lots arose around many areas of the country, credit from banks was tight and interest rates were still sky-high. Poor people needed cars, however, so "previously owned transportation reclamation engineers" such as myself put used cars on their lots with a suggested down payment price and then carried the paperwork or the "note" themselves. The trick, on a $2500 car, for example, was to get the $900 that you "had into it" as the down payment and then to receive regular monthly payments from the purchaser. Of course, a great deal could go wrong with this little scheme. The car might break down, making a buyer reluctant to pay. They may lose the job they claimed to have had even after I verified it by phone. That phone call, of course, may have just been to one of their lying friends (and the buyer never *was* employed at all). Often the car was stolen, vandalized or totaled and deadbeats who don't make their car payments usually don't pay their insurance premiums either…so, at best, I was stuck picking up a wreck from the impound yard. If they did make regular payments, however, I would dutifully report their faithfulness to the credit agency as they began to rebuild their credit, and actually make a profit on the car since every ensuing payment after the "downstroke" was all "gravy" for me.

The cars on my Detroit lot were from my repair garage next door. I bought them from customers who were hesitant to put any more money into repairs and just wanted to "get out of it" and go purchase a newer car. The problem I ran into after a few months is that *this* situation only happened about twice a month, and I could sell four cars off the lot in a good week. This necessitated my buying cars from newspaper ads, auctions and other sources. This also meant that I had too much money invested into each car to finance them all myself, no matter how much money I netted every year.

I asked for a little help from the credit union next door and they said yes…with just one little ass-covering condition. I would have to guarantee each loan myself, in essence becoming the co-signer on every loan. I readily agreed, knowing that every time somebody defaulted on their loan I would just send the repo guy over, give him his two hundred bucks, and resell the car off my lot. This was a terrific business strategy until I had my first delinquent customer and made my first call to a car repossessor. He promised to get the car that day and thanked me for my business. Two weeks later, I called again to inquire and to give him two more addresses of "no-pays." I received apologies, excuses, promises and reassurances. Two weeks later, growing impatient, I called another repossessor. My first choice had been shot doing a job and was undergoing multiple surgeries as doctors tried to save his leg. My second choice was even less successful than my first, and twice as hard to reach. January of 1983 found me in the car repo business with about ten deadbeat customers driving around on wheels that I was paying for and that belonged to me!

I grabbed all of the easy ones first, cruising past houses and apartments early in the day with the keys in my hand, occasionally finding the car unprotected at their job site. Even when I didn't have the key, my mechanical background made "popping" door and ignition locks fun, exciting and satisfying. On a couple of occasions, the deadbeat would come running out and cough up hundreds of dollars in back payments on the spot, especially if I was co-driverless that day and had my wrecker hooked up to his bumper.

But not every deadbeat let their car go willingly. If I was doing a daylight repo and needed a few minutes to hook up, I could be confronted by an irate deadbeat, especially in the hot weather when open windows made the slightest noises dangerous. I received invaluable advice from an L.A.P.D. sergeant buddy who explained that in a domestic confrontation (or any other kind), he was taught that soft words and logic only escalated a situation. I, too, found that when being screamed at by an agitated deadbeat (or their parent or boyfriend), my yelling back at top volume would usually back them down enough to give me the time I needed to get the car and go. Having a leather-lined set of vocal cords bestowed upon me at birth went farther toward saving me than any guns or dogs that I brought, although I was pretty sure I owed the female Dobe a steak dinner at least twice. Yelling loudly and clearly at a deadbeat also gave me the chance to explain my case to any neighbors that might be watching and considering their own involvement.

Deadbeats unwilling to give up cash or car would go to great lengths to secure their car and retain possession. Steering wheel locks couldn't stop a tow truck, but on this pitch dark night the rusty LTD parked behind the Honda was putting a damper on my operation. I could feel the body of the hook touching the rear axle of the LTD as my shoulder brushed against the corroded bottom of the rear trunk and rust rained down on me, forcing me to close my eyes. Groping with the hook, I eased it around the axle. In a strange way, I had started to feel secure underneath the old clunker but as I shimmied out from under it, my heartbeat kicked up yet again. In the open air once more, I jogged across the street, purposely looking ahead and never turning my head.

Years ago, I was working my way through college as a store detective at a department store called Korvettes. The head of security was a retired Berkley (Michigan, not California) detective named Jack Vananen. Jack had a pot belly, the bulging eyes of Rodney Dangerfield and Don Rickles' hairline, but Jack specialized in one thing. He specialized in people watching. During my training period, Jack and I sat up high behind one-way mirrors and looked down at people. Teenagers, mothers, executives and retirees all shoplifted from their favorite departments. During my twelve-hour shifts I spent ninety percent of my time doing one thing. I watched their eyes. Even the pros would look out of the corner of their eye before they stole. The amateurs would often turn their whole head, eyeing salesclerks with such concern that they were often offered assistance (this was back in the '70s, when service still existed). Jack called this guilty habit "rolling their eyes," and it was a sure-fire prelude to a crime. Once I spotted a shopper rolling his eyes, I never took *my* eyes off his hands. I'd watch him through every nook and cranny of the department, and if nobody else spooked him, I'd watch him steal.

I'm not sure where Jack is today, but his coaching got me through many potentially messy situations because I always looked as though I belonged there. Even as I jogged back to my silent-but-running truck, I never glanced around. As I backed it up to the dark, rusty hulk that blocked my prize, I steeled myself to pay attention to the chain and nothing else. Creeping down the driveway dragging the LTD, I wrestled it over part of the lawn and the curb and then into the street. With the chain slack again, the hook practically dropped off the axle. Moving quickly, I gathered the chain and popped back into the driver's seat of the truck, coils of chain and hook on top of my legs, and the idiot male Doberman's muscular haunches crowding me against the door. I shifted the wrecker into reverse and backed through the night to the Honda. After a quick hook-up, the Honda's back wheels were in the air. Using my key, I unlocked the door and shifted it to neutral. Walking casually but quickly toward the driver door, I reached the steering wheel to hoist myself in when...BOOOOOM!...an explosion erupted on the other side of the truck.

4

RETAIL BILLIONAIRES AREN'T born with their market savvy. It evolves gradually over the many years that it takes them to not only learn what the public wants, but the methods they'll use to sell the public on the notion that they're receiving it! These retail hyper-achievers are in reality master psychologists. A master retailer tries to outguess his competition and at the same time tries to determine what a fickle public will buy in the ensuing weeks, months or even years. A master retailer sometimes views the consumer as the opponent and his cities and towns as the arenas. They watch for weaknesses. They watch for patterns in style and taste to indicate what might be purchased the most frequently…and at the same time they try to determine the upper limit of what their customers will pay.

A masterful Olympic wrestler circles his opponent; waiting to charge him in a quick move and drop him so that he can impose his strength and his will until his opponent succumbs. The master retailers' objective differs slightly. Instead of getting the consumer to succumb by committing to a big "one time" purchase, the master looks for the chokehold that allows him to dip into his opponents pocket again and again. "In-store Credit Cards," "No Payments, No Interest for Two Years," "Incredible Clearance Sales," "Free Delivery" and "Closed till 4 p.m. so that Markdowns can be Put into Place," are examples of only a few of a famous Detroit area retail billionaire's arsenal of tricks. The Master's every thought involves striving to keep his chokehold on the savings, income, and repeat business of his opponents, all the while expanding his empire and strangling his competition until they wither and die.

After forty years of practice and evolution, Maxwell Lexington was by far the most successful retailer in Michigan. Like a surprising number of Grosse Pointe residents, Max was born in Detroit. His father was a hardworking salesman who would come home at the end of a long day and tell his two sons, "Boys, when it's been a good day and you've made some money, you deserve a couple of drinks, but when it's been a rough day and it's finally over, it's time for a couple of drinks." As a young man, Max was tall and athletic with clear blue eyes that even then seemed to pierce any façade and probe into your head until you gave up your thoughts just to be out from under the intense scrutiny. The industrious teenager worked a paper route and various sales jobs as he began to learn about the consumer psyche. Even then his jutting jaw, steady voice and matter-of-fact manner of speaking made the sale more often than not. A stint in the army had the young man practicing his networking skills until he landed the cushiest job on the base…driving the top brass around to meetings and parties.

After his military obligations were over it was back to Michigan and the retail business. For an extremely heterosexual man, Max had an enduring fascination with cloth and textures, with style and function and with wood grains and glass. He had a gnawing need to know what was happening in other parts of the country and even the world in these areas. An impeccable dresser, he found that a perfectly coifed image would put a potential buyer or his family at ease long enough for Max to ascertain what buttons he needed to push to effectuate a sale (and to calculate the maximum amount of money they were willing to spend).

By the age of 26, Max had mastered the art of selling. "Listen," he would say, "nobody, I mean nobody, ever walked out of my store without buying something!"

Anyone who has ever walked in back of a large building for any reason has probably passed a fence-enclosed area containing a huge greenish, humming metal box. Inside that box is a large power transformer with miles of copper wiring, buzzing away as it supplies power to the building's air conditioning systems, lighting and office or industrial machines. Molecules vibrate in the surrounding atmosphere and electromagnetic waves and pulses charge the immediate area. Even in his later years, even after he'd had too much to drink (which could be often), any observer standing too close to Max could feel his huge brain sending out analytical shock waves, especially when he wanted something. If one didn't become too unnerved, he might also hear faint clicking and tapping noises emanating from the large gray and white maned head. The noises were nothing more than a mechanical adding machine built into his cranium, quickly tabulating dollars and profit margins as his mind encircled his opponent, waiting for the right moment to pounce hard and make them do the Master's bidding.

At 29, Max and his salesman brother struck out on their own, leasing retail space at first and trying to develop connections with every possible supplier. Incredibly long hours and a constant advertising blitz brought enormous success as Max bought out his brother and built new stores to his own exacting specifications. Motivated sales staff were greeted warmly by name every time Max visited a store in his growing chain. Max could make a five-minute conversation with any employee seem like he was telling the man his private, innermost thoughts. He would lower his voice and speak in a low, guarded tone that caused one to hang on every well-thought-out word as though being told who JFK's real killer was. This inside-scoop, keep-it-under-your-hat manner of speaking made each employee feel as though he was part of the inner circle, and that terrific things were about to happen. This sense of belonging and promise was further fanned by the usual company rallies, newsletters and a loosely adhered to policy of promoting from within. Spotless company-owned delivery trucks, with the company name emblazoned across them, were driven by hundreds of loyal, strong men. Should one of these strong men falter he was immediately contacted; not by a gruff supervisor, but by one of five company psychologists expressing heartfelt concern over why the man was late that day or why he seemed hung over, angry or short with a customer. The psychologists were intended to be a *de facto* extension of the boss himself, reaching out with a helping hand when needed and making sure that the Teamsters Union didn't get its hooks into his 700-man delivery team.

This whole "group hug" image that Max carefully cultivated was bolstered by a number of different things. Max's huge family of eight children, by the 1960s living in their first home in Grosse Pointe Farms, may not have been a calculated publicity move but dovetailed nicely with the whole "be a part of our family" image. Max's company paid for the Thanksgiving Day Parade that ground its way down Woodward Avenue in Detroit. Children's homes, cancer centers, hospital wings and huge church donations burnished the "family" image to a high luster. A boat well at the world class Grosse Pointe Yacht Club held several different boats over the years, each bigger and more suited for entertaining family, friends and company execs than the last.

The stores in the chain grew to ten, then to twenty and finally fifty. Sales were driven by half-price sales that weren't, clearance sales that occurred every day, twelve-hour sales, President's Day sales, Fourth of July sales, and weekend only deals that were still available on Monday. Massive markdowns on items that had never been for sale at any other price, gimmicks, tricks, half-truths, price manipulations and borderline misleading ads were dreamed up by a marketing department given carte blanche to massage reality. A trusting public flocked through the doors.

Competitors howled to anyone who would listen, but the flow of cash to the state Attorney General's campaign, and to the Governor and to the occasional judge was steady and dependable. Calling the local Better Business Bureau with a complaint was futile, because its funding depended on Max. Local newspapers might do an occasional human interest story, but they relied heavily on Max's advertising dollar and weren't about to rock the boat.

5

MY HEART CEASED beating and acid poured through the knots of my stomach. A huge, fat man in ugly boxer shorts stood on the front porch of the house with a shotgun pointed in the air. He had just let off an overhead round in my direction, sending my female Dobe into a barking frenzy and turning my guts into one giant acidic blob.

His yelling was drowned out somewhat by the snarling of the Dobermans, but I gathered that he wasn't too fond of my mom, and he thought I should set the Honda back down. My small semi-automatic poked reassuringly at my leg, but I paled at the thought of how outgunned I was. Leaping into the wrecker I dropped it in drive before I even closed the door. Lurching forward with the Honda attached, I maneuvered past the LTD's front bumper and into the street. Slowly accelerating and trying to hunch down somewhat, I wincingly expected the next shot to shatter my back window and take the top of my head with it. Nearly deafened by the Dobes, I felt a surging in my chest as my heart started back up, pounding at the front in an effort to get out. The next round never came, and soon I was several blocks away, my throat suddenly dry. I quickly formulated a plan in case the LTD appeared in either of my side view mirrors. It never did, and gradually my heartbeat slowed and my internal organs began to return to their original places.

During tonight's weekly brush with death, my throat had gotten too dry for me to swallow, but a cold soda from a party store was out of the question. Anything cold that went into my stomach caused pain, dull at first but radiating around my abdomen until I was doubled over with cramps. The same would occur on an empty stomach, so I needed to eat something every hour or so. A physician that visited my repair garage regularly with his Porsche hinted that I was well on my way to my first ulcer. Since stress seemed to aggravate the whole digestive situation, and I'd just had a year's worth in one night, I decided that sleep was out of the question.

I'd had a "consignment" car deal go south on me recently, and the actual owner of the car had been hounding me daily. In the days before caller ID, avoiding him was tough, and I needed to resolve the situation soon. I'd met John Pessak, a building contractor, a year ago when a friend sent him to my repair garage for engine work on his four-year-old Pontiac Bonneville. John wanted to sell the car, and one of my mechanics needed a car. Young, impulsive and wearing too many hats, I had a nasty penchant for being lackadaisical about paperwork. My mechanic gave me $1000 and promised me $3000 more over several months. I asked John if he'd take $3000 over a few months, and he agreed. A month later, my mechanic quit, packed his tools in the car and took off without paying another dollar. Two months passed and John, getting madder by the day, started showering my office with phone calls. No one had any paperwork, but John still had the title so he called the local Detroit Police precinct and reported the car stolen. He named Mark Steel as the thief. In the early '80s, the Detroit Police were not exactly renowned for their citizen complaint follow-ups, so I wasn't in immediate jeopardy. Although I'd hoped to eventually resolve this in civil court, nobody enjoys being prosecuted for receiving and concealing (car theft), and the time had come for some action.

During my last phone barrage from John, it occurred to me that if I simply repo-ed the car I could give it back to him and still be up $1000. I told John I'd misplaced the keys, and he alluded to a spare set hidden on the outside of the car.

I dropped the Honda off inside a yard, locked the gate, and returned to my car lot to get my porter to take me to the mechanic's house. After the previous night, I suddenly felt the need for a human lookout. Upon arriving at the mechanic's home, I saw that the blinds were drawn and the car was in the middle of his driveway! I found the keys and drove off, waving my porter goodbye and heading off to home for a nap.

As I drove along the service drive of the Southfield freeway, calming myself once again and chuckling at the ease of the repo, I was stopped by a red light at an intersection. Aware that there was no license plate on the back of my (well, actually John's) vehicle, I had elected to avoid the actual freeway and any inquisitive Michigan State troopers. In spite of the remote possibility of any Detroit Police car being around, I looked back constantly in my rearview mirror.

A black car, barreling up the off ramp toward me, caught my eye. Transfixed, I stared as his hood, bumper and grille loomed ever larger in the mirror, hoping he saw both the Bonneville and the little yellow Gremlin next to me…600 feet! 500 feet! 400, and still EIGHTY miles per hour! My GAWD! I thought, *this is gonna hurt*! I shot a look in front and the intersection was clear…300 feet, 200 feet! One hundred! I stomped on the Pontiac's gas pedal. The car impacted the Gremlin first and then me and my Pontiac, one car length ahead by now, a moment later. The Gremlin shot forward, smashed from the rear all the way to the front fenders. I was sucked backward into my seat by the force, and the Pontiac and I ended up in the middle of the intersection with my foot back on the brake. The noise was overwhelming…and then it stopped.

I couldn't believe I was alive! I put the Bonneville in park. My eyes were riveted to the gas gauge, knowing that a sudden plunge of the needle meant a rupture and possibly a very loud noise accompanied by a nice warm fire. I also noticed my engine was running! Other cars were stopping to gawk at the mess, and I got out to evaluate the wreckage.

My sneakers crunched on broken glass as I arrived at the back of the Pontiac. There was a strong smell of hot antifreeze steaming from the front of the wrecked car behind me. Only the left rear of my ride appeared to have been buckled, and a quick glance at my left rear tire showed that not only was it still holding air, no crunched metal threatened to inhibit it from rotating. As I approached the rear trunk, a strong alcohol smell entered my nostrils. I assumed it was coming from the ten gallons of blood spilled by the dead drunk guy lying face down all over my trunk. Bright red as it flowed down the side of my car and just starting to drip onto the pavement, the blood made the car look like it had been vandalized by a Sherwin Williams salesman. I'm certainly no forensics expert, but judging by the massive blood loss and the missing rear half of the man's head, I was able to mark the time of death at fifteen seconds ago.

I have no idea why, but ever since my store detective job, I noticed that whenever I faced a nasty situation (such as a large shoplifter wanting to go home instead of jail), my thoughts came to me more rapidly and clearly. My head was crystal clear right now because this moment had an extremely nasty edge to it. I believed that the CCW (Concealed Weapons Permit) for the loaded gun in my pocket had expired, I was driving a stolen car and there was a bloody dead guy on my trunk. Staring down, I briefly considered asking the dead guy if he wanted to exchange insurance information. Of course, I knew the answer would be no because it was obvious he didn't intend to make a claim.

On the other hand, my car was still running, traffic was light and no one had exited their vehicle to approach us yet. Never once looking up or around, I grabbed the collar of dead guy's jacket and the belt at the back of his pants and heaving as hard as possible, swung him off my trunk. He offered me no assistance at all as I deposited his torso back on the wreckage of his own car, but I hadn't expected any. Still never looking up, I strolled back to the Pontiac and got in. *What a car!* I marveled to myself. The driver door still closed tightly as I dropped it into drive and gently accelerated. It still had that smooth big-car ride as I turned down the first residential street that I came to. Some witness/do-gooder began to follow me, but I maintained a steady twenty to twenty-five mile per hour pace through one residential block after another. I knew Joe Citizen wasn't going to be turning in my license number simply because I had no plate. I wasn't about to stop this fine, loyal car for any reason and after about a half mile, Mr. Witness gave up and turned to go back to the scene. Slowly cruising through one beautiful, ramshackle neighborhood after another, I heard the sound of sirens waft through the air. They grew pleasantly fainter, and I continued my little drive.

An hour later, the Pontiac was neatly tucked inside a small garage and I began a stressful sojourn of news-watching on TV. Channels 2, 4 and 7…nothing at noon. Nothing at six either. Watching the 11 o'clock news, barely awake and functioning, produced the same. The morning *Free Press* did not mention anything and neither did the *Detroit News* or any of the TV stations.

After washing the crunched Pontiac thoroughly, I returned it to John Pessak. Not wishing to upset him before bedtime, I left it in his driveway around 4 a.m. I later heard that he filed an insurance claim and made out fine. So I concluded that everyone was happy—except for possibly the dead, drunk guy.

But I wasn't fine. Two incidents like this within a four-hour period had much larger ramifications. Even though I ran with the Dobermans (not to be confused with "Dancing with Wolves") nightly and lifted weights, my pre-ulcerous condition, not to mention my profession, was threatening to bring me down at the tender age of twenty-six. Then there was also my newborn son and his brain-dead mother to think about. She had resumed smoking and drinking with a vengeance, and sat at home with little Matthew cradled in her arms, blowing smoke into his developing lungs as she watched television. As his asthma worsened and he fought one virus after another, struggling for breath with every gasp, I realized that a job of some sort for my wife was going to be the best excuse to get my son into the safe haven of day care. Any sort of day care would do. If Michael Jackson *himself* was running the day care center, my son would be in better hands.

Fate intervened, and two days later my prayers were answered. Two Middle Eastern gentlemen entered my office and asked me if I'd consider selling my business as a going concern. They'd been working at their father's party store down the street, watching my business prosper for some time. The fifty-hour weeks that I appeared to be putting in seemed much more attractive than the seventy-five-hour weeks that Pops required.

6

SUMMER LAURIE LEWIS was adopted forty years ago by Marvin and Eleanor Lewis, a middle class couple in the western Michigan farming town of Hillsdale. The details of her placement there by a Virginian adoption agency are and will forever remain a mystery. The "birth mother trail" ends somewhere near Norfolk where a local judge has erected an impenetrable legal firewall more to protect (according to a private investigator) the father, "a former employee of the federal government" than the birth mother. Summer's spiritual, analytical, God-fearin' mother exposed her to as many facets of life as a small town could effect. Dark haired and very pretty, the young girl played volleyball, basketball and softball with the same verve that she displayed in her English, Psychology and even her own Astrological studies. Already as a teenager, these sports produced a young woman who walked with a casualness and surefootedness that combined to produce an aura of confidence and coordination. Her rapidly blossoming figure and increasingly regal features were mesmerizing, but it was the perfectly balanced walk that helped Summer create the illusion of floating into any room she entered. A strong chin and large, almond shaped brown eyes, highlighted with a queen-like but perfectly formed nose, completely complemented her full lips and huge set of perfect white teeth. Her sensuous features blurred up close though when one noticed her flawless Italian skin with the tightest pores ever bestowed on any goddess deigning to reside on this planet.

At 5 feet 7 inches, Summer wasn't quite tall enough for the haute couture runway and while her slender, defined legs would have complimented any outfit, her huge, natural breasts would have made her seem almost out of place in that environment.

Her first real job in a law office fifteen miles from her hometown at the age of nineteen introduced her to the world of business and money. It also introduced her to a wealthy, powerful, much older and very married attorney. Work became group lunches, group lunches became just two for lunch, and checking for messages when he was away from her slowly turned into friendly and then soul-baring conversations. Dinners and gifts, and long weeknights "at the office" quickly followed. Summer, once filled with college and modeling aspirations, saw her twentieth birthday arrive while pregnant and living in a small house. She was supported by the distinguished fiftyish attorney and waited eagerly for his twice weekly visits, or whenever his alibis permitted him to see her.

After the birth of her son and the recovery of most of her figure, Summer half-heartedly pursued sporadic modeling and endorsement jobs. The "liaison" continued as her lover's children entered college until the year that his and Summer's love child was to turn six.

At first it was just a bit of uncharacteristic forgetfulness from the laser-like legal mind of her beloved, but the forgetfulness grew more encompassing until a light weakness in one side and a hitch in his gait prompted a visit to his doctor. Tests and retests mounted as his symptoms worsened. By the time his speech slowed and his vision blurred the results (and the second and third opinions) were not promising. The magnificent, questioning brain that had propelled him to the top of his law school class and earned him a cadre of well-heeled clients and friends had been invaded by a malignant tumor.

Summer watched, in horror, as chemo and radiation caused the former college athlete to waste away to a shell. With family and friends at his bedside, the still undeclared Summer found it nearly impossible to communicate with him and harder still to visit him.

He died without ever knowing of her efforts or her angst. He also left Summer alone with their six-year-old son, a sporadic modeling career, and facing impending eviction from her small home as his estate attorney gradually figured out her status.

Summer had known that she was adopted since the age of four when a brain donor of a Sunday school teacher had explained to her what adoption was and how it applied to her and her family. Since her adoptive father's demeanor was very reserved to the extent that many children would interpret his behavior as being cold, Summer's search for a warmer, nurturing father figure had begun at a very early age. The mature lover that she found at nineteen years old had played many roles at once. Now he was gone, and Summer felt abandoned and desperate.

7

I KNEW THE balance of the land contract held on my two buildings and car lot by heart and tacked an extra $75,000 onto that (today's equivalent—about $200,000). Twenty-four hours later, I was unemployed. Of course, there had been a couple of tense moments at the closing in my office. I sat behind my soon-to-be-ex desk with Doug, the land contract holder, nervously sitting across from me. The father, his two sons, and about eight cousins sat and leaned around the office as well. There were no lawyers, not much paperwork, and eyes shifting around everywhere. Doug's $30,000 payoff sat on the desk in wads of twenties. My $75,000 sat in bigger wads in front of the father. The father and I were screaming at each other over he and the sons' hesitation at taking over the credit union's imposed liability.

If it came to blows I was confident enough of my chances against the old man and his two sons, but the eight cousins really had me concerned. Hell, I thought, the small Beretta in my pocket only had seven shots and God only knew what kind of heat they were packing! It was at this moment that my personality began to re-evolve. The clouds parted, and wisdom shone down on me for the first time. My hot-headedness was aggravating this situation because I was trying to negotiate from a position of weakness. I sat down, swallowed my pride and apologized to the old man. Focusing my gaze on the two sons, I explained that signing the paper meant that thousands of dollars of cars were out there waiting on peoples' driveways for the taking. I pitched harder.

"I didn't just go out and take these cars back because these (deadbeats)…er, people, were my friends, and I felt sorry for them…but if the business were to change hands and someone else were to call in these debts, there is nothing I can do about it." I pitched harder still. In fact, the piece of paper from the credit union represented a huge hidden asset of this business! The sons bought it. The father caved moments later. A few minutes after that, I was walking to my car with my money in a shopping bag. Once again, everybody was happy. Besides, I thought, the father didn't really look all that old. He might be able to conceive a couple of more times yet if the repo aspect of the business didn't work out for his sons.

In the last three years I'd had enough near misses to last a lifetime. But the spring of 1983 found me 26 years old, semi-retired and determined to be in the best physical condition of my life. I ran sprints three nights a week. I did one armed push-ups, chin-ups, and hit the heavy bag frequently. My stomach problems were soon a thing of the past. The rays of wisdom continued to shine, and I sold the last of my motorcycles. I joined a small, hardcore gym near the little house I'd bought in the suburbs and went there regularly in the afternoons. The steroid monsters that worked out there needed a "spotter" to help lift heavy weights off their chests and treated me like a long-lost friend. I found my wife a job selling repair work at a car dealership and hung out with my young son until I found an excellent day care facility.

My arms grew steadily larger, and my chest and shoulders drew covert stares from fourteen and fifteen-year-old boys (the age group that's most impressed by that sort of thing).

I subscribed to fitness and bodybuilding magazines. I received newsletters and medical updates, downing protein drinks and amino acid tablets by the jarful as I read. Since I neither smoked nor drank, and wasn't too crazy about needles, staying away from the muscle building drugs that my hardcore workout buddies were injecting was pretty easy. It was even easier after the afternoon that found me spotting a Mr. Michigan winner in the gym when something burst way up in his sinus cavity. As he sat up, blood poured out of his nose as though someone had turned on a faucet. The manager and I hastily crammed parts of a towel up the guy's nose and other arriving friends pulled their car up for a frantic trip to the hospital. Later on I heard that he survived but that they had to pull part of his face off to operate on the affected area.

I frequently noticed surgical scars at the top corners of men's chests, near their armpits. Massive doses of anabolic steroids had resulted in the chest, or pectoral muscle, strengthening or building much faster than the ligament that attached it to their arm. When bench pressing incredibly heavy weights, these tendons would sometimes tear off the bone and the chest muscle would bunch up in a ball underneath their skin. Internal bleeding from this "pec tear" would leave unbelievable bruises in their arm and torso. Prompt surgery would involve stapling the tendon back onto the bone and post-op called for keeping the arm in a sling for a couple of months. After a year, the only outward sign of the injury was the surgical scar, but if the man was ever able to lift weights again, he avoided bench pressing.

The anabolic steroids made a young man even more aggressive and almost impervious to pain (the body's warning signal that something is wrong). Injuries would occur right and left when heavy weights were stacked on joints that had already been stressed for hours that day, or for the seventh day that week. Knees that had "blown out" or had ligaments torn from the bone (or were about to) were tightly wrapped in tape or gauze so that more weight could be added to the bar on the man's back, increasing the resistance as he squatted down, leg muscles and veins in his neck bulging.

Naturally, this often resulted in hideously painful back injuries as discs herniated and popped out of place from their spinal columns.

Steroid users also suffered from "site infections"…infections that originated at the place where they injected themselves with the drugs. Huge cysts formed on their backs, shoulders and chests leaving crater-like scars after they burst. Site infections weren't a problem when the "roid monsters" at the gym were taking steroids orally, but blood in their urine *was* after they developed kidney cysts or cancerous tumors.

Many steroid users experienced a rapid growth not only in strength but in size as well, resulting in some dandy stretch marks across their chest, shoulders and back. Sometimes purple but often just a deep red, these ropelike scars would snake out the sides of their tank top and often down their arms as well.

Anabolic steroid use also dictated "cycling" the drugs…using them for a period of weeks and then staying off of them for a time. This gave the internal organs a chance to recover and hopefully prevented the body from getting used to them. As might be supposed, many users ignored scheduled breaks, or substituted other types of steroids in the hopes that gains would start anew. Since very few doctors would prescribe steroids for athletic or bodybuilding purposes, most of the drugs available were from "black market" sources. Until new laws classified them as a Schedule IV controlled substance, Mexican pharmacies supplied many of the bodybuilding steroids that were simply smuggled across the border. Customs dogs didn't alert to them because they weren't marijuana or cocaine, and the smuggler often had a prescription signed by a Mexican physician as a precaution. A huge source in the U.S. was students from veterinary colleges, sneaking drugs meant for horses out of the labs and selling them. As the feds tightened the noose a little at the border, counterfeit steroids became more commonplace and bodybuilders often became frustrated after injecting themselves with vegetable oil or popping aspirin tablets…and not getting the expected results.

To a guy who never even tried pot, the prospect of all of my blood being pumped out through my nose was alone reason enough to never try steroids. I was content to build my physique gradually.

After three years of retirement I was starting to get low on funds. At six feet tall and 225 lbs., with only ten to twelve percent bodyfat, I was very satisfied with the results from my health regimen but knew I needed to get serious about a career again. I applied at an upscale bar/restaurant as a guest relations engineer, specializing in patron entries and crisis intervention. Some might interpret this as being a bouncer. Friday and Saturday nights, the only two that I worked, were the busiest. Jumping into the occasional drunken brawl was exciting and (since I trained like a heavyweight prizefighter anyway) pretty easy. But the most rewarding part of doing crisis intervention (or altercation impediment activities) was that hot-looking young waitresses, who normally ignored me as they flirted furiously with the rich guys, suddenly noticed me. Even a sudden commotion might be overlooked above the din of the band but the cocktail waitresses, arms upraised and pointing with a constipated look on their faces, caught my eye quickly. Usually very crowded on weekends, we ran a waiting line outside the main door in order to control the number inside and placate the fire marshall. Two out, two in, four out (well...maybe eight in if somebody was astute enough to give me the "money handshake), was the general rule. A twenty dollar bill was always welcome and would turn any shmoe and his entourage into one of the local celebrities that we were instructed to whisk in without waiting. Two hundred dollars in "tips" in a five-hour night was a welcome addition to my hourly wage.

8

WINDSOR, CANADA, IS immediately across the river from Detroit. For years, the code phrase "Windsor Ballet" is the term that men from the Detroit metro area use to describe the gentlemen's clubs found in this otherwise low-key Canadian city. Only twenty-five minutes from Grosse Pointe (if you took the tunnel), the clubs' main attraction is that the patron can be served alcohol while the female entertainment performs not just topless, which is already legal in Detroit, but bottomless as well. Some of these clubs are far more upscale than the others but the theme remains the same.

It didn't take much of a sales pitch from a girlfriend in her hour of crisis to find Summer crossing the river to the largest, most discerning club in Windsor. The manager of the club realized in the first nanosecond that he had an incredible moneymaker sitting in his office. This one oozed sex appeal in spite of her nervousness. Her smile, while somewhat forced, lit up the room. Even the wall clock seemed to stop to observe this intriguing, beautiful woman. He'd have to be *very* careful about how he handled this filly. Maybe just a Monday night at first, when it's not so busy...definitely wouldn't even bring up the word *audition*. Why was she doing it? Gotta get that question answered fast so he can pitch her from that angle. No track marks, eyes clear and steady...not even gonna mention a drug test. Dressed expensive, like somebody's been taking care of her. Incredible skin, nails, teeth...wow, can't be sick with anything, especially not with that damn AIDS virus...so it can't be medical bills. Some kind of runaway? Not at 25, no way!

33

Gambling problem maybe? Nah! Somebody forcing her? No bruises…doesn't look like she's ever had a bruise in her life! Oh, well, just turn on the charm, promise her a semi-private dressing room and give her the spiel about the big money involved if she developed a regular clientele for herself.

Summer, a very light drinker, needed several drinks that Monday night to step onto the stage and into the glare of the spotlight to begin her three-song set in front of a dozen bored and distracted men. As she stepped up in tiny top and thong, the men sat bolt upright on their stools, eyes riveted to the gorgeous creature slinking around the stage. First dance was always with a "costume." Top always comes off on the second dance and that's when the tips might start. But even "cheap Charlies" were coming to the stage before the top came off and handing her fives, as if they feared she might not stay for the second dance. A deep breath now, a flick of her wrist behind her back and the top drops down during the second song. Her perfect breasts greet the air under the hot lights and she notices the total concentration of the few men in the room. A new wave of nervousness engulfs her entire digestive system as the second song ends and the third song begins immediately.

This is the moment that she drank four Bicardi rums for, and her senses still weren't dull enough. The third song she requested was Joe Cocker's "You Can Leave Your Hat On," but Summer had the sensation of entering a tunnel when the music seemed to start dulling and softening. Her vision narrowed under the bright lights as though she were peeking through a keyhole. Cavorting from pole to pole, she was more aware than ever of her body from below her neck, especially when cool air at the edges of the stage teased her large nipples and brought them to life. Hot lights near the center made her tummy and the small of her back glisten.

9

SPRINGTIME CAME AND the bar business waned as outdoor activities took precedent. One evening, I was getting in an uncharacteristically late seven o'clock workout at the little gym near my house, and it was crowded. I noticed a skinny guy with glasses laying on a weight bench doing everything wrong. Red-faced from lack of breathing, he struggled with a bad grip and even worse form to push a bar off his pitiful, sunken chest. Suppressing a guffaw, I darted over to the little human, scooped the weight up and set it back on the rack. After all, the guy was about to expire on *my* favorite bench, and with that came the possibility that the coroner would impound it for a while for a forensic study. Instead of sheepishly slinking off, the little mortal sprang up from the bench and stuck out his hand to thank me. I felt a strange sensation in my throat. Oh my Gawd! I realized I was actually experiencing a few stirrings of compassion! It was a new and very interesting sensation, and I found, to my amazement, that it was rather enjoyable!

The thank you turned into an introduction and then turned into questions. Where should he hold the bar? I showed him, positioning his scrawny little skeleton on *my* bench. When should he breathe out? I cued him, noting that his pathetic breaths probably couldn't flicker a candle. Inwardly aghast, I suddenly found myself with a workout buddy with less than one-fifth of my strength as I guided the bar through an ideal trajectory while he pushed. It was an immediate improvement. The waif actually managed to perform a few repetitions without exploding and was getting happier by the minute. Next, I guided him through a couple of sets of shoulder presses, and he was beaming with joy! I wiped the happiness right off his face when I said good-bye. It was after eight o'clock, and I wanted to see my son before bedtime.

"Wait," he beseeched me, "don't go, I'll uh…hire you!" My entrepreneurial spirit, doused three years ago, came back to life in 1986 at that very moment.

A brief negotiation ensued, and since my base rate at the bar was eight dollars an hour, I quoted nine dollars. Trying desperately to rope in his new guru, he wrote me a check for ten workouts in advance, and a new career began. Over the next several months, other beginners at the gym noticed me and my client working out, and observed with even more intense interest as the beanpole started to add muscle.

By fall, I had several regular clients and my little business was occupying more of my time. My wife responded by drinking more, staying out all night, and dating. I found my new career somewhat hampered by the overcrowded gym I was using and an envious night manager. Without prompting, my wife came to my rescue by moving out of the house with my son and taking every stick of furniture with her. She filed for divorce the next day. This allowed me to fill the front living room with lights, mirrors, posters, weight equipment and a stereo, and soon I was running a commercial fitness training studio in a residential neighborhood.

Tara Southern lived in my neighborhood on another block. Young, attractive and smart but overweight, Tara resembled the actress Rebecca DeMornay (if Rebecca had worked in a bakery). Occasionally, I would do some discounted car repairs for Tara and her family in my garage at my home. After my wife moved out, Tara's car seemed to need repair more often than usual. After a while, Tara's car concerns turned into regular visits. In spite of other young ladies that I was associating with, lunches with Tara soon became a regular occurrence. After one such lunch had evolved into a pleasant afternoon and then dinner, Tara bluntly mentioned that she would like to become better friends. I explained that I'd always been rather shallow and superficial, and that as I got older, these traits were becoming more pronounced. I expounded on my growing training business and that the very nature of it dictated that I judge people by their percentage of body fat, their proportional appearance and their motivation to change both, not by their "inner beauty." I tried to make her understand that the workouts that had once been only a means of self-preservation through some often physically demanding jobs had evolved into a healthy, narcissistic habit. I assured Tara that while this shallowness and health obsession may not be the most attractive quality in a man, I found it far easier to just accept my severe character flaws and to use them to my advantage in my newfound career.

I had hoped that Tara would accept my lengthy answer to her request and find other guys to date. Instead, Tara took in every word and ignored my roundabout brush off. The very next day, she showed up promptly at five o'clock after she got off work. She was tired of dieting, she claimed, and wanted to begin working out with weights. I set up a routine for her, and my first female client (although not a paying one) started immediately.

The young woman had focus. She worked out every day, six days a week on legs, arms, back and chest. She worked out like a madwoman, with unseen demons prodding her on. In retrospect, she was "over-training" (as it's called), but she was unswayed by any ache or distraction. She lost a pound the first week and two pounds the second. Blasting through workouts like she was possessed, Tara got stronger as well.

Within months, she was as strong as many men, and she continued to lose two pounds a week of bodyfat.

During this time, I quit working at the bar and placed a small personal ad to increase my modest clientele. It was the right idea at the right time. Instead of one new client a month, my ringing phone brought me three new clients a *week*, and Tara and I were soon looking for a commercial storefront. We found a 900 square-foot unit in a strip mall a half mile from my house and moved in rapidly. Enthusiastic clients kept pouring in and Tara suggested the name Muscle Coach for the new facility.

Gratefully, I accepted Tara's assistance with training my clients after she got off work. Her bodyfat level continued to plummet as her physique became even more defined and her strength burgeoned. When Tara's weight, at five feet four inches tall, dropped to 116 pounds, we measured her bodyfat and were astounded to find that she'd gone from 38 percent down to 16 percent in six months! Attending her five-year high school reunion, (while I pulled a chair up for the evening to an excellent buffet table), Tara tried to reacquaint herself to old classmates. Her frustration mounted as one after another failed to recognize her. Somewhere in between the shrimp cocktail and the smoked fish, I noticed her glow as one former class stud after another hit on her. Tanned, blond and continuously smiling, Tara sidled over to me to make sure that I was still using a fork when an old classmate walked up and squinted at her nametag. "Oh...my...God...Tara, you're half!" he exclaimed, and Tara started crying with joy as they embraced.

After this whole Cinderella episode, Tara's confidence was elevated enough for her to quit her job the following Monday, and she began working full time at Muscle Coach.

In 1988, there were several ways to begin a workout program in Michigan. A common one was signing up for aerobics classes at Vic Tanny's or a large gym or the YMCA or a school. One hour a day, five days a week would often burn fat off of a participant. If they were the type that received a rush of endorphins during aerobic activity, they became almost addicted to strenuous workouts due to a phenomenon called "runner's high." A rush of feel good chemicals, released by their oxygen-starved brain into their bloodstream, masked the sweaty pain of continuous jumping, hopping, leaping and lunging. Stairclimbing machines, jogging, primitive treadmills and aerobics were all tough on the knees, ankles and hips and resulted in many crippled "aerobics refugees" searching for another method. In addition, aerobics or other cardio only kept the fat off as long as they were being performed every day. "I missed a day and gained two pounds" was a common lament.

Karate classes were popular at the time but because of the intense discipline required, an individual had to go at the pace of the whole class. Karate did not make you much stronger either (Bruce Lee lifted weights, trust me). Most classes were non-contact, meaning that students never got accustomed to being hit back. This meant that men and women would often develop a false sense of security, mouth off to a Hell's Angel, and still get their asses kicked.

Boxing, a terrific cardio exercise and a decent way to get into shape, never gained mass popularity because most people don't enjoy getting punched repeatedly in the face. Besides, beginners discovered, most good boxers lift weights. Swimming grew in popularity but most people couldn't spare the two to four hours a day that it took to dump weight using this method.

Weight (or resistance) training was snowballing in California, and large gyms were sprouting up like long lost relatives at the reading of a will. But in Michigan, the choices were far fewer. Vic Tanny's was around but packed wall-to-wall at night, with a reputation for broken equipment and a "pick-up joint" atmosphere. Large gyms were sparse, intimidating and instruction or assistance non-existent. For a beginner, watching and copying another beginner was dangerous and time consuming. How-to books talked about 1000 different exercises but never discussed which ten were the most effective or how much weight on the bar or machine was the right amount. Home equipment could be found, but was rather crude and usually tossed into a dark basement corner and ignored.

Yet people gradually realized that lifting weights, while still having a bit of the old "musclebound" myth attached, was the answer to many health concerns. Yes, they got dramatically stronger, but their metabolic rate sped up even when they weren't working out, and they lost fat…permanently. They could "target" a specific area, and change the shape or appearance of it. They also noticed that they got sick less often as their immune systems reached new heights, especially if they got enough rest in between workouts.

If an individual decided to spend two years and thousands of dollars figuring out what series of exercises worked for them, they usually gave up in frustration or injury. But if they stumbled across Muscle Coach or the only other personal training studio in Michigan twenty miles away, they could get a handle on a new regimen in two months for a few hundred dollars.

Housewives, doctors, and executives signed up. Accountants, psychologists and salesmen came three times a week. Construction foremen and attorneys, brides-to-be and their mothers, heart patients and machinists attended regularly. Fathers signed up their sons and daughters to give them an advantage in sports. I raised my prices, recruited more staff and proposed to Tara. I counted, cajoled and counseled as clients came and went.

10

A CROSS MACK AVENUE, the neighborhood consists of neat Detroit bungalows and the well kept buffer community of Harper Woods. Harper Woods, with its upscale homes and watchful police department, is actually a safe place to be; except for one fly in the ointment. Eastland Mall is a fairly modernized, completely enclosed mall that was once a favorite destination of Grosse Pointers for many years. Only five or six minutes away from most sections of the Pointes, Eastland was a thriving collection of shops and anchor stores, jewelry kiosks and movie theaters, with a finely managed and highly profitable Marshall Field's (formerly Hudson's) in the forefront. Twenty years ago however, even the Detroit gangs needed a safer place to hang out. Legendary fights broke out at the theaters, and the violent movies on the screen got blamed. Car thefts occurred at the rate of two an hour, and the auto makers got blamed. The auto companies improved the ignition locks and added other anti-theft devices, and the car thieves became carjackers. Wealthy shoppers were driven or forced to drive to their ATM machines at gunpoint. Many brave Grosse Pointe ladies refused to give in and continued to patronize the center until incessant pressure from their workaholic husbands, frustrated at their inability to accompany or protect them, forced these intrepid souls to venture farther and farther away from the "bubble" (as many referred to it) in search of designer clothing. For many years, it was an interesting, albeit embarrassing, statistical anomaly that this tiny, clean bedroom community on the Detroit border had one of the worst per capita crime rates in the nation. As you enter the Eastland Mall lot today you are reminded of a guarded police state. Security cars cruise everywhere, eyeing the few remaining cars up and down as they enter the vast and nearly empty parking lots from 8 Mile Road. Elaborately uniformed security guards goose-step in pairs through the mall, mace, handcuffs, and billy clubs hanging from their belts while talking on their radios to other guards marching through now sparsely populated sectors. At most suburban malls one has to keep from snickering at the police academy rejects that stroll or lounge in their ill-fitting security shirts and ties, chatting up teenage women. At Eastland though, the guards, like the few people that still shop there, have attitude! There's little doubt that even bumping into one guard (provided that one under six feet tall could be found) would bring hundreds of others raining down on you...their billy clubs slamming on the floor while they yelled "hoo-hah" in unison. But it's too late now for Eastland Mall. Its reputation is forever tarnished. Its fate is sealed.

11

HOOKING FIRST ONE long red thumb nail under the side strap of her thong bottom, then whisking it away only to have her other thumb find the opposite strap to stretch and tease, Summer had the room in a trance.

And then the point of no return, both thumbs at once pushing the straps down relentlessly on both sides, over the hips and midway down the long, tan, smooth thighs. Then the move she had practiced in the dressing room…stomach doing flip-flops, her back to a pole, she stretched her arms up over her head and grabbed the pole. Shaking her right leg forward, just a little, while keeping her toes on the wooden stage, then moving it back, then the left thigh, and moving it back, and slowly repeating again and again sent the straps inching down her legs as though on a mission. Gravity and motion tugged at the center part of the thong, pulling it down with the rest, revealing her, dark and closely cropped. The bottom finished its sliding descent to the stage and she was moving again, stepping and slinking, smiling and teasing, long dark hair getting damp and moving across her shoulders. At last, the song was over, and a dozen men were clapping and howling like a hundred and twenty. Summer scooped up her "costume" and dashed quickly to her dressing room. Nervousness, adrenaline and relief had cleared her head and Summer stood in front of the huge mirror in her room, inwardly marveling at the power she had over the men out there. Fifteen minutes later it was confirmed when she reappeared and the men were oblivious to the next woman dancing on the stage, motioning and gesturing to Summer for a private "table dance." The men, almost in unison, plied her with twenties, fifties and even a C-note for the privilege of viewing her close up on top of their table. Before the night was over, fifteen men had tipped her one thousand dollars altogether, many paying more than once, just for the way she made them feel during a five-minute dance.

The following Friday and Saturday, with bachelor parties and prowling businessmen filling in many more seats and tables, brought Summer a two thousand dollar night with half the effort. Frantic men *clamored* for her attention and all seemed willing to outbid men at the other tables.

The establishment's gross revenues, already good, ticked upward steadily as word spread of the management's new "discovery."

Summer, working two to three nights a week for four hours a night, brought in more money than most Fortune 500 CEOs. Lines formed outside on the nights she danced, and throngs of her loyal followers showered her with money and propositions. Seven months went by, and Summer had a substantial savings account and a beautiful, huge apartment with a new BMW parked outside. Expensive clothes hung in her closets, and jewelry lay strewn on dresser tops. But her seven-year-old son, who now had security, if not a father, began to question where his mother went at night. When the mothers of other kids at his school were tucking their children in...why, he wondered, did he say goodnight to a babysitter?

After seven months, the smoke and the noise and the adulation were taking a mental toll, numbing Summer's senses and causing her to consider other options before this life owned her completely. Besides, she reasoned, she could always go back if she failed elsewhere, and sooner or later her son, perhaps informed by a schoolmate or overhearing a phone conversation, might put the truth together.

Offers were presented to her every night that she worked. Marriage proposals—often alcohol-induced—but just as often not, were an hourly occurrence. Offers of jewelry and furs were easy to turn down because she had all of that and more. The management's strict anti-dating policy combined with her own leeriness of any man that would patronize her employer precluded any liaisons with customers. Summer assured herself that as long as her work and her social life remained separated she could walk away from this gig at any time with her self-esteem intact.

Separated, that is, until the Greek God walked through the main door and sat down at the table next to the one she was performing on. He was 6 foot 4 inches inches tall and over two hundred pounds with the athletic physique of an Olympic statue and the confident stride of an emperor. Charles Sevalas was 32 years old, unmarried and tired of dating Grosse Pointe debutantes. With short, curly hair and rugged good looks that enthralled every young woman he met, Chuck's deep voice and quick wit charmed prospective companions faster than Emeril at a hunger strike.

After years of selling real estate, Chuck was in business with his three brothers developing strip malls, trailer parks and anything else that involved buying land and collecting rent from tenants. Their closeness and ambition in the Pointes was legendary and their business surged even as the oldest brother, well-known for his sexual eccentricities, was in the process of being bought out by the other three.

Chuck, here tonight to meet a client, had caught Summer's eye as soon as the glow of the stage lights had reflected off his smile to the waitress. Summer, dancing topless for a regular customer on a table in front of the stage and stealing the limelight from the other girls as usual, had Chuck transfixed from the moment she appeared in his line of sight.

As Chuck and Summer stared at each other, (she now barely gyrating), his hand slowly and absently spun his glass around on its coaster. Paper objects between them seemed to begin smoldering…a napkin, a small menu, a straw wrapper on the floor…nothing combustible was safe in the powerful energy field created by their gazes.

Another minute went by and the song ended. A $20 tip from one of the men seated at her tabletop dance platform was absently palmed as Summer stepped down and floated to Chuck's table.

Dispensing with any greetings as she sat down, his pointed questions received incredibly astute answers and a mini-barrage of questions and "what-ifs" in return. An hour passed, then two, and the pair soon communicated with each other as if old, intimate friends. Worried looks from the manager filtered through the smoke but were ignored by his star's engrossed attraction.

Exactly two hours and ten minutes passed and both abruptly arose, he to seek the valet and his Mercedes sport coupe, and she to change into street clothes and meet him out front. Fearful of upsetting the most sensational hire he'd ever made, the manager merely observed and asked a bouncer to subtly report back.

Summer stepped into the idling Mercedes and thirty days later, she and her eight-year-old son were residents of Grosse Pointe Park. Her manager's sinking feeling was confirmed when she failed to show for work and no longer answered her phone.

12

Late on Saturday afternoon, I was waiting for Ben. The other trainers had gone home and, after Ben's workout, I would too. Ben pulled up in a sporty 5.0 Mustang and dragged himself into the gym. Tall and soft looking with a little pot belly, Ben looked like an Adolf Hitler with light brown hair and creepy Charles Manson eyes that stared right through me. Ben was a machinist who relocated from Ohio for better pay and knew no one in his new town. He spent his time listening to horrible rock music (Jimi Hendrix plays and sings the Star Spangled Banner) and re-enacting army battles (with little plastic soldier men) by mail with other geeks. Ben lived in a small apartment and was shunned and avoided by neighbors and co-workers alike.

Halfway through Ben's workout, I asked him what his plans were for the rest of the weekend. Ben replied that after this he was going to go home, stick a gun in his mouth and kill himself. I laughed politely until Ben assured me that he wasn't kidding. He said he had no friends or family and no prospects of a girlfriend. (Geez, even Charles Manson had a girlfriend, I thought) as I tiptoed over to the desk, wide-eyed, to call a shrink who worked out with me and ask *his* advice. The shrink didn't answer, and I soon realized that a somewhat compassionless college dropout had the last twenty minutes of Ben's workout to save his life. I thought for a minute and decided to give it a shot. I told Ben about another client who'd had tremendous success meeting women through personal ads. I "sales pitched" like a mad man. The ads were cheap and elicited tons of calls from gorgeous, lonely babes, too timid to place their own ads because some weirdo might call. Ben confided that he'd tried responding to some of those ads with little success. I was treading on thin ice but kept going.

"You gotta make 'em come to you, Ben," I coached. "When they read your ad they get to know ya a little bit before they call!"

"I don't have anything to put in an ad," Ben sighed. (The guy didn't exactly project a "can do" attitude.)

"That's not true," I countered. "You like sports cars, you're tall and you're employed in a 'Big Three' automotive-related field!" I still had his interest! I took a deep breath, grabbed paper and pen, and started writing the ad. I kept up the chatter. "Y' know, you're also still into rock music (inwardly I winced), when a lot of guys are into this rap stuff…women hate rap! And you're also a history buff when a lot of guys just sit and watch sports!"

I finished writing the ad, never looking up or rolling my eyes, being as nonchalant as possible. When I handed Ben the finished ad (even filling in his home phone number from his workout card), I felt a small shiver at the thought of my "Joe Amateur Psychologist" attempts. Ben stuffed the ad in his pocket, and we finished the workout without him saying another word. I'd already learned the hard way from selling cars that you have to know when the sale has been made, and then you have to be careful not to talk your way back out of it. So I dropped the subject, scheduled him for next week (provided he was still breathing), and bade him goodbye.

A few days later, Ben came in and thanked me profusely during his workout. He had gone home, placed the ad, and had scheduled three dates already! In amazement, I congratulated him (and yes, I saw the side business opportunity here but was too busy). Two months later, after not hearing from Mr. Casanova for awhile, I received an excited phone call from Ben begging me to be his best man in one week. He also needed a videographer and could I be of assistance? Stunned, and not wanting to miss the chance to meet whatever was crawling out of the tar pit to marry Ben, I agreed.

After a fifty mile drive to a small town's church, I received another surprise when Ben introduced me to a shy, fairly attractive, Hawaiian looking woman. Ben was wearing an ill-fitting suit and she a simple wedding gown. I felt a tad awkward as I filmed the quaint ceremony while handing the preacher the ring when cued, but Ben was insistent.

There were drums and amps set up in a small reception area in the back of the church and a clueless Ben howled self-composed rock and roll love songs into a mike. The thirty or so guests, tearing at dry fried chicken and meager sandwiches, stampeded out of the room, obviously concerned about hearing loss. The bride and I stuck it out, but I was laughing too hard to film her as she held her face in her hands. I peeked outside to an empty parking lot, and, not knowing what decorum, if any, was required at a twenty-minute wedding reception, found the preacher hiding in his office and said good-bye.

A year later, a very much alive Ben stopped by my gym and assured me that, while he was no longer married, he was still dating often.

Meanwhile, business overflowed at the gym, and after one year we opened location number two. Tara and I got married, and one year after that we opened personal training studio number three.

Weeks after that, Tara, adeptly managing the newest studio in the Muscle Coach chain, turned up pregnant. Despite my protestations that I was sleeping when it happened, Tara insisted it was mine. Tara's increasing girth and my inability to manage more than one studio at a time forced us to close the most recent arrivals in our chain and eventually retreat to a single large location, a half mile down the road from the original.

Tara gave birth to Rachel Faith on November 22, 1991, after I organized a very well received "birth lottery" among the clients. As the winners with the closest entry to guess Rachel's gender and birth weight, Gary and his wife were showered with free workouts, clothing, tanning booth time, protein drinks and bars and a sumptuous dinner out with Tara and myself. To reciprocate, or perhaps because he felt we had a blossoming friendship, Gary told me that Chrysler stock was around $10 a share and I'd better buy some immediately. Two weeks later, he was working out when he announced that it was at $14 a share and he'd re-mortgaged his house (he was just a middle manager at Chrysler), betting it all at that price. A week later he came in to work out when the stock was at $16 and began screaming at me when I admitted I hadn't yet acted. Gary weighed about 140 pounds and wasn't too imposing but if he felt this strongly, I thought, perhaps the least I could do is phone my broker. I purchased a chunk at $16 and then again at $18. I bought again at $21 and started buying on margin at $23, where I recommended it in passing to a client named Dennis during a workout. Two days later, Dennis informed me that he'd bought 10,000 shares. I got a little pale when I realized that Dennis had spent nearly a quarter of a million dollars on a tip from his personal trainer, but was able to relax a bit when the stock climbed to $27, where I too, bought more.

Gary, Dennis and I all sold somewhere in the low sixties and Gary, at age 42, began planning his retirement party. Tara and I were sitting in church with one-year-old Rachel, when the preacher began speaking about life passing us by without our knowing it. We looked at each other and put up posters announcing the closing of our wildly successful business the very next day. Clients cried, yelled and stomped out, but two weeks later we were unemployed and traveling.

Trips to California, Florida and anywhere else that I could find a hardcore gym rekindled my passion for working out and bodybuilding. While traveling solo in California one week in May, I decided to visit a friend in Redondo Beach. At 10 a.m. he went off to work, and I was off to a local gym. By 10:30 a.m., I was seated upright on a workout bench doing a shoulder exercise. The bench faced a huge mirrored wall, and several hardcore bodybuilders were at benches on both sides of me, pumping, sweating, lifting and flexing. As I stared into the mirror, I noticed a very pretty female bodybuilder working out on a bench immediately to my left. Tan, blond, and very focused, her arms and shoulders rippled as she thrust a pair of 40-pound dumbells repeatedly into the air. After noting with relieved satisfaction that the pair I was using were more than twice as heavy, I managed two more repetitions before nearly having a shock-induced stroke! This woman on the left wasn't just some pumped up pretty bimbo. She was Tonya Knight, one of the top fifteen female bodybuilders in the world! Her physique graced the pages of bodybuilding magazines. Her posters were advertised in these magazines as well, with my personal favorite being the picture of her wearing just a saxophone. Lacking the steroid-ravaged skin of many of the hardcore women (yes, women bodybuilders take banned male hormones…don't be naïve!), Tonya had a flawless quality and symmetry to her body that should have made her the reigning champ. My heart fluttered like a little girl at a Backstreet Boys concert. She looked concerned as my dumbells crashed to the floor and I didn't blame her. I was suddenly very unsteady, and she was barefoot. Another quizzical look from Tonya and I realized that she was about to move to another bench before I threw up on her. I needed to proffer some sort of explanation, and it had to be quick.

I blurted out, "Sorry, I just realized that I left a soufflé baking at home and it's about to burn." Even someone meeting me for the first time would instantly observe that I don't look anything like a soufflé chef, but the Iron Priestess didn't even smile.

"You'd better get home then," she replied testily.

"Oh, it's too late now," I sighed. "I live in Michigan."

An eyebrow arched, her shoulders dropped, and the bodybuilding goddess laughed! I pressed on.

I told her "don't worry, that's my last set. I heard that over-training the shoulders can cause deech spefects, but I bon't delieve it!"

She rolled her beautiful eyes and giggled. We talked for awhile in between sets until she got up and announced that she was hungry, eyeing me expectantly. I was ecstatic! Six more words, and I'd be eating lunch and maybe dinner (and who *knew* what that might lead to) with this magazine fantasy woman! And then it hit me. Doh! I mentally slapped my forehead. I'm married! Instead of saying, "Me too, what's good around here?" and being allowed to spend money on this muscular enchantress, I mumbled something about meeting a friend for lunch. With a shrug of her shoulders she was gone. I'd like to say that I've never had one regret since. Yes, I'd definitely like to say that. Not one, nope, never.

In Florida, I met up with Bobby and JoAnn Baricci. Bobby was a chiropractic doctor near Orlando. They had a successful clinic and a couple of physical therapy centers for accident victims that were practically printing plants for cash. JoAnn and a secretary ran the home office and billing department from their three-story million dollar home in a gorgeous gated subdivision. JoAnn was able to care for their three-year old and newborn while attending to the office, swimming pool and Jaguars as well. Bobby ran nightly, lifted weights, moussed his hair and kept his tan dark. Bobby was 5 foot 8 inches, very trim, good-looking, and a dazzling dresser. With his ear glued to a cell phone,

Bobby counseled patients and searched for new therapy center locations while he paced his office and the aisleways of his clinic. With his dark eyes, slim face and high cheekbones, Bobby oozed with a practiced charm and a quick, well rehearsed laugh that fooled its recipient into believing that he found them charming as well. Dr. Baricci had a simple plan that grossed millions every year. He would take out quarter-page advertisements in newspapers. His smiling countenance and those of several happy, satisfied patients and their endorsements would be featured prominently in these ads. The quotes in these ads would invariably mention God or faith and would draw in anyone with a spiritual bent that suffered from back pain. Once at the clinic, Dr. Baricci and his staff would quickly weed out all the unfortunates without health insurance, give them a ten-minute therapeutic massage, and politely, but quickly, boot their ass out the door!

The insured patients that were left were *definitely* going to need as many x-rays and spine adjustments as their plan would pay for. When that phase of insurance ran out, they suddenly needed weeks and months of physical therapy at one of the centers that Dr. Baricci recommended (and secretly owned). Thousands of dollars later, when the therapy center could no longer bill the insurance company because of payment limits, the patient was pronounced cured…whether they felt better or not. Fifty thousand dollars in insurance checks would roll in every week, but were seldom deposited into company bank accounts. Deposits would have to be reported to the IRS, and taxes would have to be rendered. Dr. Baricci found this prospect to be very distasteful. There was also a chance that an audit would reveal that Baricci Christian Chiropractic (and Faithful Therapy Centers) were owned by the same guy, and this was a felony no-no. Because of this, Dr. Baricci spent a very pleasant hour each day driving his Jag convertible in the Florida sun, visiting one check-cashing storefront after another, endorsing check after check with various rubber stamps. The five percent surcharge meant little compared to actually paying taxes, and Bobby arrived home at night with his Armani suits and Jag glove compartments brimming with cash.

Bobby was driven and intense. Even in a relaxed state he was like a coiled spring, waiting to release energy. Some of this energy came from his workout and part of it came from the gallons of caffeinated diet Pepsi that he guzzled. Part of his boundless hyperactivity, however, was derived from the lines of cocaine that he snorted when able. JoAnne Baricci, at 5 foot 3 inches tall, was Italian looking with pouty lips, jet black hair and an unusually photogenic face. She was top heavy but dressed to minimize, rather than flaunt. They were a stunning couple together and happy photos adorned mantels and countertops at their mansion.

After the newborn boy turned six months old, Bobby didn't come home one night. He explained to JoAnn that he'd had a very hard day and went for a long drive. As he was driving and praying, he claimed that his cell phone had died from an equally hard day and that eventually he pulled over at a rest stop to sleep. JoAnn was livid. Bobby had had many unexplained absences in the last several months, and in spite of battery chargers everywhere, his cell phone had been dying more often than a stand-up comic on the funeral home circuit. But at least his excuses prior to this were creative and believable, and JoAnn, running a treadmill of exhausting 18-hour days, might have had suspicions but little time to explore them. After this night's ridiculous alibi, however, she found the time. The billing secretary went on overtime, and a nanny was quickly found. With her moments of freedom, JoAnn found herpes medication in Bobby's parked Jag. She noticed that Bobby had stopped paying for anything with a credit card and that phone bills from the clinic no longer came to the house. Condoms in the locked desk drawer of his office seemed unnecessary when JoAnn herself was on the pill.

Juggling four businesses at a time, Bobby was a list maker. He'd rough out the list in his head on his morning run and when he got home, write it down before his shower. A portion of the day was spent attending to the list, crossing off items as necessary or adding to-do's that could be combined with tomorrow's list. Sometimes JoAnn's corporate tasks were spelled out in faxed copies of the list from Dr. Baricci's office. JoAnn hadn't seen any lists lately though and, suspicions on full alert, began to wonder why. The private investigator she hired to tail her straying husband suggested that she begin "dumpster diving" through daily trash from his clinic office. She and a girlfriend/lookout began doing so on a regular basis with stunning results. Letters about pending investigations from the State Attorney General's Insurance Fraud unit were crumpled and discarded or unopened. Receipts from women's clothing shops and a local apartment complex lay amid chiropractic newsletters and obsolete patient files.

Each trash bag usually contained one of the doctor's missing lists as well, sometimes in sixteen pieces but just as often in a wadded-up ball. One of the retrieved lists had ten items. Number one: a reminder to call on the expected delivery of a new x-ray machine. Number two: check with a commercial real estate broker about a vacant medical building. Number three was quite disturbing. It detailed figures necessary to complete a money order to a life insurance company. But this company wasn't the one that JoAnn mailed the monthly premium to for her two-million dollar policy (so that the kids would have the best care if God forbid something happened). No, this list indicated a monthly premium of *five times* that amount and a completely *different underwriter*!

But item number four made the blood from JoAnn's head drain to her feet. Armies of goosebumps formed on her skin in the 90 degree heat of the parking lot behind the office. Item four, duly crossed off, reminded Bobby of a date two weeks pending, to meet Carlos and Ramon in Miami, about the "JoAnn situation." He also reminded himself to put $2500 in cash in an envelope prior to the meeting. Since a statewide problem at the time was the flood of mariels and other violent prisoners being released from Castro's prisons (and finding their way to south Florida), JoAnn ran to hire a private investigator. Her private investigator, a former FBI agent, assured her that her concerns were justified. A "hit" could be purchased for as little as $500...more if one desired a quality job and a few days notice in order to establish an alibi.

Two days later, fighting waves of fear, disbelief, and rage, JoAnn filed for divorce and a protection order based on Dr. Baricci's discarded but thorough written list. With the good doctor residing elsewhere, she encouraged me to take up residence in the third floor of the mansion. JoAnn moved as many relatives into her mansion as possible while the divorce and criminal investigations got under way. She also became a much better shot with her newly purchased .38. I was growing homesick for my daughter and found my way back to Michigan.

Once back in Michigan with Rachel, "Beauty and the Beast" videos and Barney filled our days for a while after Tara accepted a corporate job at a multi-billion dollar investment firm.

But cheering for Gaston, only to be repeatedly disappointed, and hoping that Barney would fall on a live hand grenade got old after a while, and I found a need to do something useful and yet cautious. Powerboat racing seemed to fit the requirements quite nicely.

"What could be safer?" I reasoned, "than blasting across a lake at 115 m.p.h. in a super charged, tunnel hulled boat that barely touched the water?" Life vests were not called life vests in power-boat racing. They were called "cadaver retrieval" vests. The safety helmets were connected by intercoms that could be easily unplugged if your co-driver's screaming grew irksome.

I had met my friend Doctor Mike through one of my gyms. He was a master's ski champ on hiatus because of a shoulder that dislocated painfully and frequently every time he skied. One of his clinics was two doors down and I began to work out with him three times a week. We not only fixed his shoulder but because of his athletic background and some decent genetics, built him an unusually muscular, tapered physique for a 50 year old man.

After Tara and I closed Muscle Coach, Dr. Mike was in between wives and found himself with too much money in his bank accounts. While we remained workout buddies and hung out often, Doc became obsessed with going fast on the water...very fast on the water. One hundred thousand dollars later, he was the proud owner of a thirty-one foot catamaran or twin hull, "go-fast" boat. Unfortunately, the 100 m.p.h. promised by the builder wasn't possible. Not only did it "max out" at only 87, but it broke down constantly, cracking engine blocks like victims of an egg toss contest for the blind.

While my boating experience prior to 1993 was limited to smaller powerboats and sailboats, my mechanical background in engines suddenly became of great interest to Doc. He knew that he needed to "set the hook" first. We drove twenty minutes to the marina. The 31-foot race boat was in a storage rack in a huge garage with others. A monstrous forklift grabbed the gleaming white craft with the stunning graphics and giant, colorful decals on the hull sides. My heart filled with lust as the boat, shimmering in the sun, was gently set into the water and tethered to a dock. Dr. Mike agilely hopped into the driver's seat and fired up an engine. Like an angry T-Rex, the boat thundered to life, shaking the marina and everything in it. The second engine shook the earth and sky as it fired up. Everybody within 1000 feet craned their necks to determine the source. My eyes were wide and my body was permeated with an inexplicable desire. I cast off the lines and we rumbled down a canal out to the lake. As Doc gradually opened the throttles, the beast leaped out of the water, passing smaller craft at 40, then 50, then 80 miles an hour. At 85 our cheeks flapped in the windshieldless breeze, eyes tearing in spite of sunglasses being embedded into our surrounding orbitals. We pulled out goggles and put them on, stopping the tears and allowing us to finally check the gauges. We screamed across the waves, watching for slower boats. Of course, *all* the other boats were slower, and Doc could see that he had me hooked. He slowed down and turned back to the marina. Could I install a more efficient exhaust? Would I be able to put in a better camshaft? How about superchargers and a spread bore carburetor to pour more gas into the engine during a race? Sunlight glinted on the water as we coasted into the slip at the marina. Now that the hook was set, Doc began to reel me in.

"You could use it during the week," he offered, "as long as it runs for me on the weekends. And I'm not in town every weekend," he cajoled. "You just keep track of your hours. I'll pay you every time you tell me to."

By now, I was totally snared in his net as he tied up the loose ends. His nephew would be my assistant, running for parts, cleaning up any messes and bringing me lunch.

Doc had already related tales of woe about weekend boating disasters during our last few workouts. After operating and stitching all week while praying for a sunny weekend, Doc would phone one of his "Boat Bimbos" and head out to the marina, which was over an hour from his house. Loading on coolers, towels, any relatives and the Bimbo, Doc would quickly run through the starting procedure. Often both engines would fire right up, much to everyone's delight. But almost as often, one wouldn't start, and Doc would be mortified and embarrassed. If both did start, the ride was usually very short, abbreviated by one mechanical breakdown after another. The end result was usually a frustrated and apologetic Doctor spending the remainder of the weekend trying to make amends to all concerned.

My task was quite simple at first blush. I was to make the boat faster by bolting on high performance parts to the engines. I was to make the boat more reliable by rewiring some items and substituting heavy-duty mechanical parts as necessary. It was, in reality, an expensive process of trial and error, with brief test runs out on the water followed by an hour and a half of pulling a still-warm engine out of the boat. We would take the engine in my cargo van to the workshop in my garage, knowing that after several greasy days we would begin another destructive round of testing.

We eventually sold the boat without ever finishing a race. Dr. Mike, however, would go on to purchase a more reliable boat in the spring of 2001 and win the first race that he entered!

13

CHUCK HAD JUST purchased the stately brick house with the sweeping roofline and four-car garage in The Park that year. The deceptively large basement came in handy immediately for the myriad of workout machines and weightlifting equipment he'd bartered for in a deal with an expiring gym in a building his company purchased.

Aglow with the sensation of being in love for the second time in her life, Summer set upon the enormous task of not just turning the house into a home, but into a showpiece befitting an up-and-coming real estate mogul and his beautiful soon-to-be bride.

Each room's wood floor was carefully sanded and restored. Every wall in the house was repaired or prepared by skilled artisans with textured paints to give the house an "old money," ornate feel. Quotes were gathered on a huge in-ground swimming pool for the backyard and an outside Jacuzzi.

Wedding plans also evolved rapidly as Summer, always quick to make friends, solicited advice from mothers at her son's new school. With her son in a private school nearby and worshipping Chuck's every word and move, the torn, ragged edges of Summer's life were being mended rapidly. Summer also began to make a splash on the Grosse Pointe social circuit. Chuck's friends and business associates, intrigued by his new trophy fiancée, gathered around her at every opportunity, making her a much more conventional center of attention than she had been several short months ago. With love, security, adulation, friends and a bright future all within her grasp, Summer began to speculate about family. How many children would be appropriate? How best to meld everyone in with her adoptive parents one hundred miles away? Where should the new nursery at the house be located?

And then the whispering started. Chuck and his three Greek brothers had always been close. In business, who could you trust more than family? Even the buyout of one of the brothers was going along amiably. But they all knew…they *knew* how he met her. They knew about her son and her past liaison. And they did not approve. This little tramp wasn't good enough for their brother or their precious standing in the community. They did not approve of her or accept her and the whispers that spoke of her past and found fault with her prior decisions. They found new flaws in her personality, her words and her plans. Ignored at family gatherings and ostracized at every opportunity, Summer sensed a growing chasm of unacceptance and distancing. The family's "Anti-Summer" dominoes continued to fall…Chuck's mother, aunts, and uncles began to withdraw. Finally, Summer noticed the first warning signs from Chuck. Wedding plan decisions that needed his input went unresolved. Family visits were sans Summer. Purchases of expensive household pieces were put on hold. With the handwriting on the wall and the tide turning, Summer was furious at the ostracism from Chuck and his family. In a rage she gathered up her son and moved out.

Chuck made lame attempts to reconcile, but, blood being thicker than water, lost momentum and immersed himself back in the family business. Summer, her heart broken and dreams crushed, leased a nearby condo and evaluated her situation. She loved everything about the Pointes, from the quaint stodginess of the tree-lined streets to the coffee shops and salons. She had no intention of leaving the area but knew full well that a return to her old career would never allow her to be accepted. A chance meeting at a party had resulted in a job offer from a short man whose original wealth was derived from distributing beer.

Mot Montgomery was married, had three children and was known in the Pointes as a front man for money that nobody wanted to know the source of. Always in the market for long-legged beer poster models with larger-than-life smiles (and racks), Mot gave Summer carte blanche to run an advertising campaign as long as her gorgeous physique appeared in its ads and posters.

Of course, this new position required a certain amount of mentoring from Mot, but it did not require sexual trysts between Summer and Mot at weekly intervals. A dozen unsatisfying (for Summer) interludes later and the future North American marketing director missed her period. An anomaly, nothing more, she thought. Stress...or maybe it was her body's reaction to an emotional shutdown whenever the pale, tiny, entrepreneur climbed naked on top of her. Summer soon found excuses not to be alone with her boss, maintaining that her son and her closest girlfriend suddenly needed her undivided attention. But the avoidance was too little too late and Summer missed her period the next month as well. She broke the news to Mot after he initiated a conversation at lunch about their recent "lack of closeness." His stunned silence after her announcement was foreboding (to say the least), and resulted in an early end to their noontime conference. One week later, a memo on her desk indicated that her job performance was slipping and that steps "might be needed to correct it." Two weeks later a marketing consultant was brought in to "correct the situation." Summer's replacement was cold, stern, and abrupt and could barely hide her disgust for her beautiful but pregnant underling's plans. With tears of frustration streaming down her cheeks, Summer resigned and went home to brood. But the brooding turned into anger and indignation, and after a week an increasingly self-righteous Summer began to call Mot's office.

Another week of increasingly adamant calls and Mot, suddenly back from a "business trip," returned her call. Threats and innuendo peppered their conversation, all dutifully recorded by a newly bought attachment to Summer's phone.

Quickly the tables turned. A man on the rise, respected by the

Grosse Pointe community and several hundred employees, happily married and adored by his children, was suddenly being held hostage by a small cassette tape, safely stored at Summer's best friend's house. The initial offer of $100,000 was judged to be low. After two days, a messenger delivered a check for $200,000, and once the funds had cleared, Summer's pregnancy was terminated as promised.

For two years, Summer traveled, made new friends in the Pointes and played soccer Mom. Men would search for a take-a-tab machine as they lined up to ask her out, and on occasion she said yes. But Summer was still in love with the tall Greek god.

The god's life had continued on, too. His company grew, and he and his brothers scored one real estate coup after another, adding important pieces to their empire. But the women that Chuck met seemed like vacuous girls compared to the inquisitive, exotic creature he'd given up. So eventually it re-began with a phone call, then another, and finally they met for coffee. The next week they ate dinner together, and finally the separated lovers realized that they could no longer exist apart.

Chuck spent a long month mediating with first one brother and then another. A stubborn uncle finally acquiesced and a favorite cousin agreed to try to accept Summer and not to judge her. After years of negotiating for new properties, Chuck's powers of persuasion were honed sharper than ever before, and he persisted with his family members. Even his mother had seen the vacant stare, the half-heartedness of his movements when family was present, and began to give in. Everyone noticed the gleam back in the family scion's eye and agreed that perhaps they'd been a bit closed minded. Another tryout might be in order. The woman *did* seem to love Chuck with all her heart. She told anyone who would listen that she was *determined* to make him a good wife. She also seemed to have *some* money of her own, she wasn't about to move away and most of the younger nieces and nephews were quite attached to her.

Within months the wedding was on again. The largest reception hall at the Yacht Club was reserved, the family's favorite priest was sufficiently compensated and in mid-April 1992, the good father rendered his blessing.

Summer spent the next eight glorious years being a mother, housewife, lover and confidant. The interior of the large old house in "The Park" was her domain and her canvas. Decorating it was her passion and her expression of self. Each carpet selection was agonized over. The proposed function and exact configuration of each piece of furniture in every room was first imagined, with its exact, final position visualized before it was sought after and then finally purchased. If a piece could not be found it was commissioned and then custom made. The interaction of every furnishing with the wall treatments, artwork, and lighting fixtures was taken into account. The flow from room to room was evaluated and small "collections" (walking canes, candles, pottery, old binoculars, etc.) were situated in each room to stimulate spontaneous conversations among antique aficionados.

Chuck and Summer's presence at social functions was in greater demand than ever. Chuck—witty, handsome, and worldly—was complemented perfectly by Summer's increasingly relaxed and charismatic manner at Grosse Pointe parties. Summer's cadre of friends grew yearly, and morning coffee klatches always included several of them.

Summer swam in their huge in-ground pool or walked with friends for exercise, but the endless restaurant and party food and the morning scones helped her put on three or four pounds a year. Dieting was boring and it was frequently sidetracked by the variety of social engagements. Even at thirty-five pounds overweight, Summer was still exciting, exotic and beautiful. She was content with her house, her marriage and herself until a chance review of one of her old modeling portfolios prompted a conversation with a tennis-obsessed girlfriend. The week after, Summer signed up for tennis lessons at Lochmoor Country Club, for years a favorite haunt of Chuck and his family. Summer's natural athletic ability enabled her to be competitive in the novice league in her first year, and by the second her ability to follow her instructor's suggestions vaulted her to a level not normally visited by a beginner. Summer's newfound passion and her son's love of the game drew the two closer than ever, and his proficiency at it compared to his peers became a growing source of pride for her. Evan was now 19 and beginning his first year at college. Chuck had adopted him long ago, and only smiled when people who saw them together for the first time remarked at the amazing resemblance. With Evan away at college, Summer's third year of competitive tennis was spent sizing up prospective opponents, finding their weaknesses and then beating them. The tennis lessons and tournaments, unfortunately, did little to help Summer shed her unwanted pounds. This realization was partially offset, however, by the designer tennis outfits. Each ensemble was carefully selected to distract the eye away from her growing derriere and emphasize her tan and still cellulite-free legs. With her long dark hair bobbing and swaying in its ponytail, Summer still cut a breathtaking and arresting image as she covered her court in quick and fluid movements.

14

M Y WORKOUT OBSESSION continued during my hiatus. By November of '95, the urge to open another gym became overwhelming. Better exercise equipment and a new high-protein diet philosophy gave me an edge over the ever-growing competition.

As I got older, my average client seemed to get older too. One of them, a 280-pound tire store chain owner, came to me one day and confided that when he rode his big custom $50,000 Harley Davidson motorcycle, people assumed he was a tough guy. But in reality, he intoned, he was just a weak fat guy. He really didn't mind being fat, he assured me, "Hell, I weighed 200 pounds when I was 12 years old!" But he wondered if I could at least turn him into a strong fat guy? I promised him that I could and of course, I did. For quite a while his friends came to me too, and from 5 p.m. to 6 p.m., three days a week, I directed a bunch of rich, fat (but strong) bikers through their workouts.

Many of my clients this time were older, such as the head of Wayne State University's chemistry department. People recovering from strokes and cancer surgery found their way to me through testimonial ads that I ran in newspapers, or were referred by physicians that I worked out with. Dr. Dan, "The Hernia Man," sent me a few, and a cardiac surgeon sent me more.

Clients retained me to help them pull off weight they gained after giving up smoking. Executives would find clever ways to ask me if I thought they were drinking too much and I'd find politically correct ways to say "yes" if I thought it was true. I pulled 100 pounds off of a 325-pound nanny who glowed with appreciation until I turned her down for a date. I struggled to find the cause of 340-pound female bank manager's weight problem during her workouts even as she looked me straight in the eye and said "just salad, no dressing or croutons," when I asked her about the day's lunch. Her friend, standing nearby, jumped in minutes later to whisper about the half-bakery the manager ate for breakfast, the two dozen donut snack (that wasn't considered a part of lunch) and the nightly double pizza habit. In spite of her obvious lying I got 20 pounds off her in a month, but she quit my gym and put it back on with a redoubled eating effort. She eventually had bariatric surgery and now weighs 180 pounds with one-fifteeenth of her stomach still functioning.

The local high school's cheerleading coach approached me at my studio and asked if I would work with a large group of 17-to 18-year-old cheerleaders for $2000. Business was excellent and I couldn't resist the obvious punch line. I replied, "Sure, but I can't get the $2000 until tomorrow!" The coach, appalled, stomped off in a snit.

Some of the younger clients that I did have at my studio, Peak Physique, were cop wannabes. An extensive physical test involving push-ups, chin-ups, running, "the body drag," and obstacle courses was required before a recruit could enter the academy. Written and oral psychological tests were required afterwards to judge a candidate's propensity for violence and his or her moral character. I knew I'd be of no assistance in the latter but I was so useful at preparing candidates for the former that I never had a student fail.

Although the physical tests for women were slightly less demanding than the men's tests, few women could pass without months of preparation. I derived a fair amount of satisfaction from starting a female client at ground zero (basically as weak as a newborn infant), and gradually building her strength over three to six months until she was quite strong and very coordinated.

Dan Cikota, a local Sheriff's deputy who had done unusually well at my studio and broke several strength records as he sailed through the academy, referred Terri the cop to me. Terri Regis, at 5 feet 9 inches, was tall, slim and beautiful. Her long, ash blonde hair was normally corralled in a huge ponytail and topped with a baseball cap. Her almond shaped eyes could open wide to emphasize a point or squint suspiciously to verify a fact. High cheekbones and a small, perfect nose completed a surprisingly photogenic package whenever she removed her cap and ponytail holder and shook her head until her long locks flowed. Terri had been a police officer for two years and was college educated in psychology and criminal justice. Aggressive, focused and ambitious, Terri was determined to move up the promotion ladder as quickly as possible at the medium-sized suburban police department that employed her. At 25 years old, Terri was already a damn good shot with her revered Sig Hauser handgun, but realized that her resume would need extensive additions (and quickly) to leap ahead of other patrolmen in the competition for a sergeant's rank. Terri's city of Waterford, Michigan, was located in Oakland County near the County Courthouse. Oakland County maintained a SWAT team of fifteen specially trained officers drawn from surrounding police departments to act in extreme crisis or hostage situations. Sniper rifles and heavy body armor were fitted to each member. The potentially long hours incurred during a standoff or the need to knock down a door or quickly subdue a suspect demanded a substantially higher physical standard. Terri's written application was immediately accepted, which meant that she was smart enough. She was subsequently informed, however, that there were no female members on the SWAT team. If she aspired to be on the team, she'd be required to meet the same strength and agility standards as the male candidates with *no* gender allowances.

These demanding tests were more rigorous than those imposed on male candidates at the rookie academy. Terri, a standout high school athlete who still played on several men's softball teams, already ran like the wind. But she didn't have the raw upper body strength that many male athletes possessed and she was obsessed with altering the situation.

Over a six-month period, we used a machine that simulated pull-ups until she could pull herself up on a bar (with equipment on if necessary) many times over. Her back muscles flared out in a V-shape when we practiced, and other clients would pause their conversations to watch. At the end of our program, she could lie on a bench and push the equivalent of her body weight into the air repeatedly with just her arms as her chest muscles flexed and heaved under her tank top. Shoulders bulging, Terri could heave weights over her head that few men could. Her long muscular legs grew even more sculpted as she squatted to the floor with a heavy weight across her back. At 5 feet 9 inches and 130 lbs., Terri had five percent bodyfat and now moved so fast that I became apprehensive about racing her in my parking lot. There were 99 other candidates—all male—for the six open positions on the team. Some of the officers prepared by eating donuts while Terri ran sprints.

Officer Terri Regis placed fourth in the fitness tests out of the 100 SWAT applicants and joined the team. She also worked as an undercover narcotics investigator, a private bodyguard for celebrities flying into town, and a squad detective. After seven years as a police officer, Terri was promoted to Sergeant, thirteen years ahead of schedule.

Donna Colson weighed 180 pounds at 5 foot 8 inches tall but did not sign up at Peak Physique to lose weight. At 30, this smiling, pleasant lady had very sparse, curly hair. Intensive chemotherapy after brain surgery for a malignant tumor had left her in remission but walking with hesitation. With her ready smile, renewed zest for life and determination to return to her computer job full-time, Donna was a favorite client of my eleven (by this time) trainers and mine. She laughed and joked her way through leg presses and upper body workouts alike. As she improved her strength and coordination, she was also good for business, inspiring healthy but timid clients to keep attending. Donna's gait improved dramatically as she lost weight, claimed her energy back and became reinvigorated at work. Not shy about taking advantage of her accomplishments, I talked behind her back at the gym, goading on clients with her story (if *she* could do it, so could they), and business boomed. Donna inconvenienced me slightly when she had a relapse after a year and required *still another* round of brain surgery and chemo. But, six months later she staggered back in, with co-workers not only paying for her workout packages but passing the hat for a trip to Hawaii to be taken after I got her strength up again. Smiling and grunting, Donna's first two welcome back workouts went well, with clients practically applauding every repetition. She missed her third workout after her friend called to say she had been readmitted for some tests. She died two weeks later. A friend flew her ashes to Maui and spread them on the waves. For someone that seemed like such a nice person, I thought that Donna had acted very inconsiderately. I still think about her…and miss her.

Of the eleven fitness trainers I employed at Peak Physique, only two were full-time. Betty, a 45-year-old divorced mother of two, was my day manager. She worked from 9 a.m. to 5 p.m. until I strolled in to take over until 9 p.m. Betty, like my other good trainers and myself, was fixated on her looks and quite narcissistic. She had undergone several plastic surgeries in the past five years to keep herself fresh for her boyfriend Paul. Paul had inherited a multi-million dollar company and was feverishly rearranging the assets before he filed for divorce from his wife of 20 years.

Tim Raven was my other full-timer. Bald and bespectacled, Tim was a 40-year-old, $7,000-a-year housepainter and musician who had lost a million-dollar recording contract when two of his band members showed up at a trial recording session stoned on heroin. Depressed and feeling betrayed, Tim satisfied his artistic bent by building an amazing physique. His wide shoulders looked as though someone had stuck half a cantaloupe on each end.

Tim worked from noon to 9 p.m., which suited him fine as he didn't awaken until 11 a.m. Tim spend a great deal of the $40,000 I paid him that first year at the tiny Italian restaurant next door. He would typically arrive at 11:30 a.m. and place his lunch order. To spare my clients the aftermath of his late morning duties in *my* gym's bathroom, Tim would grab a magazine and, while waiting for his order, park himself in the small restaurant's restroom instead. Sometimes the miniscule room's ventilation system would be simply overwhelmed and the restaurant wouldn't smell like fresh pasta anymore. On one such occasion the owner came in early as Tim exited the restroom. Yelling and screaming, with tears streaming down his cheeks, Benito chased Tim back to my gym, and lost his best customer. During a little confrontation, I tried to explain to Benito that, similar to the bottle return law, Tim had purchased a product at his restaurant and was just returning the unused portion. Benito didn't buy any of my "Render unto Caesar what is Caesar's" speech. The quick-to-over-react restaurant owner suffered a heart attack two weeks later, which left him considerably less excitable upon his return to work.

My best part-timers were not only absorbed by their quest for physical perfection, but worked for me in spite of it being financially unnecessary for them to do so. Nancy was tall, blond and beautiful with a deep, smokey voice and an even deeper spirituality. Applying for the job after a spat with her husband, Nancy drove 120 miles roundtrip for what amounted to three five-hour shifts every week. A capable and encouraging trainer, Nancy continued making the journey for two years after Hubby moved back in. As winter ushered in gloomy days and early nights, I purchased a halogen floor lamp to accentuate a black and white figure study hanging above my gym's reception desk. As Nancy stood near the light one evening, the combination of halogen and fluorescent rays wafted across her pale skin and striking blue eyes. Tim and I stood with our mouths agape, staring and murmuring as we tried to puzzle out why this thirty-year-old mother of two looked like a sensuous and desirable goddess whenever she stepped near the desk. We eventually figured it out and changed the entire gym's mixture of lighting until we had the perfect combination throughout. Thanks to Nancy, everyone looked a little better during their workouts.

As a used car dealer I had learned that, for me, no deal ever went down perfectly. A buyer might pay me the full asking price for a unit, but I'd later find that his deposit check had bounced. A workout client might pay me for months in advance, and on the second workout I'd discover that showers and soap seemed to be forbidden in his culture. If I was washing my car on the driveway and a herd of Jehovah's Witnesses came tripping towards me, they would veer away when my Doberman stood up and stretched. But five minutes later, while inside to get some lemonade, that same dog would toss her cookies on my living room carpet. My shallowness and superficiality, coupled with my penchant for looking at everyone first as a lump of clay that I'd mold until it was more pleasing to the eye, resulted in hundreds of clients. I worked from 5 p.m. to 9 p.m. Monday through Friday and was making a very comfortable living. But Tara, always very introspective, grew more spiritual still and finally had enough of me. She and my gorgeous daughter moved out, and this caused me to take a long pause. Maybe there was more to life than a relentless quest for health and strength. Perhaps my purported long-term goal of squeezing as many vigorous, productive years out of the time allotted to me on this planet was in reality shortsighted. Was it possible that I was ignoring the things that really mattered? Did I appreciate the closeness of a family? Was I ignoring the spirit that moved through a small church as members of the congregation linked hands and combined their voices in prayer? Some time devoted to my spiritual future might be redeemed a hundred fold when it mattered most. Maybe a long overdue inward reckoning was in order. Shaking my head slowly, with no idea where these foolish thoughts were coming from, I signed the divorce papers. To console myself, I moved to the lake and bought a huge offshore boat.

The ride to the gym was substantially longer, but three of my trainers had opened negotiations to buy me out. Two different well-heeled clients did the same, and soon I was involved in a very pleasant bidding war. Naturally, the highest bid won and, six months after my divorce, I was again retired.

15

THE YEAR 1999 dawned with Maxwell Lexington, a Grosse Pointe retail billionaire, at the top of his game.

The money flowed in torrents back to Max. An entrepreneur's heart can't help but leap when he realizes that after all of the sweat, hours, risks and moments of doubt, that he is actually worth a million dollars. Max personally grossed about $1 million a week, which gave him a net income of $3,570 an hour, twenty-four hours a day, seven days a week!

The offspring benefited mightily from the money spigot, with trust funds that paid $250,000 a year commencing on his or her thirty-fifth birthday. An upscale retail chain employed two of Max's sons. It was purchased in the mid 1980s, but eventually bit the dust in a cloud of (actual) clearance and going out-of-business sales.

Living in the most famous house in the Pointes—a house that he had helped supervised the building of—was very satisfying. The mansion was set on seven impossibly expensive acres on the most well known street in the Pointes, and guarded from the riff-raff by the required stone walls. With its elaborate landscaping, and iron gates, the house resembled a 25,000-square-foot castle. Neighboring lakeside mansions, with their long hedged driveways, seemed like older starter homes when compared to the monstrous turreted sandstone-colored showpiece of Max Lexington and his wife.

Automobile traffic slowed regularly on the street as gawkers craned to stare at the behemoth for sign of life from its residents. Pleasure boats from the lake floated as close to the back acreage as the shallow waters would allow. Tennis courts, a putting green, indoor and outdoor swimming pools fed by a carefully crafted stone waterfall, Jacuzzis and fountained ponds with koy lent the heavily landscaped grounds a recreational flair. The twisting, winding driveway began immediately after the card-coded, motorized gates and meandered until it disappeared under an archway that connected the main house to the servants' quarters. The garages housed all manner of Mercedes, Rolls and Jaguars, hand-washed, detailed and refueled early each morning by members of the grounds staff. Once inside, the visitor found himself overwhelmed with wide marble hallways, winding staircases and huge but comfortable rooms filled with imported furniture and motorized TV screens (not to be found in any of Max's retail stores).

Greeting and assessing all visitors at any of several intercommed and "alarm system interfaced" doors was the house manager/butler. An American born but London butler-school-trained former waiter/ hairstylist, Robert (not Rob, never Bob!) was a forty-something man with close-cropped, receding hair and a small mustache. Efficient, polite, with a hint of casual, Robert's walking style, quick movements and "you're intruding just a little" demeanor reminded the regular visitor of Gomez Adams on a half dose of Ritalin.

At 5 feet 11 inches tall, Robert's waistline would grow or shrink depending upon his love life. If things were going well with Brian (the house manager two doors down), Robert's "tummy" would obscure his belt-line just a little bit. If the two weren't speaking, or if one or the other was having "commitment" problems, Robert rejoined the spa, hit the treadmill and was usually too distraught to do anything more than "just nibble."

Fastidious and naturally attentive to detail, Robert's rapport with the maids and the conga line of maintenance and repair men that came and went each day was good, provided that no mistakes or delays were noticed by the owners of the house. His talents in the area of garden party planning, bill paying, cooking and phone screening were outstanding. That's not where his talents ended however. The lady of the house adored him for his sarcastic wit and for his ability to help pick out the perfect outfit for the evening's soiree, flicking off any pieces of dust or lint, whether real or perceived.

If Robert did have a flaw, it was his total intolerance to any offspring under the age of eighteen. Since Max and his wife Elizabeth lived in the palace alone, and the youngest of their eight children was thirty, this might not have been a problem but for the thirty-one grandchildren. A huge playroom with every manner of game, doll house, and pinball machine would keep the little ones occupied during the parents' visit but the room's proximity to the potential tragedy of the indoor pool was poorly thought out. A prolonged visit from any of the grandchildren would render Robert increasingly agitated and snappish.

In the elaborate workout room, wooden lockers each sported a parent or offspring's name on a plaque with "and family" etched underneath those of the offspring. But this homey touch misled an infrequent visitor as to how often the offspring and "family" visited as did a wooden placard along the winding drive proclaiming that "hugs and cookies" were available from doting grandparents at any time.

In one of the huge living rooms on the main floor, an expansive, hand-painted mural filled most of one wall. In the foreground of the mural was each of the Lexington's eight grown children standing next to their mate at the time the mural was commissioned. Standing in front of or next to their parents were each of Max and Elizabeth's twenty grandchildren. When Max proudly showed guests the mural, they couldn't help but wonder if the artist was still taking commissions in the Detroit area or if he was still in good health. Due to the ongoing need to update the mural (with new grand-children being born yearly and with Max's own children divorcing and remarrying periodically), the natural inclination was to surmise that yearly additions and subtractions to the mural might provide a steady stream of income to the artist. These questions were never voiced out loud in Max's presence, however.

Most mansions have an impressive front entranceway, and Max's was no exception. Several times, on visits to Europe, Max and his wife had stayed at an old but famous five-star hotel in London. Max had often admired the elaborate chandelier that hung in the lobby; so much so, that when he read in the Wall Street Journal that the hotel was being razed he "moved heaven and earth" to procure the chandelier. It now glittered and shimmied over all of the guests that passed through the main door of the mansion, having been carefully shipped from Great Britain and cautiously restored to its former splendor.

Max's Florida penthouse condo was nothing short of spectacular. It was wrapped around the top of a fifteen-story structure and afforded an impressive view of both the ocean on one side and the Intracoastal waterway on the other, with security guards bowing and waving to Max, ever mindful of their Christmas tips. The condo was also a haven that one of Max's daughters could go to get away from it all during a painful divorce and substance abuse recovery process. Her husband had originally been in Max's employ, but became a pariah when he had the audacity to branch out and compete against his father-in-law. Max's shit list had a special slot reserved for the man.

A tiny fraction of Max's money went to operating a three million dollar, 82-foot Italian Yacht, discreetly docked in its Florida berth, with captain and crew at the ready 24/7. None of Max's income was needed to operate the fleet of eight private jets, since the aftermath of 911 guaranteed waiting lists of busy executives clamoring to lease a hassle-free ride to their next meeting or vacation.

The huge house in Northern Michigan's most upscale development had its own smaller 50-foot yacht and a soothing waterfront view. This gorgeous, large hideaway with huge exterior windows to take in every molecule of the amazing view, was accessible from Max's Grosse Pointe residence in just over four hours door-to-door. When Max needed to start vacationing in a hurry, a jet whisked him there in forty-five minutes. One phone call sent a 550 mile per hour jet from Max's fleet to meet him at Detroit City Airport, a short car ride away. Courteous, uniformed pilots stood awaiting the opening of the security gate that allowed Max or his driver to drive to within fifty feet of the plane. Baggage was hustled out of the trunk and onto the plane by the crew. No lines or detection devices hindered anyone as they stepped up into the plane and seated themselves. Within minutes, engines were restarted and the twelve-passenger jet was roaring down the runway, nose pointing up, the trip begun and Max already half-asleep. In the winter, a three-hour plane ride landed him at a small private airport in Boca Raton. After another ten-minute car ride to his condo, Max was watching waves and seagulls instead of ice and plow trucks out of his windows.

16

IN THE MID 1980s a show appeared on TV called "Miami Vice." It featured stylish cops chasing stylish drug lords around Florida on huge go-fast boats. As I look back on the show via reruns on cable, it also featured some pretty hokey plot lines. But the incredulous lifestyle presented every week apparently had a lasting effect on me. The two main cops the show revolved around were so overly dramatic that I found myself rooting for the drug lords with increasing regularity. My frustrations grew as episode after episode passed with the drug lords and their enforcers constantly failing to kill the cops with hand grenades, car bombs and mac 10s that spat out thirty bullets per second.

Stymied by the bad guys' poor marksmanship and the good guys' lack of credible acting, I eventually quit watching. But in 1998, I bought a 42 foot "deep V offshore" and kept it on a hoist in the canal in back of my home. After a year of roaring around the local lakes with a carcinoma-dark tan and the "Miami Vice" theme song ringing in my ears, I suddenly decided to become a grown-up again. Somewhat inhibited by a non-compete clause relative to the sale of the gym, and intrigued by anecdotal accounts from friends of their experiences in Grosse Pointe, I resolved to get the entire community into shape. Since I was reluctant to commit to establishing a new gym and somewhat unsure as to where to locate it within the community, I decided to convert the 49,000 residents one step at a time.

I placed display ads in local papers advertising my services to anyone with fitness equipment in their home or with access to a

79

local gym. I found that the Pointes, where I could find a hair salon on every block, weren't exactly littered with public workout facilities. My friend Doc, always helpful, suggested a career deviation to become a manicurist or hair stylist. But after a few responses to my ads, I found that several of the houses and mansions that I visited had at least some rudimentary equipment. When a client was serious and yet equipmentally-challenged I would lease workout machines to them on a "to own" basis.

Clientele slowly increased and within weeks I had six or seven regular "stops."

Trish lived in Grosse Pointe Woods. A drug company rep who shared a $200,000 two-story bungalow with her husband, Trish was pretty with a grown cherub's face and smile. Trish was also 70 pounds overweight. Her basement harbored a usable weight machine and enough miscellaneous bars and benches to piece together an effective three-day-a-week routine.

Over several months, we worked out with every major muscle group. We talked about and agreed to make adjustments to Trish's diet. Weigh-ins revealed little progress. Trish's clothing stayed tight, without any of the usual loss of inches that most women experience at the onset of their workouts. I got out my psychologist's hat and put it on. We talked about her childhood and her relationships with her divorced parents. We talked about her taking care of her invalid mother until the poor woman's death. Discussions about her sporadic dating prior to her marriage revealed few clues. Finally, after we began discussing former jobs, Trish alluded to a "difficult" employment situation that occurred when she was 18. Working her way through college at an advertising agency, Trish was befriended by a vice-president of the company. Eager for advancement and enticed by the corporate perks that the 45-year-old executive enjoyed, Trish began to accept social invitations. A night of underage drinking at a company stadium suite led to Trish and her "mentor" being alone in a limo on the way back home. Drunkenly groping and cajoling while his strong hands unclasped and shifted her clothing, the number two man in the company raped the young intern. Guilt-ridden but too ashamed to confide in anyone, Trish anguished over the incident for days, too embarrassed to even show her face at work. Days turned into weeks, and Trish was let go for non-attendance in a certified letter from the company lawyer. Bright and personable, she quickly landed another job at another agency. Immediately popular with her new coworkers, Trish needed a way to ensure that the horrific experience of the last employer would not occur again. So, perhaps without knowing why, she began to eat. It worked. Ten pounds later, Trish felt a little less attractive. Twenty pounds later, she sensed that social invitations from coworkers were proffered less frequently. Forty pounds later, the former 110 pound high school cheerleader had a protective suit of fat hiding her from "lecherous old men." When I finally met Trish at age 30, she had gained a security-enhancing 70 pounds for a total of 190 pounds at 5 foot 3 inches. Her husband accepted her the way she was but encouraged her to diet. Raiding her pantry and refrigerator and confiscating high calorie groceries had no effect on Trish. She had become adept at closet eating for years now, and found other, more clandestine ways to pack in the carbohydrates. Eventually, through diligent, secretive and unrelenting snacking, Trish managed to replace the ten pounds we took off together and ended her workout program.

My cell phone has a myriad of options. Not particularly high-tech by today's standards, my cell phone can nevertheless remember up to 50 numbers and match a name to each. The phone's caller ID will remember the last twenty calls. It has three games programmed in. I can press a button, speak a name aloud, and my phone will dial the number for me. My cell phone can emit many different sounds. The "ringer" options that I can select from alone total twenty-five. When I receive a call, I can elect to have the phone ring normally or I can listen to a marching band erupt on the little speaker to alert me to a call. With a little pre-programming, each person that regularly calls me can be assigned their own ring, or tone. A cop friend's call, for instance, might be a few bars of the theme from "Dragnet." A call from my second ex-wife might initiate a few bars of "When the Saints Go Marching In" until I answered. But if I'd had any inkling of the future as my phone rang on that fateful Friday in May four years ago, I would have matched the caller's number to Ricky Martin's "Living La Vida Loca" because my simple existence was about to become quite crazy indeed.

"Hello, Maaark Steel please," I heard in a nasally male voice.

"This is Mark speaking."

"Yes, this is Mr. Lexington, and I understand that you're a personal trainer." The voice was unusual but clear, nonetheless, and commanded attention. The caller ID showed a number from Grosse Pointe Shores, with the smallest population of the five boroughs and yet the highest (by far) per capita income.

"I am. What kind of exercise have you done in the past?"

"Oh, we've had a trainer come to the house for years. Mrs. Lexington and I have everything we need in the basement. It looks like a regular gym. We have more than enough equipment."

I launched into a mild pitch about resistance training and its link to permanent weight loss.

"That sounds real good Maaark." He said again, "This is Mr. Lexington. Why don't you come by the house for an interview on Monday?"

An interview? Well, aren't we special? I thought. I hadn't been on the applicant side of a desk for over twenty years. On the other hand, it didn't sound like my fee would be a problem nor did I anticipate having to supply heavy machines and lug them inside.

"Of course. Would sometime in the morning be possible? Perhaps ten o'clock or so?"

"Let's see." Voice muffled by hand over receiver, "Hey Babe? How's ten o'clock Monday to interview Maaark Steel?" Louder now, "He's the trainer"…still louder, "The trainer!…I said, how's Monday?" A minute goes by, the responses too muffled now to hear. The missus must have walked into speaking range. "Yeah Maaark," he returned to me, "Monday's fine, how about ten o'clock?"

"Why sure, Monday's good with me, about ten o'clock." *Oh*

brother, I thought, *we might have some communication glitches coming up fast.*

"Just come right to the home, on Lakeshore, this is Max Lexington. Ring in at the gate. Robert will let you in."

Slowly, like an apparition appearing out of a heavy fog, the reality of who I might be talking to began to define itself. Was this? Naw. I would think someone would call *for* him. But, well, maybe he occasionally hires somebody himself? Didn't I read something about the house a few years ago? How many stores was it? Was it ten? Was it twenty? I saw a lot of delivery trucks with the name Lexington on the side…better be thorough…he may be reluctant to leave a home phone number.

"Uh, Mr. Lexington?" *That sounded confidant!* "You probably don't get asked this much, but what's your address there?"

"It's 777, so we're set at ten?"

"Oh, yes, ten is perfect."

"Fine, then, just ring at the gate, and our house manager Robert will let you in."

"Perfect, see you Monday." I hung up. I should have been excited. I should have been a little nervous. Because of the constant TV and radio ads, this was arguably the most famous man in Michigan. Like many people I was always a bit star-struck whenever I met somebody even marginally famous. But soon after the initial contact, I could always count on my shallowness taking over as I began to appraise them. At the first meeting I would estimate bodyfat percentage, check for pectoral muscle, look for hints of the size and shape of their upper arms and covertly evaluate the fit of their pants. Any other data concerning who the person was, and what they might have accomplished, was not even a part of the equation. So I mentioned my conversation to the girlfriend, and we hopped onto the boat for the rest of the weekend.

Monday morning rolled around, and I woke up fifteen minutes earlier than necessary. After all, I thought, this was an important interview (for some reason) and I should be dressed appropriately.

Perhaps a suit would be required? Required, perhaps, but both

of mine were in need of a trip to the cleaners, and that opened
other cans of worms such as ironing a shirt and my lack of dress
shoes. Maybe a knit golf shirt with some nicely pleated pants?
Unfortunately, a stop at a waterfront Italian restaurant and two large
pizzas on Sunday had left my waist at 33 inches. The pants I had in
mind sported a 32-inch waist.

In just one hour, I'd be standing in front of a man who had
hired thousands of people in his lifetime, or at the very least hired
the people who hired those thousands. Every loose thread on me
would be noticed. He might own suits that cost as much as my
entire current wardrobe. This man sat on director boards of other
large companies, hiring and firing CEOs. This man donated millions
to charities and was in many cases the sole insurer of their continued
existence. If he insisted on signing all of his employees' paychecks
himself, it would be so time consuming that they could only be
paid monthly at best. My every movement would likely be
scrutinized, noted and catalogued. My body language, analyzed
by groups of technicians behind one-way glass, would probably
be diagrammed in grids to look for subversive patterns. Fully
expecting to pass through metal detectors to gain entry into the
mansion, I would have to divest myself of anything that might set
one off. The clothing decisions I made in the next five minutes
might affect the rest of my life.

I chose the light blue jeans, a newer pair of tennis shoes, and a
tight-fitting yellow T-shirt. While admittedly the jeans had a few
washings on them, the T-shirt was not only form-fitting in a color
that flattered my tan, it had a snazzy little pocket over the heart as
well!

Five minutes early, I buzzed in at the front gates.

"May I help you?" a cold, disinterested male voice inquired
over the speaker.

"Mark Steel to see Mr. Lexington," I intoned, trying to sound
equally disinterested. A long pause, some rustling, a longer pause
followed by muffled murmurs and finally the huge wrought iron
gates began to swing open from the center where they touched.

"Park on the side."

I slowly drove along the bending, turning asphalt drive, noting the putting green and tennis courts off to one side. Prepared to stop for armed security guards patrolling the grounds, I received instead a squinty but not overly hostile "once over" from a chubby man with a rake as he paused and looked up.

As I approached the main house a fountain, positioned in front of the long stone stairs that cascaded from the front door, sent a huge pattern of droplets upward. Each stream of droplets was bent and contorted by a light breeze. A circular drive around the fountain and its koy-pond base was obviously not the side of the house, so I continued to the right. I idled underneath an archway that connected the main house to what appeared to be a combination garage and guesthouse. I slowly crept around the side until my progress was halted by two parked construction vans. They blocked in still another van and two economy cars that were parked further up. I parked my car and got out, scooping up a fat file folder from my now empty passenger seat.

There were three garage doors to my left. Suddenly the left one started to open. I walked over to within thirty feet of the door and peered in. A somewhat portly gray-haired man, dressed in a white tennis shirt, shorts and shoes stood in a doorway that led from the back of the garage section into the main house. The man's voice echoed through the garage, "Maaark, right on time, c'mon in buddy," as he waved me around the Mercedes station wagon parked in the left space.

The man, his ruddy face tanned and his shock of white-gray hair combed back, pumped my hand and said, "I'm Max Lexington." Speaking up, I told him it was a pleasure and followed him down a long hallway. Seemingly out of force of habit, he pointed into each room as we passed, offering a short explanation of each one's function. The hallway ended after the tanning room and emptied out into a 20x40 square foot room dimly illuminated by windows at the far end. As my eyes grew accustomed to the room, I peeked around the circular staircase in the center. A large multi-station piece of equipment of early 1990s vintage occupied half of one wall. Two stair-climbing machines—one new, charcoal-colored and expensive; the other white (and not expensive), were in the middle. A rack of dumbells, two workout benches, and some as-seen-on-TV ab and thigh machines made of white tubing fought for recognition in the center of the room. Floor-to-ceiling mirrors covered half the walls on either side. Fastened between the mirrors of one wall was a wooden exercise rail. Hip high, it looked like the type that ballet dancers use to stretch and practice on.

Somewhat let down by the equipment shown to me and the relative darkness of the room, I followed the slightly bow-legged billionaire up the circular staircase. We climbed into a large den, dominated by a huge, blond wood desk. The expected bookcases lined two walls. Ornate furniture was arranged neatly everywhere and all the end tables were covered with framed pictures of family and thickly bound portrait books stacked three and four high.

"Please sit down," Max motioned as he sat behind his desk. "Babe, the trainer's here," he yelled towards the bottom of another circular staircase in the corner of the den. A short, pleasant looking woman with short blond, carefully-coifed hair began her descent down the staircase as I cast around looking for a place to sit. Sofas aligned perpendicularly to the desk made a stereotypical interview difficult for the interviewee.

Elizabeth Lexington was pretty, with a curiously wrinkle-free countenance for a woman who might be in her 60s, I thought. Wearing taupe-colored shorts and a dark blue V-neck short-sleeved blouse, Mrs. Lexington scampered down the staircase with ease. Her compact, athletic legs were somewhat pale but had a smoothness that belied her age. A brief welcome smile flashed across her face and she bounced to a sofa across from me. We both turned our heads, mine to the right and hers to her left, as we returned our attention to Max, who was partially obscured by a reading lamp on his desk.

"Maaaark," Max said. "As you can see we have a complete gym downstairs. Now we had a trainer until recently but he told us his wife was leaving him and he was too upset to continue."

"After we paid him, that is," Elizabeth interjected testily. *Oh wonderful*, I thought. *Nothing like starting off on the wrong foot, especially on the tail end of some other guy's scam.*

"Mike was a good guy," Max said as he shot his wife a look. "He just developed some personal problems when his wife took off. He has a two-year-old son that she left him with. Do you know Mike Evans?"

My eyes opened. I thought, *no, why, do you know everybody in your business*? Besides, it seemed to me that if I were suddenly the sole support of a two-year-old, I'd need a job more than ever. Something about Ole Mike's story smelled fishy already. But as I mulled it over, Maxwell Lexington probably *did* know everybody in his business.

"No, I never met Mike Evans," I replied. My answer seemed to satisfy Max and he leaned back in his chair. At least now I could see his eyes. He talked about his battle with his weight and his tennis game. He briefly expounded on how fit his wife was and how it was almost embarrassing for him (she smiled) when she woke up early every morning to attend her aerobics class or ride her bike.

I had learned long ago to let a potential client talk. I learned more about their past programs (and what they supposed their current fitness level to be) by listening than by asking. Besides, when they caught themselves in contradictions like "I don't eat badly, but we did have pizza late last night," they were embarrassed in front of me rather than defensive.

As I listened to Max talk, pausing for an occasional nod or word of agreement from Elizabeth, I realized that they had no plan. On the other hand, most Michigan couples in their late sixties considered a weekly walk in the summer and regular TV watching in the winter to be sufficient. I considered Max's awareness that he needed something besides weekly tennis a damn good start!

Now it was my turn. The T-shirted trainer trying to "sell" the master salesman. A slightly rusty salesman stepping up to the plate against a legendary businessman who'd seen every huckster imaginable parade through his office. There was a brief moment of mental circling as the former car salesman eyed the most famous entrepreneur in Detroit. Pulses of energy emanated from the large brain housed inside the huge head…probing…searching for a chink in my skull. Echoes of advice from a friend rang inside the back of my head. *"If people like this like you then you're set for life." "One rich couple liked their chef so much they left him in their will!" "If you get in good with one family then all of their friends will want you too!"* I looked down and opened the slightly tattered manila folder that I'd brought with me. The innocuous looking folder contained a three-year history of a family of physicians that I'd been working out with. It contained much more than just a few charts of recordings of the weights that the husband and wife lifted and the amount of times they did it. I had noted every weigh-in and every workout date. Physical limitations were recorded based upon their medical histories. Current medications and their dosages were duly listed. Meal contents were catalogued, receipts for new equipment were retained and even applicable newspaper articles were included.

Max's eyes widened perceptibly as he quickly examined the complete if somewhat shopworn "case histories." I kept it short and sweet, and when I was through, the billionaire looked up at me and said, "Maaaark, you look like you're in great shape too."

"I practice what I preach, Mr. Lexington." *A minute-and-a-half total. Did it. Closed the deal*! We briefly discussed my rates and two minutes later we were beginning our first workout in the lower level of the three-story monolith. Mrs. Lexington, already strong and coordinated, jumped to each new exercise with energy. Maxwell Lexington was more tentative and less familiar with the motions than I might have first believed. He was also very interested in the constant interruptions from Robert the house manager. The periodic but incessant ringing of their multi-lined home phone never stopped and would prove to be a constant distraction during the ensuing years.

17

MAX HAD A humble, subtle way of boasting about his jets and his other amazing luxuries. A short story about a wealthy associate who had emphatically explained the business need for such an item would segway into assurances that Max had originally purchased a less extravagant item. (In this instance, meaning he started with a smaller jet). A litany of the benefits to the company would then ensue, followed by a history of the upgrades to the fleet and the justifications for such. Then followed the heavily veiled boasting when Max mused aloud about how spoiled he was, as if to convince the listener that should it all disappear tomorrow he wouldn't be troubled a bit (but instead might be a bit relieved).

My "old money" clients in the Pointes seldom had a need to boast, but every "new money" client seemed to have an urgent need to do so, once they deemed the recipient of the boasting out of their league, of course.

Max's boasting covered every aspect of his life, both public and private. He was truly "grateful" that the house manager laid out his clothes in the morning. He was "blessed" that breakfast was made and waiting when he got up. He was "spoiled" because members of the four-man ground crew hand-washed the cars every morning, gassed them up, and brought his Mercedes around to the front door. He was "fortunate" to have three maids constantly cleaning the mansion and doing laundry. The litany went on, repeating aloud the time he believed the weekly manicurist was due, or wondering if the masseuse could come on short notice in the house's private massage room. A standing joke at Christmas was a recitation of decorating the twenty-foot pine tree in a living room and climbing the scaffolding to place the star. In actuality, a three-person decorating crew spent two weeks at the task. An elaborate manger, the size of a coal mine town row house, loomed inside the front gate and was "especially beautiful" every season. Warranty work or mechanical problems with the cars were of no concern after fleet mechanics at Headquarters drove over with loaners to whisk the offending vehicle away to the dealership until it could learn to behave. Dry-cleaning vans and huge tree-trimming trucks jostled for room in the front driveway while contractors and pool maintenance vehicles fought for parking in the back, and Max Lexington was thankful for it all.

While Robert was in charge of keeping Mr. and Mrs. Max Lexington organized at home, all business lunches, charitable obligations, social functions, interview requests and thousand of other business details were capably handled by Max's oldest daughter, Bertha. Known and feared company-wide as the one who had the boss' ear, Bertha was identified by outsiders as well as Max's "right hand woman." If the Cardinal needed money, he called Bertha. If an old friend of Max's needed a loan or a shoulder to cry on, he phoned Bertha first. She screened charities, hospitals, yacht and car salesmen, real estate brokers and event organizers. While the company president Dale Ladd handled the day-to-day sales operations of the corporation's four-million-square feet of buildings, it was Bertha that often seemed to be the power behind the throne.

Max Lexington's morning drive to Corporate would be spent on his cell's speakerphone with Bertha as she briefed him on his day's itinerary. His Friday briefings often included a selection of black-tie affairs to be accepted or turned down as his mood took him.

Forty-nine years old and divorced, with a rapidly developing smoker's voice, Bertha lived in a huge Grosse Pointe Shores colonial with her boyfriend of seven years, Joe. Joe was a barber, owned a tuxedo, and knew thousands of jokes…he was respectful to Max and adequate enough to be seen with Bertha at social events, but Joe was *not* a marriage threat that Max need be concerned about.

Christmas shopping for Bertha's gift and those of his other daughters was simplified by a trip to Saks Fifth Avenue. After Mr. Lexington sat down, racks of dresses and furs were wheeled out by eager store employees. Styles were discussed and fretted over, available sizes and colors were expounded upon, and selected items were altered, wrapped, billed to Max, and shipped to each daughter's home. Some years the theme was jewelry but the process was similar. Max was "extremely grateful" that this shopping method was an option for him, and reminded me every Christmas.

Max Lexington's yacht sucked up more money than a bordello on an aircraft carrier. A broken propeller on Max's three million dollar yacht ran $25,000 in parts and labor. Regularly scheduled maintenance on a yacht engine (and there were two) was $25,000 per engine. A professional hull cleaning runs into the thousands. Breakdowns in electronic navigational systems must be repaired by a specialist at an outrageous hourly rate. At forty miles per hour a hundred-foot yacht's two engines can burn 300 gallons of diesel fuel per hour at two dollars per gallon. When a boat consumes one gallon in twelve seconds to push 150,000 pounds against water resistance for only one-eighth of a mile, even a ten-mile-per-gallon Hummer seems like an economy car.

At $75,000 per year, insurance is a bargain. A smart-shopping yacht owner can find a Florida boat well for only $12,000 a year. A boat well at an exclusive club or resort (at $350 per day), will leave the yacht owner with $128,000 less to contribute to his stock portfolio every year. Keeping the outer hull clean and polished is only $5,000 a year, but quadruples if the boat is removed from the water (to have it done right).

Every yacht over sixty-five feet in length must be piloted by a licensed sea captain. A "one hundred ton" license is the most common but still doesn't guarantee the captain to be competent, prompt, dependable and a non-drinker. The going rate for a yacht captain is $1000 a year per foot of boat. Thus the captain of a one hundred-foot yacht can expect to gross $100,000 per year sans bonuses and benefits. Most yacht captains are responsible for overseeing the extensive cleaning and repair operations and many have an engineering or mechanical background. Many large yachts, however, employ a full time engineer. A first mate and his/her salary is standard and crews of up to six and their salaries are not uncommon. Many yacht owners will order the captain to sail to a particular destination and then jet to that location once the ship has arrived, meanwhile incurring fuel and travel expenses without ever setting foot on their own boat.

All of the above expenses, and many that I've omitted, can add up in a few short years to equal the original cost of the yacht. The majority of yacht owners only actually use their boat for a total of four weeks a year. The captain and crew, although expected to travel on short notice, are usually just on standby enjoying the sun and water. Max Lexington once confided in me that when he died, he'd like to come back as his yacht captain.

"Curb appeal" was the term that Max used to describe the stares and finger pointing that were directed at his boat as it pulled up to a dock or cruised slowly down a waterway past houses and outdoor restaurants. Smart knit shirts with the boat's name and crisp khaki pants were required of all crew members, and added to his boat's curb appeal.

After a short tour of the boat's sumptuous yet tasteful five-star hotel interior, Max would eagerly ask the overwhelmed visitor what they thought, never once getting a negative answer. Polished teak, gold fittings and the finest fabrics, material and furnishings filled every living area, as well as five bathrooms. Outside, the white hull and huge black stripes were reminiscent of a giant, powerful killer whale...with radar and a multitude of antennae masts perched on its back. The yacht certainly had curb appeal.

18

BODY WEIGHT WAS an obsession with both Mr. and Mrs. Lexington, and our morning ritual always began with a weigh-in. Almost a mini-marital contest in and of itself, the weigh-in occurred while each recited their caloric transgressions from the previous day. The fact that many omissions occurred was apparent when one spouse "ratted out" the other if they forgot about anything from candy to frozen yogurt. If Max or Elizabeth was down a pound there would be much chortling and hrrmmphs of satisfaction. If one of them was up a pound, however, an immediate dietary review would commence. But if *both* of them were up a pound that morning, a spontaneous review of my workout plans for them and the frequency of their workouts might occur instead. I bought them a digital scale for the workout room that I knew to be 100% accurate so that the statistics gleaned from the weigh-ins would never be in dispute. Tuesday workouts were infrequent when Elizabeth worked as a volunteer in the premature infant ward at the local hospital. Saturday mornings were usually not possible while she taught retarded adults at a Catholic school. Mr. Lexington's workout schedule was sporadic at best, with tennis partners, business meetings and trips and forays out to breakfast or lunch with the "missus" all taking precedence. Many times my car idled at the front gates while Robert explained over the speaker that the scheduled workout would not be possible. My frustration mounted and my interest in the pair's success waned. The appointment calls grew fewer during the summer months until finally they stopped.

Two months went by without any word, and then in late fall of 1999 my phone rang. Their bodies hadn't magically transformed into living Greek statues during my absence and would it be possible to start up again? During the next several workouts we discussed possible improvements. Each time I was asked, I replied with as much tact as I could muster that, for such an impressive house, the workout room was quite dungeon-like. With sporadic natural lighting inhibited by tall hedges around the windows and very dim bulbs in the few electric lights available, the room could be positively dreary and uninviting. In addition, the equipment was of an older design and somewhat limiting in what we could do with it. After a series of discussions and meetings (unpaid of course) and pouring over catalogs of the most modern and current equipment the industry offered, we agreed on six sparkling new pieces. Their arrangement in the room alone was the subject of two meetings, and sizes and measurements were forwarded to the head designer for the Corporation. Colorful but tough-fibered carpet was chosen and powerful new lighting fixtures were ordered from U.S. and German sources. The day eventually came when we could no longer use the room for a workout. Painters, carpet layers, and electricians had taken over with a vengeance.

Lochmoor, a nearby country club located in Grosse Pointe Woods, was visited frequently by the Lexingtons. While its excellent golf course was seldom utilized by Max Lexington, its tennis courts would find him at a regular Thursday morning foursome whenever he was in town.

Sunday morning brunches in the tasteful dining rooms were always satisfying and the omelet chef very accommo-dating...turning egg whites into a gourmet repast. A large glass-walled area on the second level of the tennis house housed the treadmills and machines of a spotless workout area. Televisions tuned to cable news channels hung from every corner. The Lexingtons and their faithful trainer journeyed there on several occasions while their home exercise room was under invasion by the contractors. After two weeks, the facility at the house, while far from finished, was deemed marginally useable again.

One cold December morning I stood at the side of the huge house, vapor emanating from my lungs as I watched the middle garage door slowly rise to allow me in. I expelled the remainder of my air in a gasp! A brand new, gleaming, black Rolls Royce occupied the space that, up until yesterday, had been claimed by a black BMW sedan. Jaw hanging, I circled the Rolls while Robert stood in the small doorway and rolled his eyes. "It's just a caaaar," he said impatiently. My drooling was hampered by the relatively dim light in the garage. I stepped backwards through the doorway and into the house, nearly treading on a clearly unimpressed Robert's foot.

During the workout I remarked several times about the Rolls to a beaming Max. I touched on my teenage fascination with British cars to explain why I was overwhelmed with the center garage's current occupant. My questions about the car drew mostly shrugs and blank looks. On my way out, Mr. Lexington paused at the small doorway as the outside garage door slowly groaned open.

"Y' know Maaark, Mrs. Lexington and I are going to the season's first Christmas party Friday night. Would you be interested in driving us in the Rolls? We'll pay you hourly of course. If you are interested, maybe you could come by tomorrow with your girlfriend and take her to lunch in it or something. That way you could get used to driving it."

The master of persuasion had struck. Thirty seconds start to finish, and I was hooked and reeled in. Did he think I couldn't see what he was trying to do? Was he under the misguided impression that I was so enamored with 6000 pounds of British metal, rubber and leather that I would stoop to being a chauffeur just to get my hands on it? Did he expect the second most successful trainer in Michigan to forsake all career plans to kowtow to a rich guy with a $225,000 Rolls Royce Silver Seraph just because I'd probably never have the chance to drive one again?

"Of course I can drive on Friday, Mr. Lexington."

"Okay Maaark, that's excellent, Buddy."

"I'll call Robert in the morning and arrange to get the keys for a lunch time test drive," I said.

"Fine, Mark, fine, and the Missus and I will see you tomorrow afternoon to work out."

As I left, I was already mentally listing the things I'd have to do before lunch tomorrow. The Rolls required a certain look…my usual blue jeans and T-shirt simply wouldn't suffice. No, if I were to be seen about town in a new Rolls, I needed a look to go with it. Fortunately, I had a new pair of black jeans, unworn, sitting on the shelf with the tags still on. Next on the list, the perfect shirt. The light gray T-shirt, barely worn, came out of the drawer afterward. While accentuating the biceps without overstating the pectoral development, the muted color of the gray shirt was the perfect choice for an early winter drive in the Rolls.

After wardrobe selection, I needed to alert the girlfriend. Very tall at 5 feet 9 inches, with narrow hips that added the illusion of endlessly long legs, Natasha would be perfect for the passenger seat of the Rolls. Her long blond hair and wicked toothy white smile were undeniably compatible with the image I sought. The wide, tanned shoulders and back of her female bodybuilder's physique would be somewhat obscured, I realized, by the long leather coat she'd insist on wearing. But Natasha, with no bodyfat, chilled somewhat easily in December. As much as I enjoyed watching goosebumps popping out from her bronzed skin and through the clingy tops she favored, I didn't want her shivering to spoil any of our entrances. I made sure the camera had film and phoned Doc to set up a workout and a lunch with him and one of his favorite bimbos.

10:30 a.m. the next day saw me and Natasha charging up I-75 to Doc's newly purchased gym. I felt like the most fortunate man alive as the 322-horsepower behemoth floated over the concrete. A clearly impressed Natasha, smiling seductively as she sank into her hand-stitched leather seat, assured me that my luck would continue well into the night.

Doc's gym was thirty-five miles away and, after figuring out all the knobs and switches, we settled into a routine of counting up the double takes from other drivers. My race boat buddy had purchased a 13,000 square foot World Gym franchise after the previous owners fell behind on their payments to the bank. Although not much more than a diversion from his usual surgical obligations, Doc's gym was already past the break-even point due to his business savvy and his gregarious nature. An entire side of the weight room was lined with huge glass windows, and I pulled the purring Rolls into a parking slot in front of them.

Doc had brought an unusually top heavy brunette woman with him. She had a penchant for being tied to an eyehook while wearing just a thong and being spanked as a prelude to further activities, and Doc was quite fascinated with her. The lady was wearing black skin tight leotards this morning and a thin, cotton, midriff-baring top...stretched to its absolute limits. Natasha and I, suppressing grins and threatening to check the woman's fanny for redness, didn't mention the Rolls and began our one-hour leg workout. Pausing every minute to check on the car, we watched members occasionally leave the gym and slow down to gawk as they walked by the car. But Doc, focused on his 315-pound squats (and his girlfriend's every move), never gave any indication that he noticed the Rolls.

Noon rolled around and we discussed a lunch destination. We agreed on a local Greek restaurant that featured $5.95 entrees and plastic water glasses. As we ambled out into the parking lot debating about which car to take, Doc stopped in his tracks. "Oh wow, somebody drove a new Rolls here." Grinning sanguinely, I hit the "unlock" on the remote entry. Suavely sidling up to the back left door, I opened it and held it open while Natasha, smiling, did the same on the other side. Looking at us in disbelief, Doc and his girlfriend slowly got in. I spent the short, careful ride to lunch trying to convince Doc that it was high time that I moved to a little nicer class of car and that the four doors of the Rolls made double-dating easier. The restaurant we selected was actually quite appropriate as the row of windows adjacent to the parking lot allowed me to keep tabs on the car. Doc's persistent inquiries about the car's true owner were ignored at lunch and, as the waitress approached, I looked at his girlfriend and announced, "I think I'll have the melons!" This seemed to divert everyone's attention, but a couple of days later I called my friend and 'fessed up.

As Friday night rolled around, I once again grew concerned about wardrobe requirements. With no foreseeable way out, I broke out one of my suits. The excitement of being reunited with my Rolls again was tempered somewhat by my apprehension about bringing my gun with me. Ever since my first meeting with Max and his wife I'd been very careful about never bringing a weapon into his house. That very act, it seemed, would violate some unspoken trust that he placed in me. All other employees, from the manager on down to the lowliest gardener, were subjected to thorough background checks and drug testing. While I would have no problem passing either (and in fact only consumed two drinks in an average year), the fact that I wasn't even approached said a great deal about the trust that was wordlessly conveyed.

But following that same line of thought, I concluded that it would be far more serious if Saturday morning's newspaper headlines reported that the well known billionaire and his wife had been car-jacked (or worse) in a new Rolls Royce while I was driving. My favorite "carry piece" was a .45 caliber Beretta loaded with hollow point bullets. It fit snugly in a shoulder holster under my left arm and the suit jacket actually covered it perfectly. I arrived at the house ten minutes early and, with Robert gone for the day, Max himself buzzed the gate to let me in. Max also answered the front door himself, and seconds later I was ensconced in a sofa in the office/den. The oldest daughter, Bertha, was upstairs with her mother while her boyfriend Joe was in the den, drink glass in hand, waiting to finish the joke my arrival had interrupted. Max laughed sincerely at the joke's conclusion and then, with a brief glance in my direction, picked up his drink from the desk. During many morning workouts the topic of "too many" the night before had been broached by Max himself but occasionally by Mrs. Lexington.

Did I detect a tiny slur in Max's speech? Perhaps I was mistaken. A couple more jokes from Joe, and I heard footsteps resonating down the spiral staircase. Mrs. Lexington and Bertha, smiling, made a sequined-gowned entrance into the den. Well-rehearsed "wows" emanated from Max and Joe while Joe approached Elizabeth to kiss her cheek. Excusing myself to be the first to the car, I held and closed the doors for the parents and Bertha while Joe sat himself in the front passenger seat.

The Rolls rolled smoothly forward and I managed to get through the front gates without sideswiping the fountain or the stone retaining wall. Calming down now, I mentally went over my route for the tenth time. Only fifteen miles away, the restaurant/banquet hall was also located only a quarter mile from Max's corporate headquarters. As a lifelong resident of the area, I knew exactly where we were going. Max felt compelled nonetheless to bark out the occasional direction or traffic warning. Arriving without incident, I noted with satisfaction that the facility valets hopped to the Rolls four at a time. After some fumbling, Max rolled his window down and explained that his driver would stay with the car. A spot directly outside the main door was cleared, and I backed the Rolls regally into its prime slot.

For the first hour I read a *Time* magazine while latecomers checked out my car. After the tenth, "It's a Goddamn Rolls!" I got hungry and walked across the street. After four more hours, a nap and several cell phone conversations, partygoers began to filter out of the building as running valets retrieved their autos.

Twenty minutes later I decided to check on the boss. Dodging women in gowns and men in tuxedos, I threaded my way through the garland festooned hallway toward the glittering banquet hall. Max was partially blocking the doorway, drink in hand, with an entourage of four women, necklines plunging, laughing and hanging on his every slur. "Oh Max!" mixed with laughter as the billionaire completed his story. Every few moments one of the group would venture a light touch to his arm. Members of the little group would eventually be found and pulled toward the main door by their companions, with one of the latter sometimes pausing to shake Max's hand. They were immediately replaced by other gowned admirers, and Max seldom stood alone. For a brief moment though, he *was* alone, and Elizabeth swooped down from hiding, taking his now empty glass and setting it on a nearby tray. Max, who usually walked with a purposeful (if bowlegged) stride, now zigzagged erratically down the hallway, pausing every ten steps to say hello or good-bye.

After all four were rounded up and bundled into the idling car, a high pitched squeal broke out near the main door. "Max, don't leave without saying good-bye to me!" A drunken lady in fur slapped the window glass with an open palm. Already in drive, I shifted back to park again. Max fumbled again with the switch, gave up, and I rolled down the window with my switch. The strong stench of whatever the lady was drinking blew into the car and mingled with the breath of the other occupants.

"Max!" (piercing now, with the window down). "Oh my gawd, this is a fuckin' Rolls Royce!" She received a sharp prod from her male companion. "Oh, excuse my French! Ha ha ha!" The obnoxious woman was practically crawling in through the open window. "Max, you can't go, I gotta have a ride in this!"

"Mimi, I…" Max, looking dazed but amused, glanced around while I waited for instructions.

"Hi, Elizabeth, oh please Max, I loooove this car, take me just around the lot!"

Who was this woman, and why was Mr. Lexington even waiting this long, I wondered? Then, to my utter shock, Mrs. Lexington, with a roll of her eyes and a nudge to her daughter, said "C'mon Bertha," and swung open her door!

Stepping outside to wait on the sidewalk, Elizabeth and her daughter chatted as though nothing had happened while a drunken Mimi exclaimed, "Are you sure?"

Mimi lurched around the open door and got in. She managed to get the door closed and with a nod from Max, I drove around the parking lot with Mimi squealing in delight as though on a ride at an amusement park. Joe leaned back in his seat, inebriated and reactionless, while Mimi leaned all over Max in a way that seemed far too forward and familiar. We made two rounds of the large parking lot's perimeter, and I stopped the Rolls near the patiently waiting ladies. Mimi got out with high-pitched thank yous and a kiss on Max's cheek. The women got back in with Bertha exclaiming, "Dad, what was that about?"

"You've got me, babe." he replied and after the doors closed again I headed for the house.

On the ride back, I discovered that Joe had a passable singing voice as he and Max switched from Christmas carols to drinking songs. Eventually Joe soloed on a few country tunes while everyone guffawed. Unfortunately, Joe's extensive imbibing at the party hadn't been useful to his memory, and many of the lyrics to his songs were either forgotten or groped for in laughing pauses.

As we pulled through the gates and wound around the drive, I was careful to avoid Joe and Bertha's car parked in the circular drive. Everyone tumbled out to goodnight hugs and kisses as a half-asleep and tipsy Bertha handed a wobbly Joe the car keys from her purse. With a final wave they got in her car and careened off into the night together. Slurring, Max thanked me profusely and sincerely for getting them home safely. I had an awkward moment as he turned to face the long stone steps to his front door, wondering if and how I should help him negotiate them. But Max quickly turned his full attention to making the ascent, with Mrs. Lexington gripping his arm as if she alone had the power to prevent a tumble from beginning. They made it to the top and I jogged to my car on the side and left.

19

DURING LULLS IN workouts I would occasionally ask clients about the most famous person they'd ever met and the circumstances surrounding the encounter. If I turned it into a contest, I usually fared well enough because I'd once met Arnold Schwarzenegger at a bodybuilding show. During one of the many mornings when Max's hangover prevented him from joining the workout, I played the game with Mrs. Lexington. After I posed the question, she looked pensively at the ceiling for a moment.

"Well, I met the Governor, but who hasn't? And I met President Bush *while* he was President. Oh, I guess it would be Pope John Paul." Whereupon Elizabeth sidled over to a cabinet drawer, and after rummaging briefly, pulled out a large envelope containing some 8x10 glossies of herself and the Pope engrossed in conversation. She handed me one triumphantly. I've never really enjoyed that game since.

The weekend following the party was the Governor's Christmas Ball in Lansing, the State Capitol. I agreed to drive the Lexingtons and received a map that Bertha had faxed to her father with a time and date. The formal invitation was in Elizabeth's purse, and the three of us set off on the seventy-some mile drive to the Governor's mansion. The Rolls glided over the roads and as I drew closer, I glanced down at the map to reaffirm our freeway exit. None of the ramp signs matched the map, and I sailed about five miles past the exit. Turning around, I took a different approach. I ramped off this time when I *sensed* that we were close to our destination, but found myself surrounded by dilapidated houses and cockroaches. Driving the state's wealthiest man and his wife around in a delightfully seedy neighborhood, I confessed my puzzlement. "I can't help you Maaaark," said the directionally challenged billionaire in the back seat. *Lost in Lansing, how special,* I thought. As I reached for my cell phone to try to call Natasha and her Mapquest-ready computer, I stopped at a well-lit gas station and decided to humble myself as the hour grew later. Leaving Max and wife locked in their own car, I asked the lady behind the bulletproof glass for help. A nearby patron, dressed in some natty third world attire, offered up that the street I was looking for had been changed to "Martin Luther King Boulevard" some years ago. "Dat map is wrong man," he assured me. Of course it was…. I remembered driving on *that* road, and ten minutes later we were easing past parked limos, Mercedes, Cadillacs and Lincolns, many idling with their drivers half asleep.

At the gate, two plainclothes State Troopers with crackling radios approached the Rolls from either side. Max rolled his window down and said "Max Lexington…sorry fellas, we're running a little late!" Max's trooper looked across at mine and almost in unison, they waved us in. As I drove us around the large circular drive to the main door, I noted the absence of any other cars. The protocol was quite clear…drop the passengers off at the main door and either turn the car over to the valet or try to find a spot out in the street with the others.

"The Governor said he had to get up early so I don't know if he'll still be there or how long we'll be, buddy," Max said as, stiff from the ride, he lumbered out of the back seat. Having just spent the last fourteen years listening to people speak and then reading in between the lines, I summoned up all of my skills and clearly heard, *"See if you can get away with leaving the Rolls right where it is."*

I turned off the headlights as the couple entered the mansion through a huge set of wood paneled doors. Leaving the parking lights on, I backed up about thirty feet and idled. After some more time had passed, I turned on the stereo, leaving the magazine I brought untouched and the car's interior lights off. After five minutes, a plainclothes guard walked around the corner, appearing out of the shadows to notice the purring Rolls. He drew his hand to his mouth and spoke for a full minute on his radio. After apparently receiving his instructions, the man began walking toward my car. Not sure if he'd be able to see into the darkened car, I grabbed my cell phone, opened it and put it to my ear, pretending I was busy. If he was going to challenge me it would be soon, and I'd already decided to force the issue a bit by agreeing to move and then reneging after he left. The fake cell conversation could be anyone...the Boss...the Gov...he'd never know. But the trooper stopped several feet away, stooping slightly in an attempt to peer in. Looking out of the corner of my eye, I was careful not to acknowledge him. The next move was his. He stood up straight...and walked away. I *loved* this car.

A few minutes more and, emboldened, I snapped on an overhead map light and began reading. Ten minutes later, another member of the Governor's security detail returned, spoke briefly into his radio and then disappeared. An hour of reading and actual cell phone calls passed. People began to appear in the windows of an addition off to one side of the house. I could see waitresses darting about with serving trays. I opened the door and strolled, stretching a bit, to the vicinity of the windows. Peering in, I spotted Max and Elizabeth sitting down at a table, just starting on some salads. I knew this gave me at least one hour and possibly two or three. The protein bar I'd brought held little appeal at the moment as my stomach rumbled, and I was doubtful that a dinner invite would be forthcoming from inside anytime soon. I decided that the Rolls had been discussed by the security detail and they had decided to grudgingly tolerate and accept it. It was probably already a familiar part of the driveway (like the Christmas-light-festooned bushes) and would no longer be questioned. I ambled back to the gleaming car and got back in. Headlights now on, I dropped it to drive and went in search of a high protein, low-carb dinner. Four miles away I came across a fish and chicken carryout. Fifteen minutes later I traced my route back to the "Gov's Crib" with dinner in tow. As I neared the gates, I knew another test awaited. If stopped, I would explain that a cellular summons from the boss necessitated my re-entry. No guard stepped out to challenge me. I coasted past, and an hour later partygoers began to filter out. Some waited for their limos to negotiate the driveway, but most made the trek down past the gates and into the street. Max and Elizabeth walked to the Rolls, accompanied by a couple they met inside. The couple ooohed and aaahed as I opened the doors and I received the very first warning sign that my beautiful Rolls and I wouldn't be together forever.

Turning to step in, Max remarked, "Jim, you don't think this is too much, do you?"

Jim replied, "Oh, heck no, Max. You worked hard all these years; you've earned this!" I gave Jim a big smile but resisted the impulse to hug him.

On the ride home we played Christmas music off the selection of CDs that had been stored in the trunk. Several more times, and much to my chagrin, Max questioned aloud the pretentiousness of the Rolls.

"So, Maaark, you really like this car?" Max asked for the thirty-fifth time, as though he had bought it for me and I wasn't appreciative enough.

"This is a beautiful car Mr. Lexington." I replied for the thirty-fifth time.

"It sure has a smooth ride, doesn't it Mark?"

"It just glides, sir," I replied for the twenty-fourth time.

"So you think this one's a keeper?" (As if he gave a rats-glutes about what I thought).

"Do you mean Mrs. Lexington or the car?" I deadpanned. They both laughed. Max asked me to turn down the volume. Soon the wine and dinner took hold, and Max was snoring loudly in the back seat.

But the handwriting was on the wall. Max had 4000 employees.

It is the nature of all employees to feel overworked and underpaid. Many attempts to unionize his 500 truck drivers had been made by the Teamsters locals over the years to no avail. But these attempts often had to be thwarted by Max himself, who regularly addressed driver meetings replete with free dinners and drinks. At these meetings Max would speak personally and "from the heart" about the teamwork and sacrifices that made a great company and the "family" of employees that made him so darn proud. But Max had a growing concern that some "family" members were aware of his $225,000 Rolls after rolling into work in their Ford Escorts and worried that widespread knowledge of his flashy indulgence might open the door for the dreaded "union monster." Max confided in me that he could never allow the despised union to organize any aspect of his company. If it happened anyway, he warned, it would provide the impetus he needed to accept one of the periodic buyout offers thrown at him from Warren Buffett, the multi-billionaire stock investor.

The first time we talked about Warren's buyout offers I was mildly surprised, but not floored. Surprised because Max seemed to enjoy not only the financial trappings of success but the attention and recognition that it brought. At the Legatus (a Catholic fraternity of movers and shakers) meeting, Max was not only welcomed warmly but also had his advice sought openly. Name-dropping to a hostess or manager was a guaranteed entry into any crowded restaurant, receiving their best tables despite having absolutely no reservation. The Grosse Pointe Shores police patrolled past the gated house with such regularity that they resembled the rounds of a private security company. Nor was I surprised that Max would confide in me about the potential of buy-out negotiations occurring. Max had a way, even when we were the sole occupants of a room, of lowering his voice and leaning in to me slightly, as if to share a secret for the first time. But I knew that among his wife, sons, company president, and close friends that talk of the buy-out negotiations was old (and probably frequent) news, as the 70-year-old billionaire hedged and hawed about giving up his empire.

What did surprise me were the details that I got about the famous and all-knowing Warren Buffett's personal life. Max would drop his voice when we were alone and speak in hushed tones of the 69-year-old investor, worth at least 37 billion, and the longtime "arrangement" he had with his mistress. A former French waitress, the mistress lived with Warren in Nebraska, where his offices were. According to Max, Warren's wife resided quite happily in California surrounded by her friends and family. Max was starting to speak to me more often and in more detail of the practicality of this situation. Max was impressed by the arrangement because it prevented Warren's financial empire from being divided in divorce court and squandered.

I was especially surprised when Max spoke *wistfully* of Warren's matrimonial situation, and said it was best for all concerned. I suspected that Max didn't discuss his envy of Mr. Buffett's private affairs with his wife or close Catholic friends. I did find *myself* getting asked more frequently whether I would ever marry again (as though I should be setting an example for a man with his 50th wedding anniversary fast approaching). His question did, however, cause me to consider the radically different paths that he and I had both taken until we met.

20

MAX HAD A relentless business drive and a long and enviable record of achievements. He strongly emphasized the importance of his family and his church in his life. Max and I couldn't have taken more divergent paths to our acquaintanceship if we'd sat back and planned it.

Bartenders and hairdressers are notoriously beset upon with the personal problems of their clientele, and I had become inured to the constant barrage of confidential information whispered to me by my clients every day. But as I continued driving Max around after an evening of drinking, or when the destination was a less desirable area of town, the snippets of discontent began to take on the makings of a torrent. According to Max, his children were spoiled, and he wished he'd made them struggle for success more. His relationship with his oldest son, Larry, had been a series of shouting matches after the newly minted MBA had graduated and tried to touch the reins of the family business. A working truce had developed between the two by the time my employment began, but words that could never be taken back had been exchanged, and Max still needed to vent about it now and again. The second of Max's three sons, Ben, had battled drug and alcohol problems in the past and Max's involvement in his treatments and therapy was now reduced to mere concern as Ben excelled in his management position at the company. Max's youngest son, Nathan, was an officer and TV spokesman for an upscale subsidiary of Max's company, and the billionaire received some solace from the daily phone calls he received from Nathan regarding day-to-day operations. But Nathan had three young children with his wife Lu Ann, and their upbringing was an area of concern for Max. Grandpa's worries in this area weren't relegated to their bedtimes and snacks either. One gloomy day, I was driving Max down Jefferson to an afternoon meeting when he received a frantic call from Nathan. His three-year-old son (and Max's favorite of the twenty grandchildren) had fallen near the fireplace and his pajamas had caught fire. The family managed to put the little guy out quickly, but still looked to the patriarch for medical advice. The rest of the ride, of course, addressed Nathan and Lu Ann's decisions in general, and I wore both my listening and Dr. Spock hats.

The morning workouts that saw Max moving about slowly with a hangover were becoming more frequent. So were the calls from Robert canceling them, leaving Mrs. Lexington and me to work out by ourselves. Elizabeth's workouts would be constantly interrupted by calls from one of her daughters or members of the huge Grosse Pointe social network looking for a spectacular charity venue (i.e. the mansion) or for a "sponsor" (i.e. a handout). Mrs. Lexington and Max received a hundred letters a year asking for money, but the one they cherished most was from a high school senior in Grosse Pointe. Mailed from her home (a $600,000 one) address, the girl explained that all of her best friends were going to Europe for their senior class trip. It would be very educational as well as fun, but this deserving young lady was approximately $3,000 shy of the funds that she would need. As a matter of fact, the entire cost of the trip was about $3,000. Because of the group discount the students received, the $3,000 was actually quite a bargain. Any amount of money that Elizabeth could forward would be quite useful, but if Elizabeth could write a check for the entire $3,000 that would be the most helpful of all. Mrs. Lexington's kindness would be greatly appreciated and the student thoughtfully enclosed a brochure detailing the proposed itinerary. Max and Elizabeth vacillated between framing the letter and hanging it in their kitchen for a good laugh, or writing the young lady back with a nasty reply.

Meanwhile, my driving duties increased steadily. The annual Detroit North American Auto Show is the ultimate see-and-be-seen event in the Metro area with the charity-themed opening night raking in millions at $350 a ticket.

Opening night means bumper-to-bumper limousines vying to get close enough to the main entrance to disgorge their occupants. It means hundreds of Detroit cops concentrated in one area, not only to direct traffic but to keep any opportunistic riff-raff away from the furs, jewelry and thick wallets.

Opening night in January, 2000, found me inching along in a sea of limos in a hideous dark blue Mercedes station wagon packed with Mr. and Mrs. Lexington, Bertha Lexington and Joe and Nathan and Lu Ann. My beloved Rolls had been turned back to the dealer just days ago, a victim of Max Lexington's union paranoia. For day-to-day transportation it had been replaced by a new black BMW 740i. The BMW was a fine, capable automobile, but it wasn't what lured me into driving Max around initially. And driving the silly Mercedes wagon made me want to wear a disguise in case somebody I knew saw me.

After the Charity Preview ended, the plan was to have me pick the family up at the main door, but the police wouldn't let the ridiculous little car into the limo line. I managed to park along a side street within easy walking range of the main doors. Plunging into the slowly exiting crowd, I located Joe, who had a rough idea of the others' location. A visibly intoxicated Max seemed upset at the prospect of walking any distance in the cold to the waiting car, but the others gamely set off. After a minute of walking, a fully champagned Bertha began complaining mightily as she staggered along in the cold. Elizabeth was setting a brisk pace up front after I pointed to the street where the car was stashed. The group started to string out a bit and I elected to stay with the principal (Max) as he tripped along asking "How much farther?" with each step. The uneventful journey ended at the station wagon with Elizabeth and

Lu Ann circling the locked vehicle until I arrived with Max and the keys. With everyone finally in, a police barricade and two policemen prevented us from entering onto the main drag. As I shifted into reverse and mentally prepared a zigzag route down side streets, Max reached his breaking point and yelled, "Stop the car!" The billionaire lurched out and angled toward the surprised officers with his outstretched arm lined up for a handshake. We witnessed a brief introduction and soon the cops were moving the barricade aside to let us pass. I saw a satisfied smile cross Elizabeth's face, but little was made of the police courtesy and soon all of the passengers were singing and laughing their way home as I picked my way up Jefferson through the limos.

During the next week's first workout session Max brought up the subject of my full-time employment.

"Maaark, Elizabeth and I feel as though we have a need for someone like you who can wear a lot of hats. You've been our trainer and our driver for a while now and we're thinking of spending a lot more time in Florida on the Yacht and at the condo." I grew very attentive as I saw where the conversation was going. Max kept pausing to ask me if I loved boating, and when I'd reassure him that I did, he would continue. "Elizabeth likes you, don't you Babe?" He received a nod and a smile from his wife. "I like you and you've been there whenever we've asked."

I hadn't actually worked for any one company for a very long time but I felt at ease with Max and his wife and had grown somewhat fond of them in spite of myself. Having my own Rolls suddenly seemed very unimportant compared to having my own yacht, and the late model Chevy Suburban that came with the Captain's job would get me around Florida just fine. I knew exactly what "wearing many hats" would entail, and I already had the perfect first mate in mind: a pretty, 40-year-old people-pleaser who managed a small office. Michelle loved any kind of boating, was very competent and would provide the attention to detail that I sometimes did not.

"You'll need to get a Captain's license," Max cautioned, "I think it's a two-week course. I'll get Renaud Stacey in Florida to set you up." My heart jumped as the workout ended. I was to meet with Max's operations manager, Daryl Sunkett, in two days and work out the details. "You sure you want this job?" Max inquired.

"I definitely do, Mr. Lexington, I'll have no trouble passing the test for the Captain's license, and I promise you I'll do a fine job."

"Fine," Max extended his hand and we shook on it, "It's a done deal, then!"

I bounced out to my car on cloud nine, visions of yachts at their docks and nonstop sun and waves interspersed with lists of personal arrangements that I'd have to make starting yesterday.

Max Lexington's three yachts were overseen by Daryl Sunkett, an ex-college football star with an engineering degree. Daryl's main role with the fifty-store retail chain was to oversee maintenance and improvements. If a heating and cooling system acted up, the store manger called Daryl. Quotes for parking lot resurfacing, electrical repairs, repainting, re-roofing and window tinting all went through Daryl. When a new office was needed or when ceiling tiles became discolored, Daryl was the man with the plan. Daryl shared a suite of offices with his staff and that of Hal, Max's pear-shaped, "alternatively lifestyled" and perennially depressed chief of store design.

At one time or another, almost everybody has met somebody who, for one reason or another, they've taken an instant disliking to, or met someone who has taken an instant disliking to them. When I walked into Daryl's office, he loathed me instantly.

When I worked at the bar, I would often sit or stand in the entranceway, checking ID's or "running the line" that formed. Once a night or so, for some inexplicable reason, a pot-bellied, spindly-armed, fifty-something-year-old-man would approach me and critically eye me up and down. He then would feel an overwhelming need, as he squinted at my biceps, to launch into a discourse on his stint in the Marines Corp/Special Forces/Army/College Varsity Football team or any other group he thought might impress me. I would usually react with polite interest and if I was bored perhaps even ask a question or two. From this point these out-of-shape older men would break into two types. The first type would regale me with stories of a powerlifter son/buddy/neighbor/brother/gay lover whose arms were much more massive than mine. The second type would "intimidate" me by telling me that in his day, his awesome strength/special training/amazing reflexes enabled him to "chew up" or "tear apart" guys like me. I liked to put my hand on the shoulder of the second type, while smiling, and say, "Well you can't anymore!" He'd either clam up or slink away (probably to "tear apart" somebody a little smaller).

When I appeared in Daryl's office to "interview" for the Yacht Captain position, my heart sank when he stood up to shake hands. Forty-five years old, crew cut and pot-bellied, Daryl's physique was furiously making the transition from burly to fat. I was overwhelmed by a feeling of déjà-vu as the former athlete appraised me in a leisurely fashion. Since Daryl had never met me before, I had brought a photo album depicting various yachts and racing boats that I'd piloted (as a sort of visual resume). But Daryl didn't want to look at pictures or talk much about boating. Daryl's preferred topic of discussion this morning was going to be his treadmill at home and the amount of miles he was putting on it. I sensed my morning being further wasted as Daryl peppered me with questions about his diet. From there we moved on to the many facets of his tiny wife's health regimen and how incredible and devoted to it she was (an interesting twist on the "my buddy's arms are bigger than yours" routine). Operational details of Max Lexington's yacht were never introduced into the discussion, and any hint of the steps we'd take to obtaining my Captain's license were neatly suppressed. Spouting only that, "Mr. Lexington was at the point in life where he deserved and could afford the best," Daryl shuffled me to Hal's office to introduce me to the huge, myocardial infarction imminent designer.

Another unpaid and uncomfortable half-hour passed as Hal rambled about his resolve to lose weight and elicited my thoughts on a source for a new treadmill. I delivered as much pep talk as my plunging spirits allowed, but the thought of Hal walking or running was taxing my imagination to its maximum limits. I left the building knowing that Daryl wasn't going to be my ally in obtaining any sort of Yacht Captain's job.

Ed and Mandy were two of my "in-home" clients. They lived in a large, immaculate yellow brick three-story house in Grosse Pointe Park. Increasingly worried about being overweight and the health problems that seemed to come with it, Ed and Mandy began to piece together an amazing gym in their basement and hired me as their workout guide to maximize its use. Over several years, I've watched Ed turn from fat to burly as he determinedly pushed and pulled his way back into shape. Bearded and initially gruff-looking with short arms and tree trunk legs, Ed will never in this lifetime be mistaken for slender or svelte. Not content with being a fat, middle-aged man looking forward to his first coronary, Ed applied the same bullheadedness that made him a business success and willed himself into losing one hundred pounds of fat while packing back on thirty pounds of muscle. The transformation was gradual but dramatic and today Ed is one of the few men I know who is as strong and powerful as he looks.

Mandy was blond, opinionated, and completely and totally devoted to Ed and wasn't about to be left behind. Her trans-formation, begun at the age of fifty, began slowly and picked up momentum immediately after she left her corporate job. She had spent sixty hours a week working for a billionaire industrialist/ entrepreneur whose initial fame and wealth came from racing cars. Mandy talked of a driven boss who demanded 110 percent from each employee. She also spoke of a leader who would lay out a course of action to an employee and expound on every possible detail, working the underling into an enthusiastic frenzy. The underling would slowly realize that the boss intended to use him as "point man" for this fascinating new plan until his own career soared with the plan's success. Just on the verge of implementing this incredible plan, the boss would then jet off to Europe to propagate other immense deals and inspire other employees, leaving the underling lathered up and ready…but hung out to dry nonetheless.

Three days went by after my meeting with Daryl. I'd heard nothing from Daryl and Max, out of town with Elizabeth, was incommunicado. I expected a phone call after a week or so but knew better than to press the issue, remembering with satisfaction the "done deal" handshake. Two weeks after my meeting with Daryl, I heard from Robert asking if it were possible to be at the house in an hour. I said of course I would be there and after showering, happily bolted to my car for the twenty-five minute ride to the castle. Upon arrival, I learned that Max and Elizabeth were back and just wanted to work out with their trainer so I put that "hat" on instead. I briefly mentioned my meeting with Daryl and Max exclaimed, "That's right, I gotta call Daryl and get him working on things!" He went on, "We've gotta get together with Renaud Stacey in Florida and get you signed up for that Captain's course. I think it's about two weeks. Are you ready for it?"

"Oh yes sir, ready and eager!" I replied.

A week later, Max, Elizabeth and their humble driver were en route to an event at St. Johns Cathedral, a huge complex about thirty miles away. St. Johns was the headquarters of Cardinal Fiat, attorney, confidant of the Pope and benefactor of millions of dollars of Max's charitable donations. The topic turned to the sunny, spring-like weather and I remarked that I'd be getting my boat out soon.

"Hey Maaaark, that reminds me, I've been wanting to call Daryl and work out details about you and the Azimut." Max reached out. "Lemme use your phone for a minute if you would, in fact, if you could dial in a number for…" I dialed the number and Max spoke to Daryl, "Yes, I've got Maaaark in the car with me and he's ready to get down to Florida. I told him we'd set him up in that Captain's school and he'll need time to get familiarized with the boat." Max listened, "Uh, huh, yeah, uh, huh, sure, yeah, well he's crazy nuts about boats. Uh, huh sure…."

A minute went by, and I committed the cardinal sin of interrupting Max when he was on the phone. "Please tell Daryl I already have a place to stay." I received an unusual dirty look from Max, and my heart began to sink as he continued listening to Daryl. Two minutes later Max hung up.

"Daryl says that boat is much trickier to handle than most people realize. I pay him to watch out for me and he says he's just trying to protect me and Mrs. Lexington. He's worried that nobody else can *handle* that boat the way Boomer can!" Max went on, and my sinking hopes rose again. I jumped in and declared that I could handle any boat that had a steering wheel that was attached to something. Max mused aloud. "Of course, at the end of the day, it's my boat and I'll decide who the Captain is going to be. I'll give Renaud a call on Monday and we'll get you some time to get down there and practice. Relieved, I continued driving to the Cathedral and spent my down time on my cell making arrangements for Florida, giving my "in-home" clients notice that they'd need to find another trainer and that I'd be delighted to suggest a capable alternate. One month later. I was still in Michigan. Most of my clients were gone, and I had a new-found understanding of the term "done deal."

The fifty-foot Sea Ray, which Max referred to as his "small boat" was used primarily in the waters of Northern Michigan. After supervising the installation of a new interior in the Detroit area, Daryl decided to take it out for a test spin. It was one year after my unsuccessful interview, but even an unworthy and unqualified boat captain, such as myself, would have been able to direct Daryl around the rocks that guarded a small island about eight miles out in Lake St. Clair. Under Captain Daryl's capable command (I think his first mate's name was Gilligan, but I could be wrong) the ship came to a hull-rending, grinding halt one fine spring day. The Coast Guard rescued Daryl and Salvage Ships Inc. towed the boat to a repair yard for thousands of dollars of work. Mere words cannot paint a portrait of the enormous interest I had when I heard of Daryl's mishap. I fought to suppress daily urges to call and express my sympathy as one snickering local ship's Captain after another related the story to me.

21

WHENEVER I ARRIVED early in the area for my morning appointments, I got in the habit of reading the paper in front of a vacant building in a nearby suburb. A mile away from the beginning of the Pointes, the little building had been several different businesses over the years. A huge "For Lease" sign had sat in the window for many months and I brought this up to Elizabeth during a morning workout. She replied, "Oh, I can't remember what used to be in there but I drive by it all the time because that's the way I prefer to take to the freeway." Her offhand remark turned on a light bulb in my head. I had considered opening a small studio once again in the Pointes, but the high cost of a decent location discouraged me from even scouting one out. This innocuous little building, however, might have some merit if every resident of the rich and mighty Pointes were to eventually drive past it. I decided immediately that a demographic study would be in order. It would have to be precise. It would have to be accurate. It would need to factor in the specific economic situation of every driver that passed in front of the building. While the economic status of each study participant was crucial as an indicator of whether or not they could afford a personal trainer, other profiles were important as well. I needed background about their recreational inclinations, supplemented (ideally) by health aware-ness questionnaires.

After working out with Elizabeth, I grabbed some lunch and returned to the vacant building's parking lot. While eating, I watched as every fourth car seemed to be a Jaguar, Mercedes or BMW. After a half-hour the study was over. This building would do just fine.

A personal training studio would require commitment and dedication and clients would expect it to be open long hours. Warm, sunny days were fast approaching and I knew that my boat would soon be calling out to me, so twenty-five hours a week wasn't going to cut it. I needed a partner. My girlfriend Natasha was not only the strongest woman I knew, she was also an experienced and knowledgeable personal trainer. I called her and told her all about my demographic study. She thought about it for twenty-four hours and agreed. I called the landlord and began negotiations.

Shores Personal Training was ready and open in June, 2000. The clientele increased with little effort on our part as one curious passerby after another inquired. By July we had our first employee helping us work out with twenty clients. Max seemed skeptical but interested whenever he asked about the business' growth and I think he felt "let off the hook" by my new endeavor. The promises to "call Renaud Stacey" had grown few and far between as did the requests to drive for him and Elizabeth. Max referred a next door neighbor's wife to me and I began working out with her at her home in the mornings. She had been a dancer in cabarets when in her twenties and her husband, a man twenty-five years her senior, was known in the Pointes because of the huge international bridge that he owned. Until that point, I never realized that a giant bridge *could* be owned by just one individual. I learned that most of the couple's tremendous wealth, however, came from the trucking fleet that they owned and managed. Whiney and distracted during her workouts, the woman was pleasant enough to talk to until she laughed. Her strange hoots reverberated throughout the tiny workout room in her mansion like a wounded whooping crane taking flight. After several weeks, the phone calls from her maids canceling her workouts for one reason or another grew frustrating, and she quit entirely at about the time I vowed to make myself unavailable for her.

22

O<small>N A COLD</small> morning in late fall, Summer was finishing her tennis lessons with a stretching routine on the near empty courts at Lochmoor. Glancing up at an elevated walkway, she noticed a little troop of three people making their way to the glass-enclosed workout room. An older gray-haired man led the way wearing a long leather driving coat over a tennis shirt. The walkway wall concealed him from the waist down but he appeared to carry his bulk well with a presence and sureness that indicated his familiarity with his location. Following the man, blond head visible and shoulders barely bobbing over the top edge of the wall, was a short, nice-looking woman. Pinpointing a woman's age in the Pointes was difficult due to the city-wide penchant for cosmetic surgery, but the woman appeared to be about 55 or so. Trailing behind the woman, looking over the edge and down below, was another man. He was tanned and looked to be about 40 years old. His unzipped jacket revealed the T-shirted chest of a bodybuilder. Six feet tall, with a blonde mustache and short hair, the man squinted slightly as he looked around, giving Summer the impression that this was his first visit to Lochmoor.

As the three neared an outside reception table, the younger man positioned himself near the glass doorway. After a wave and a smile from the girl at the table, the man swung the glass door open and the older couple entered first. Fifteen minutes later, as Summer went to the locker room, she looked up again to watch the younger man standing near the older one while taking notes on some half-page pieces of cardboard. The gray-haired man was pulling repeatedly on a chrome bar affixed to an exercise machine.

The next time Summer noticed the gray-haired man he was dressed in white shirt and shorts and playing in a foursome on the tennis court adjoining hers. It had been an unusually rainy spring and the indoor courts were still very popular. The man was wearing a huge set of clear, protective eye goggles held in place by a black elastic strap around his head. The other three men in his group seemed to be about his age, evenly matched and equally intense. Concentrating on the ball as if in the semi-finals at Wimbledon, each of the four grunted and strained to reach every ball hit their way. The years of volley experience were apparent in all as their expensive racquets twisted and swooped as though merely extensions of the men's tanned, wrinkled arms.

Sweat poured from the head and brow of the gray-haired man and Summer observed that with his broad shoulders and wide stance, he appeared to be a human backboard, unerringly and automatically returning any balls hit his way. The gray-haired man's goggles didn't give him the bug-like appearance Summer had laughed about when seeing them on other players. Instead, they made the man seem more athletic…even a little mysterious.

Summer was in her car now. Thoughts of tennis faded into the background as she contemplated the upcoming weekend with a mild feeling of dread. A huge weekend family get-together, marking Chuck's mother's 75th birthday, was on the calendar beginning Saturday morning. The two-day affair was to be punctuated by relatives from five different states flying in at intervals all day Saturday. On the surface, the uncles, aunts and cousins were cordial and almost polite. But the obvious reluctance of any one of them—save for the female teenage cousins or nieces—to engage in any type of in-depth conversation nagged at Summer. It was probably her imagination, but when meals were served, the seats on either side of Chuck were snatched up by animated relatives, forcing Chuck's wife to find an empty chair at the "children's table." While

Chuck had kept his word, engineering and then enforcing an uneasy cease-fire for years, his iron will still couldn't change his headstrong, clannish Greek family's inner thoughts. Even the adoration and shared intimate thoughts of the teenagers gradually turned to stilted, arms-length politeness towards Summer as they matured into the adult ranks.

Her son Evan's absence from this weekend's celebration wasn't going to make Summer any closer to the clan (or was it Klan?) either. He had begged her forgiveness, but his girlfriend's sister was getting married and his attendance was critical to them. Summer had caved in to the "Please Mom, you know I love yous," and didn't raise many objections. Chuck and Summer's many attempts, replete with the best medical techniques, to have a child of their own had been to no avail. The doctors universally agreed that Chuck's procreative contributions were inadequate, but Summer knew that the whispers of the Klan said otherwise. The whispers said that Summer's unconventional past had left her barren, and it was grossly unfair that such a fine man was to be denied an heir that was genetically his!

With Evan elsewhere this weekend, Summer was slated for the first taste of what the rest of her life would be like at these affairs. She would be alone and politely ostracized.

Summer didn't notice the gray-haired man at her tennis club again until the following winter when the white-frocked and clear-goggled human backboard again appeared in the court adjacent hers. Politely pausing after her game ended to watch the older men, she heard the man's partner say, "Nice shot Max!"

A remark to her tennis partner, "Max, that was my uncle's name," drew the offhand reply, "Oh, that's Max Lexington…You know, the chain of stores…the castle on Lakeshore…the cancer wing at the hospital!"

Summer was mildly intrigued. Her circle had never overlapped with his in the Pointes and, engrossed in her own little world, she had never had occasion to put a face to the famous name. She would have been far more likely to recognize his youngest son, Nathan, in public from all of the TV commercials for the stores. *He* was practically a local celebrity and with his dark hair and sincere eyes and…well she wouldn't kick him out of bed if her situation was different!

Summer knew when men were watching her…all men…and the next few months became a little game to see if the billionaire watched her like all the rest. The rules were simple. When she arrived at the courts, she'd stand in the entranceway and gather up her ponytail while holding her racket between her knees. Subtly, and with apparent disinterest, she would check all ten courts for any foursomes of white togged old men. If any courts matched her search criteria, she would scrutinize them carefully, looking for goggled players. A goggled competitor meant no more looking until she passed that court. While approaching, she could chat animatedly with her partner, check the tape on her racquet handle or chat distractedly on her cell phone, but she could never look over! As her peripheral vision told her she was passing the court, a brief pause to adjust a shoelace or sock with a tanned leg flexing as she raised her heel would be acceptable, but any acknowledgment of the foursome would not! If the mornings schedule merely called for a tennis lesson, she would make the walk with the pro, flashing smiles and acting as though his every word was gospel.

As Summer passed the men's court, she'd wait until her senses indicated a pause in the action. A tingle at the back of her head always told her when she was being stared at. Wait for the tingle, then drop something (a wristband, a ponytail holder, anything), stoop, turn on the way up and look! Sometimes two of the men were looking, sometimes three, and once all four! But she always caught Max staring, six times in all during the following fall and winter; four times after the first day of spring. She became bolder, flashing that magnetic, knowing smile directly at him when she caught him now, watching his brow furrow slightly as he wondered if they'd met. Still, the time to say hello didn't seem quite right until the day in early April when not introducing herself would have been almost impossible. His foursome had started after hers, but their assigned courts were numbers eight and nine. While his group volleyed back and forth to warm up, a ball strayed to her feet during a break on her court. Quickly picking it up, she trotted it over to Max, flipping it to him with a smile as she said, "Hello, Mr. Lexington, I'm Summer Sevalas."

"Nice to meet you, Summer," as he stepped forward to shake her smooth, soft hand with a damp yet firm, practiced grip. "Call me Max. I've seen you here before."

With polite good-byes at the end of Max's match, Summer watched quizzically as he packed his racquet and goggles into his bag and zipped it up.

He seemed nice, she thought. Wonder if he's looking for marketing help for his stores? After all, she had experience working for the beer distributor. Of course, after giving her the check for $200,000, Mot Montgomery might balk a bit at giving her a letter of recommendation as well. That *was* in the past though, and for sure Mot must have gotten over it by now. No time to worry about it, Summer thought, because she had a busy two days coming up. From tennis she was headed straight to her nail appointment, and from there she would have to rush twenty miles to have her eyebrows waxed. Tomorrow was booked solid with lunch at Somerset Mall and an all-afternoon hair appointment. She'd be lucky to have time to breathe! Summer unlocked her Mercedes doors with the remote and tossed her tennis bags into the back seat. As she looked up she spied Max two rows away getting into a platinum S500 Mercedes.

On a Thursday morning, exactly one week after their first formal introduction, Summer arrived slightly late for her tennis lesson. She spotted Max immediately and when within shouting distance felt quite comfortable in calling out, "Hi Max, how are you sweetie?" Summer used the word "sweetie" lavishly on all of her friends, but not all of her friends were 69-year-old married pillars of the community. As the other three men on Max's court raised their shaggy eyebrows in unison, he merely nodded his head and smiled. A questioning look from his doubles partner received a shrug and a smiling shake of his head in return. Their match over, the men's eyebrows again jumped and twitched as Summer sidled over to where Max was packing up.

"Nice to see you again," she lightly touched his arm as the men's looks became stares. "If you wouldn't mind, I have a question that I'd like to ask you?"

"Not at all," he replied. She had his complete attention.

"I saw you with a personal trainer here once, and I was wondering if he works with other people or just you?"

"My gosh, Summer that was over a year ago! We were having our gym at the house remodeled! I can't believe you remember us coming here then!"

"Of course I do!" she replied. "Anyway, is he employed exclusively by you? I've got a lot of equipment in the basement, but I don't use it because I don't have anybody to work with me." Summer conveniently left out the fact that Chuck had offered often.

"Well, he used to go to peoples' houses and he still comes to ours but now he has a gym about two miles from me. His name is Mark. Would you like his phone number? I have it in the car. He drives for Mrs. Lexington and me so I keep it on the car phone's memory."

"That would be great, let me set up my next lesson and I'll walk out with you and get it."

Max watched as Summer pranced over to her waiting instructor to retrieve her racquet and make another appointment. Wow, he thought, if she lost five or ten she'd be an A-plus.

As the pair walked out to his car, chatting, Max began to get a very exciting, yet comfortable feeling. Maybe it was the fact that she never looked away when talking to him. Or, perhaps it was her animated gestures with her long fingers sweeping through the air. Every time she asked a question, he felt as though his was the only advice she would ever seek for an answer to her query. She would raise her voice an octave when she asked a question, and then lower it to emphasize a point or offer an opinion, and her manner was most engaging. Max was beginning to put his finger on it.

This woman had a way of talking to him that made him feel as though he were the only man on the planet, or at least the only man that she cared to confide in.

But while she talked and gave the impression that *he* was the only one that mattered, he found himself wanting to know more about her. Where did she live? Did she come from the Pointes? Never one to ignore a pretty woman, how come he hadn't noticed her a year ago? How old was she? She sounded well informed and worldly, yet she appeared to be only in her early thirties. Pausing for a moment to greet a friend passing in the parking lot, Max noticed that Summer went to his car and waited, no doubt in *her* mind which one was his. Max sat in his car and brought the trainer's number up, writing it on a scrap of newspaper and handing it over to sincere thank yous.

Summer skipped to her own Mercedes and got in. She'd find out more about this trainer when she called. Maybe he had a diet for her that wouldn't leave her hungry or faint.

Arriving home and appraising herself in a full-length mirror, Summer stared critically. Her friends all told her how hot she was, and Chuck seemed happy, but the weight had crept up in the last ten years, and she needed to start working it off. Outfits that fit fine five years ago were tight now. Not that she minded buying new stuff as often as necessary, and it wasn't that a lot of the extra pounds hadn't gone to her chest, but the size twelves were starting to feel better than the size tens. The perfect legs she had been so proud of were much heavier above the knees although the skin was still smooth and cellulite-free. Did Max mention that Mark was his driver too? He seemed to be doing fine without the benefit of a driver as he pulled out of the lot.

23

IF MAX HAD a public figure that he not only considered his peer but his confidant, it was Cardinal Fiat, the spiritual leader of every Catholic in the Detroit area. The Cardinal was only seven months younger than Max and possessed a keen legal mind as well as a strong spiritual faith. The Cardinal's sumptuous new living quarters were part of a Detroit suburb's palatial grounds that included an ornately redone cathedral, banquet halls and extensive offices all set on a rolling golf course partially bisected by nature trails. Max was awed by the fact that his friend, the Cardinal, held a law degree as well.

Cardinal Fiat had actually obtained a civil law degree and passed a state bar while in his mid-thirties. His Eminence was licensed to practice law as an attorney. Max often mentioned the regular calls that his Cardinal buddy received from the Pope himself requesting advice on the legal ramifications of a proposed or contemplated policy or decree.

Max would also mention that even the spiritual leader of all of the area's Catholics (and a church official with a direct hotline to the Pope) needed to kick back once in a while.

Max was at his subtle, boasting best when he talked about soaring up to his northern Michigan retreat in his jet with his holy pal for a few days of R&R together. Golfing at exclusive resorts, dining at the finest northern Michigan restaurants, and cruising

sunlit lake waters in Max's yacht were relaxing and cathartic for
His Eminence. Max was always quick to point out how much he
enjoyed doing it for the Cardinal. But Max also couldn't resist
musing aloud about the Cardinal's nightly brandy intake as the
two settled down after a day of play together. It almost seemed as
though Max's prodigious intake of Crown Royals on the rocks
was somehow justified by his spiritual and admired drinking
partner.

Many questions coursed through my mind but went unasked
whenever Max brought up details of these "getaways." Did the
drinking start with a little wine at lunch? Who drove back from
dinner and how much was normally consumed? Did His Eminence
notice the moment that Max started to slur...and call a halt to the
procession of nightcaps? I suspected that he did, which would
explain the early bedtimes that Max mentioned. But most of all,
did Max use the times they had alone together as opportunities to
confess his sins (followed by his friend's absolutions), or was it a
series of "attaboys" for Max's financial donations and an agenda
of planning for future contributions and good works? In other
words, were the billionaire and his ecclesiastical pal close because
they shared common views and goals or did the holy man feign
friendship in order to keep the checks flying out of the check book
and in his direction? And was Max, innately suspicious of any
beneficiary of his wealth, wondering if the "friendship" was based
on donations, with His Eminence more than adept enough to make
it seem otherwise?

There could be little doubt that the rich man's special affiliation
with the church through one of its leaders gave a meteoric boost to
Max and Elizabeth's social standing among Grosse Pointe
Catholics. But in case this close, private affiliation with Cardinal
Fiat wasn't enough, the couple had an ace in the hole. Over the
years, a local Catholic school and church had benefited mightily
not only from the tuition of the eight children's continuous
attendance, but from huge side offerings as well. It was common
knowledge that the entire construction bill for a separate, serenity

filled little chapel attached to the main church had been footed by the generous patriarch and his wife. The Bible teaches that it is easier for a camel to pass through the eye of a needle than it is for a rich man to enter heaven. But Max Lexington was never afraid of a little competition. In fact, he welcomed and reveled in it. He was inwardly confident that on the day of his death, in some exotic land, a camel would be getting shoved through the eye of a needle as well.

The same naysayers who wouldn't have thought the self-taught sales and marketing genius had enough business savvy to build a retail empire would also deny that his purchase of a place in heaven was possible, but Max relished the chance to prove them wrong. The Cardinal, using a portion of his friend's generosity with an eye on building not only a luxurious retirement setting for himself, but a truly inspirational place of worship and celebration for his flock, did nothing to dissuade the billionaire from meeting this challenge.

Residing with the Cardinal in these sumptuous living quarters was his right-hand man, Father Pete. Father Pete was a devoted priest in his mid 30s. God had called on Father Pete to serve with Cardinal Fiat several years ago, and the young man had proved his trustworthiness and efficiency from day one. Personal secretary, personal shopper, driver, keeper of the schedule, event organizer and overseer were just a few of Father Pete's job titles.

Weight training with his humble trainer on a $6,500 leg press machine had helped Max Lexington's tennis-ravaged knees recover some of their strength and spring. After a day of golf with the Cardinal, Max observed that the holy man was walking gingerly on a pair of arthritic knees. Braces on each did little to alleviate the pain. Max decided that a personal trainer could repair both knees and diminish the discomfort of a day of golf, his good friend's only recreational outlet. My distrust of the billionaire was growing every month, and I did *not* want to commit to the process of strengthening his holy friend's knees.

Two weeks prior to Max's new brainstorm, we had finished

filling his exercise room with $23,000 worth of brand new, state-of-the-art exercise equipment. Robert and I, struggling mightily, had managed to move a huge, old unit (a 3/4 ton multi-workout station affair) to the wide, adjoining hallway where it sat awaiting a new home. Substantial disassembly of the weight stacks, pulleys, cables, rods and framework would be required before the monstrous machine could be moved. Purchased locally, it had been assembled inside the house several years ago in eight hours by a two-man service team sent out by the exercise store. Max debated whether the machine would be shipped to his house up north, sold outright, or given to an aspiring exercise fiend. His oldest son, Larry, soon solved the dilemma by claiming the machine for his new house on the lake. Over the years, I had acquired oodles of experience in disassembling, transporting and reassembling exercise machines. I relied on my automotive mechanical background to take apart a machine and transport it in the biggest sections feasible to make the reassembly process quicker. I also found that the assembly instructions were usually misplaced long ago, and the myriad of nuts, bolts, washers and pulleys could be easily switched if removed. I offered my expertise to Max, and one sweltering June day, I was crouched in the coolness of the hallway with a toolbox. Taking only short breaks, I had the machine sections lying on the floor and ready to go in just under two hours. Feeling quite satisfied, I found Robert and asked to borrow a cargo van that was kept at the house. To my delight, Robert offered to help and, although ignorant of anything mechanical, he was very useful in dollying out the larger sections and the pounds of weight plates. Robert's value was even more appreciated when we arrived at Larry's house eight miles away in Grosse Pointe Park. The van was sans air conditioning, and we backed into the driveway of Larry's huge house sweating profusely in the noontime sun. Larry's wife let us in and showed us the winding staircase to the basement and the room that the machine was to reside in. Twisting and grunting on every step as we maneuvered the heavy parts down a narrow stairwell, Robert and I straightened up after an hour and surveyed the mass of parts sprawled on the floor. Slapping the back of my shoulder he declared "good luck!" and left me with my car and toolbox as he sped off in the cargo van. Larry's wife, ever the gracious hostess, stayed upstairs and ignored me as I went about the tedious business of reassembling the machine. Fortunately, I was able to find a basement washtub and suck some water out of the faucet before my severely dehydrated condition became fatal. Two hours later, I adjusted and tested the machine and found that each station still functioned perfectly.

As the hot water of my shower began to rinse off the grease and sweat, I contemplated a fair charge for my labor. Two servicemen for the day would likely bill $600 to $800. A bill for $400 would reflect substantial savings for the task. Billed hourly, my regular in-home rate would reflect a total of $375. I decided on the latter, so that when asked I could explain why. But the next day, as we worked out, I wasn't asked. An observation was made by Max, "Oh, you boys got that machine out of here, good!" The words, "So what do I owe you?" never left his lips either. Larry, in spite of his CEO salary and yearly $250,000 trust fund checks, didn't burn up my phone lines with thank yous or payment offers.

I was born at night but I wasn't born last night, I thought, when Max asked me to contact Father Pete. The billionaire's plan was to send his trainer over and purchase workout equipment for the Cardinal's knees as needed. Thoughts of injuring His Eminence's tender knee joints further and being immediately subjected to hell fire and brimstone (intermingled with the surety of little or no financial gain) made the phone call impossible for me to make. Max broached the subject twice more, and twice more I agreed to get right on it. And at least twice more I asked Max if Larry was having any problems with his free workout machine. He wasn't.

Max soon recommended another social acquaintance and neighbor whom he was sure would benefit mightily from my services. Ron Weevil, the "Trailer Park King," and his wife seemed easygoing, affable and open, but my workouts with them felt awkward when their probing or seemingly innocuous questions began to sound like "Judgement Day at Nuremburg." I always found it curious that a man who "dug his way up Jefferson Avenue, one shovelful at a time" was so quick and so obvious about passing sentence on others. Why was I so quick to divorce my first wife (a brain dead alcoholic who looked good years ago on the back of a foolish young man's motorcycle as long as she didn't speak)? Why did I buy such a loud, obnoxious boat (years of watching "Miami Vice" made the purchase eventually inevitable)? Why didn't I wear tennis shoes at the gym (Arnold never did in the book "Pumping Iron")? No answer was good enough for these and two dozen other far more personal questions. In just six workout sessions with the King and his Queen I learned a valuable lesson about the Pointes. When a self-made man has decided to appoint himself prosecutor, judge and jury, even Johnnie Cochran and the "dream team" could never win an acquittal after the "servant" is accused of being unworthy.

Ron kept his 118-foot Italian made yacht on the "back wall" of the Grosse Pointe Yacht Club. He had purchased it for seven million dollars and his wife had decorated it lavishly with art and fine furniture. A visitor to the Yacht Club would have his attention grabbed immediately by the huge boat upon rounding the corner of the main building. But first, a visitor had to pass muster at the front entrance.

Just inside the tall-hedged entrance of the Yacht Club is the state-of-the-art gatehouse. Outwardly finished in earthy tones, the inside was filled with the usual TV monitors, phones and two-way radios. This gatehouse, even though the gates were usually in the "open" position during the day, was staffed by not one, but two sport-jacketed guards. While they acted friendly enough when I drove past them in a newer car, I received a much closer scrutinization whenever I pulled up in my 1993 cargo van. I frequently observed that a Mercedes or BMW required little more than a smile and friendly gesture from the driver to get waved on in. I had never actually observed a guard to leave this gatehouse and attempt any kind of rounds or patrol around the Yacht Club's acreage. I guessed that the only reason that two were assigned to this post was in case one of the old buzzards keeled over with a coronary. If this tragedy occurred, the plan might then dictate the remaining guy to call 911 and continue greeting and waving to the Mercedes and BMWs.

After the gatehouse, the long, straight, hedge-lined drive eventually ended in a generously wide, valet serviced semicircle in front of the main complex. Tall, stone-facaded and quite impressive, the building oozed history. Thousands of past parties and receptions, charity balls and fundraisers, mayoral and senatorial appearances, debutante affairs and victory and thank you speeches echoed throughout the halls once inside.

In back of this historical monolith was the requisite pool and patio and to the south was the harbormaster's tower. Surrounding the building on the south and east were the wells of the members. With a rumored waiting list of ten years (more for some, far less for others), each boat well was provided with electrical power and a fresh water hook-up. A special section at the southwestern-most edge of the marina contained thirty or so wells capable of accommodating boats of sixty to eighty feet in length. Laid out like incredible, expensive ocean-going condos, many of these yachts' owners employed full-time captains and first mates to oversee the constant maintenance required, both mechanical and esthetic. With staterooms and other accoutrements to rival any five-star hotel, a phone call from the owner could result in the ship being ready to go in under and hour for a half-hour jaunt, or an extended trip of several weeks.

24

I DROVE MAX (and often Elizabeth) to meetings of a group of Catholic millionaires called Legatus. In spite of his poor sense of direction, Max liked to back seat drive whenever we drove to the sometimes obscure locations. A rapid lane change four cars ahead of me might prompt a "Watch it! Waaaatch it!" Second-hand directions obtained by phone from Bertha were relayed to me before we began driving, and they often interrupted my final review of the map I had already printed out in the morning from my computer. The ride home was usually a different story when Max was tipsy from too much wine. Elizabeth, always seated behind me, was too short to see where we were going and thankfully never contributed to my travel plan. Ever mindful of how important my cargo was to so many people, I always checked the tires prior to a trip and brought a gun in case of late night tire failure or an unlikely mechanical breakdown. We never discussed my "packin' heat" in any way, but I assumed it was on a "don't ask, don't tell" basis. Three years before I met Max and Elizabeth, a fired house employee stopped taking his medication, loaded his gun and set off for Max's mansion. Upon his arrival he prepped the house's cargo van with carpet and blankets for two bodies. He cut the mansion's phone lines just after a warning call came in from his girlfriend to the Lexingtons. He missed a secret line, however. The police arrived as he prepared to enter the house, search out his prey, and complete a bloody mission. The Grosse Pointe Shores police, hemmed into a very small community, have a response time of about fifteen seconds (which also includes throwing down their donuts and spilling out their coffee). Officers from the adjoining Pointes responded as well, and soon the grounds were awash in frantic cops with guns drawn. A short chase ensued and the psycho was captured alive. During my tenure, I was surprised that Max and Elizabeth even opened the letters of remorse that the aspiring killer wrote from his prison cell. More chilling yet was the fact that the ex-employee had also taken the time during his preparatory phase to lower the huge flag on the backyard flagpole. He placed *it* in the cargo van as well in case the blankets alone proved inadequate for wrapping up the bodies.

I always found it curious that such a fabulously wealthy and well known couple didn't have more trained personal security people surrounding them. Even I knew that a former bouncer who may or may not have a firearm handy wasn't enough. I remained extra vigilant at night or whenever we were in an undesirable area, ready to hustle my charges out of harm's way if I had to. Strangely enough, I felt even more responsibility when late one night they matter-of-factly entrusted me with the keypad code at the front gate entrance. A little thing for sure, but I knew that few others had it.

Occasionally held at country clubs or church reception halls after a service, the Legatus meetings always featured a keynote speaker. Often a Bishop spoke, and once or twice a year it was the Cardinal himself. As I waited in the lot for my passengers, I would note a preponderance of high-end Mercedes and Jaguar models with their drivers patiently reading or napping. If I were the Cardinal and looking for donations, I thought, I'd never miss a meeting of this crowd, and, in fact, might consider hiring a speechwriter and a band to pep things up.

One rainy night, after puzzling out the location of an especially well hidden mansion, I found an excellent after-dinner location in the circular driveway that enabled me to face the front door. Max and Elizabeth were still inside and a peek in a window a minute earlier told me that they would not be coming out soon. Any attendees without a driver had valeted their cars. As some of the rich and faithful meandered out, the valets were running to get their rides. A tall bespectacled man in an impeccable suit walked out the front door, looked around the driveway and waved to me. I recognized him almost immediately as Shane Bryant, the Michigan Pizza King. Growing up as a dirt poor orphan and raised by nuns, Shane started his first little pizza carry-out in his teens and had hundreds of them before the age of thirty. Max used to marvel that Shane's selling price was one billion dollars in cash and any lower offers were rejected. I also appreciated a man who insisted on nice round numbers, but the man had just taken ten steps toward my car and was now crouching and waving, trying to catch my eye. I waved back to acknowledge his presence and rolled down the window of the S500 Mercedes. Visibly upset that I didn't start the car and pick him up, the Pizza Potentate began to run toward me, and it looked as though I was about to experience an attempted car-jacking from a billionaire. A few feet short of the car Shane stopped, realized he'd never seen me before, and dashed off to wave at another Mercedes. I though about asking for a "two-for-one" coupon but quickly had second thoughts that maybe the moment wasn't appropriate.

By January of 1991, Max had been trying to sell his three-year-old Italian yacht, a beautiful but breakdown-prone 82-footer, for several months. Elizabeth was increasingly loathe to be away from her grown children, numerous grandchildren and ailing mother for any period of time, and the Florida penthouse and boat were receiving very little use. One item that was getting more use, however, was my cell phone as Max began to upset my schedule at the gym with more frequent phone calls asking me to drive. His drinking, always limited to after work, had increased to the point where afternoon meetings that started with "a couple" ended at 5 p.m. with a blitzed billionaire still aware enough to know that driving home was a bad idea. Elizabeth confided in me during Maxless workouts that there were many times, though, that Max drove home from work when he shouldn't have. Even Max himself began to make more frequent mention of his increased intake when he *did* manage to make a pre-scheduled workout. The stressful and always ongoing debate about whether to sell out to Warren Buffet had gotten to the point of protracted negotiations and exchanges of accountants' profit statements of the closely held corporation. The minutiae of the deal apparently also required the consumption of a lot of booze. Max would often go to bed at night ready to sell, only to wake up in the morning refusing to sign key papers or return phone calls. He not only confided in me, but in almost anyone that he came in contact with; his constant vacillation had almost everyone else reaching for a liquor bottle as well.

Max asked me weekly if I drank, and I once said that unfortunately, no, I did not. Puzzled, Max asked "unfortunately?"

I replied with the old adage of "Yes, unfortunately, because when I wake up in the morning, I already know that I feel as good as I'm going to feel all day. I *know* it won't improve. But when you wake up, Mr. Lexington, you're going to feel better and better as the day continues!"

Max laughed long and hard at my twist and recited it many, many times in the next year, telling anyone within earshot and giving me credit for it each time. Of course, the first five times he would have to ask, "Maaaaark, how does that go again…that part about you being sad because you felt good all day?" His excessive drinking was beginning to so consume his thoughts that it was a constant topic, and soon Elizabeth was asking me in a quiet voice if there was anything else that I could say or advise that would encourage her husband to taper off or get help. I replied that many people with far more experience than I had studied excessive drinking and its roots, but that I would contribute the best I could.

My main concern at the time was that Max didn't receive a DUI that would surely make the papers and result in mountains of negative publicity. Elizabeth vowed to call me whenever a phone conversation made her suspect impending disaster, and I promised to drop what I was doing and pick him up. I knew that part of Max's problem was the uncertainty about what the still-energetic 70-year-old was going to do with the rest of his life if he sold his business. He was also becoming obsessed with wondering about the amount of "good years" that he had left. Elizabeth's increasing reluctance to participate in many trips involving leisure activities of more than two or three hours was also an overwhelming source of consternation to Max. I knew this because he was starting to bare his soul to me more often when we were alone. His offspring's lack of personal ambition stuck in the craw of the hyper-ambitious man (a by-product of their trust fund payments, no doubt) and Max wondered if he'd made the right decision in providing for them for life. But his waning relationship with his wife concerned him the most. Sometimes, out of the blue, Max would say, "Maaaark, she's got everything she needs right here. She's got her daughters, her church, her work at the school, her work at the hospital. Every time one of the grandkids has a problem or a crisis the daughters call Elizabeth for advice and she loves it! She just loves being involved! Her life is so full with everything that she has no time for anything else!" Max went on as I began to think about how much a good psychologist would charge for these sessions. "And even though her mother is living with one of her sisters it's still pretty close by and I know Elizabeth wants to be near here when she's not doing that well. I said Elizabeth for *God sakes* we'll get a full time nurse…"

Over time, it gradually dawned on me that Max's vast wealth gave him impressive leverage in every aspect of his life. His fifty stores gave him tremendous bargaining power with manufacturers. Truck makers fought for the right to supply his delivery fleet with new vehicles. Businessmen approached him with new propositions weekly, knowing that an affiliation with the famous man would guarantee their idea's success. Even tree pruning services sent emissaries running to the mansion to bid on pruning contracts for the one hundred trees that graced the grounds. And now, Max was getting a bargain on his psychologist; he was paying a personal trainer's rate and getting house calls from an analyst at no extra charge. There *was* a small drawback with Max's money-saving idea, however. His new psychologist was not licensed to practice. His new psychologist did not have a degree in psychology. The man who listened and helped search for answers had only taken one psyche course in college, and, other than remembering a few snippets about Dr. Alfred Kinsey and some research he did on homosexuals (which Max definitely was *not*!), didn't recall a thing. His new analyst *did* have *some* previous hands-on experience with alcoholics. Ten years prior, I used to toss them out of a bar after their involvement in an altercation and gleefully count the bounces as they tumbled down the concrete steps to the street.

Because Max's new analyst had only consumed about forty drinks in his entire life, he was completely flabbergasted when somebody claimed they couldn't just stop. I'd had some limited success in my gyms in the past when clients with drinking problems began to make progress with their workouts. They'd find that a hangover from the night before wasn't conducive to an intense and energetic workout that day. They would often use the workout as a punishment for their excesses of the previous night and vow not to do it again. I was fully aware that Max was employing this technique. He would make an appointment a day or two in advance and then will himself to keep it. He would trudge though the workout in spite of the hum and pressure in his head and the 70-year-old body that just wanted to rest. As Max and Elizabeth's cries for help grew louder, I tried another tactic. Max was overtly concerned about the steadily increasing numbers at the morning weigh-ins. His expensive suits could only hide his gains up to a certain point, and his long-term health indicators were beginning to spiral downwards.

Once a week, Max would ask, "Maaark, how do the Crown Royals affect my weight again?"

I'd reply, "We store fat in various places on the body until we have an extraordinary energy demand, and then the body begins to burn fat for energy. But a controlled study has found that too much alcohol can suppress an enzyme in the liver that's needed to burn fat in men. Once the excess consumption stops, the enzyme levels rise again and fat burning, and thus weight loss, can resume."

I was required to recite this often and add any details that I could remember and inevitably would be asked, "Maaark, you don't drink at all do you?"

I'd again say, "No, unfortunately I don't…" until the cycle had completed itself still another time. For a period of time, I remained hopeful that Max's concern about his weight and health might motivate him to cut back on his alcohol consumption, but my naivete was glaringly evident when Max's drinking continued to increase.

25

W ITH A FEW months rent at my new gym paid in advance,
and with only about sixty percent of the planned equipment
in and assembled, I felt no pressing need to advertise. I would sit
at the desk reading as I waited for the occasional drive-by inquiry
to call or wander in. One evening as the twilight deepened, I sat at
the desk with my feet up reading a *Time* magazine and looking
quite worldly. I'd actually done five or six workouts that day at
our slowly growing business and was beginning to debate the merits
of leaving a little early. Suddenly, a car's headlights caught my
eye in the parking lot outside the glass front doors. A man got out
and walked towards the building. He swung the door open, and I
tried to maintain an exterior calm and prevent my jaw from dropping
on the outside. If Dustin Hoffman had a twin, it was the man
standing in front of me right then and there! Not the recent Dustin
Hoffman perhaps, but the actor as he looked in his mid-forties or
as he appeared in the movie "Rainman."

The uncanny resemblance became even more real when the
man spoke. I almost jumped when the man introduced himself as
Bob because he was using Dustin's voice! The voice sounded so
much like the movie star's that I began to look around for an
entourage or a camera crew or any indication of a prank. But as
Bob sat and talked about his boxing career and his desire to get
back into shape, I looked down to where his hands rested on the

desk. With slightly bent fingers and knuckles enlarged from years of pounding heavy bags and foes alike, Bob's hands *looked* like a boxers and *not* an actor's. Bob apparently sensed that I had nowhere to go and he began sharing sizable portions of his life story. I spoke little and soon learned of his failed marriages, his battles with alcohol and drugs, his bankrupt produce delivery business and his troubles with the IRS. He confessed to being very vain and concerned about women still finding him attractive. I didn't say he wasn't (he would have been even better looking if his nose were still on straight) but told him that I worked out for longevity first and vanity second.

I sort of saw it coming when Bob started talking about his church and how his life had been turned around by God and faith. He also talked about making plant manager at his new job at a bottle recycling plant after only three years. It sounded to me like his sixty-hour work weeks and willingness to learn Spanish, when other management prospects wouldn't, had more to do with it than his church did. Bob eventually signed up and when he finally stood up, he pumped my hand enthusiastically thanked me profusely for listening and extended repeated invitations to me to visit his church. I would have been surprised if his departure had *not* included an invitation to pray. When he *did* offer, I said that I'd think about it.

Bob attended the gym three to five times per week and made rapid gains as his workouts intensified. His shadow boxing in between sets fascinated many clients and eventually one of our female trainers. Bob and Maura began dating, and I'd like to take a moment to crow about how happily married they are (but I can't because they're not). I later pressed Bob into service as a fill-in trainer for busy times at the gym, and several of my female clients seemed to thoroughly enjoy working out with Dustin Hoffman's muscular twin. My only complaint was that Bob was too vain to wear his reading glasses and sometimes needed to guess at the numbers on their workout charts.

Blake Hytemp was a local restaurant owner. His establishment sat close to the lake at the end of a large marina and was easily accessible by boat as well as by car. Blake pulled up in his Mercedes convertible, opened the door to my gym and practically fell in sideways, as though the door was almost too much to wrestle with. Tall, thin and pale with sandy hair combed across, Blake looked like the end result if the actors John Cusak and Kyle McLaughlin mixed their DNA. At 40 years old, Blake's boyish good looks and ready laugh, handshake and shoulder grab greeting were deteriorating into a seen-better-times party boy image. Seeing only one other trainer and client in the gym, Blake pulled up a chair and sat across the desk to tell me his tale of woe. According to Blake, he had spent his life (so far) working in restaurants first as a 14-year-old busboy and later as a 16-year-old cook. He had spent the next ten years as a waiter, bartender and manager, learning every aspect of the business until he partnered up with a brother to co-own a restaurant/bar. Selling his share, he opened his own waterfront dining/drinking/nightspot and claimed to have worked sixty to eighty hours a week until it took off. Packed with drunken boaters and local marina tenants during the short Michigan summer, the bar raked in cash despite the restaurant's mediocre food. In the fall and winter, comics, contests and crooners kept business at a break even level.

Now, after ten years of toil, Blake had a huge house in the Pointes, a Mercedes sports car and a blonde auto show model as his fiancée. But age 40 had hit Blake like a ton of silverware, and he had resolved to get back some of the health and vigor of his teenage years. During his little dissertation, Blake insisted on picking up his shirt to show me his pale, sunken chest and rolling up his sleeves to reveal his thin, frail-looking arms. I was forced to agree that he looked quite pitiful and that if I were his trainer, I wouldn't injure him. I sensed that I wasn't getting the whole story and later learned that his previous workout experience with a trainer at a gym had left him flat on his back in bed for two days, practically paralyzed with pain. I had never worked out with anyone so fearful as the former high school baseball player and during our first workout readily conceded that he was one of the weakest men I'd ever encountered. Blake's relatively young age was a bonus (although his tender neck, back, and tendonitis-racked shoulders were not), and I gradually put muscle on his frail frame. Blake soon got in the habit of staring into the gym mirrors and yelling out that he was "huge!" I never did determine if his "huge!" rants were a psyching up process or an attempt at comic relief but was fairly certain that even he didn't believe it. He did believe, however, that he was extremely desirable to women and could have any woman he set his sights on.

Blake was purported (confirmed by other clients) to have the largest collection of Snoopy dolls and memorabilia on the planet packed into a gigantic room of his house. Blake's technique, when he judged the time to be right, was to invite dates over to his house to review his immense accumulation of the comic strip dog's likenesses. This disarming dating approach was extremely successful and, once the unsuspecting woman was inside the house and put at ease by Snoopy, the ending was determined by Blake and whatever fine wines he had available.

Due to the late hours of the bar business, Blake had the least health-conducive sleeping and eating habits of any of my clients. He had the unusual habit of barging into the gym's employee lunchroom and eating the salt out of the saltshakers, but I decided it didn't actually hurt his workouts and that it kept him from "hitting" on my female trainers between his sets.

The gym closed at 9 p.m. with the last appointments taken at 8 p.m., but Blake seemed to enjoy pushing the envelope, arriving at 8:05, 8:10 and eventually 8:15 to 8:30, trying to determine at what point he would eventually get turned away. When a Powerhouse Gym franchise opened three miles away, my employees encouraged Blake to join and were all very relieved when he did. He was ready to make his mark on a new gym with his new and mighty fourteen-inch biceps.

Sherri Pine was a single mother of three girls. In her early 40s and aging well, Sherri worked part-time as a nurse for a nursing outplacement agency. She had put herself through nursing school in her early 30s after her last divorce. Sherri's "girls" were 26, 23, and 18-years-old respectively and at age 39, her unmarried middle daughter had made Sherri a rather young grandmother. Sherri lived in a miniscule Eastpointe home with her two youngest daughters and her three-year-old grandson. Sherri arrived at my gym one afternoon and paid cash for a workout package with money given to her by her rich boyfriend Phil. Very pretty but worried that her top heavy and very curvy figure was finally starting to feel the effects of childbearing and gravity, Sherri realized that her infrequent aerobics classes needed to be supplemented by much more. Phil, on the other hand, didn't care as much about Sherri's body as long as she continued to tie him up at night and force him to lie at her feet while she watched TV, or led him around his back yard on a leash attached around his neck (or worse).

Phil lived in an architecturally intriguing wooden turreted house on the lake in Grosse Pointe Park. The house had multi-level rooms throughout leading to hidden, skylighted bedrooms. It was in a constant state of decorative transition as Phil's penchant for foreign travel and erotic art filled the house with nude sculptures and paintings.

When Phil used to be a Catholic priest, he had opened a free counseling center for drug addicts and other misguided souls until he discovered that their health care coverage would pay the tab if he achieved clinic status. Phil took the necessary steps to do so, quit the priesthood and opened a chain of clinics across the country. Small and slight with a reddish, ruddy face from twenty years of wine and yachting, Phil's dates with Sherri consisted of fine dining and nightcaps followed by impassioned pleas for her to spank him while he wore his thong (or less). Sherri agreed to each session with a reluctant roll of her eyes as she continued her bar circuit search for a more normal millionaire to take care of her so she could stop working once and for all.

Sherri's workouts at the gym progressed quickly, and soon, with her medical background as a natural advantage, she was working for me part-time at night. I introduced her to Rob Shasta, a former race car driver turned millionaire construction contractor who came to the gym faithfully to have me rehab a post-back-surgery body. Sherri and Rob's eventually volatile relationship was the classic result of a possessive woman's determination to move into her boyfriend's large new house colliding with a recently minted millionaire's reluctance to break off all contact with his former girlfriends.

Sherri's hours at the gym quickly increased, and soon she built an enthusiastic female clientele in the morning hours that I had refused to open up the gym for. With the weekly gross steadily increasing and the ability to boast of a staff of eight trainers, I felt as though I should spend more time at the gym and assist Michelle, by now my full-time manager, with the day-to-day operations and more than two hundred weekly workouts.

Max, however, had other ideas. I fielded calls on my cell phone from him or Elizabeth asking for safe transit home until he could sober up. I still rented limousines for family fetes and outings and was often putting in full work weeks followed by working weekends. Michelle, compact and attractive with tiny hips and curly brown hair, would open her hazel eyes wide in panic as I would click shut my phone and explain that I had to go. Michelle, Sherri, and the other trainers would then take over my clients as best they could as I sped away.

Just as I was thinking of resigning from this inconvenient situation, Max called one night and explained that he'd had a few too many "pops" but had promised Elizabeth that he'd pick her up at the airport upon her return from a granddaughter's wedding in St. Louis. I rushed over before the billionaire changed his mind and decided to negotiate the twenty-minute trip to the airport while impaired. Max himself buzzed open the gate which, as I expected, meant that he was in the enormous house alone. Over the previous several months, I had been with Max when he was in far greater states of inebriation than tonight, but I had never seen him as morose and melancholy as he seemed right now. As I sat in the den, he presided at his usual position behind his desk, half-heartedly shuffling papers without focusing on anything. A Crown Royal on the rocks glittered and sloshed amid its cubes, and my eyebrows raised not only to find him drinking alone, but to see him still in his business suit hours after leaving the office. I listened as Max sighed over the usual monologue about Elizabeth's happiness and contentment.

After twenty minutes, a glance at his Rolex caused Max to stand up from the desk and announce that we had better leave. After donning his coat, the lonely-at-the-top poster child walked over to the full service bar off the den and topped off his drink! Other than a recent limo trip when eight family members topped off before going to the car, I had never seen Max carry a drink outside. We walked out the front door as the bitter cold hugged us and sought a direct way through our coats. I stayed in close proximity on the long, hard steps ready to grab an arm or step quickly in front to avert a possible fall. We arrived safely at the bottom and settled into the frigid Mercedes. I breathed a sigh of relief as air from a still-warm engine cascaded through the vents and glanced over to check the status of Max's drink, noting with satisfaction that it hadn't spilled.

On the way to the airport, Max talked incessantly about his jets and the fine, motivated pilots who flew them. He elaborated about complex financial arrangements made with hangar owners and partners that left him with a minimal financial obligation and yet a maximum stake in the company. Starting at square one, Max told me how having the jet spoiled him and how very lucky he was to be able to use it to send his daughter-in-law and grandchild to a holistic children's center in Toronto for medical treatments.

"And then there's Robert," Max went on, as I considered opening the driver door and flinging myself onto the freeway to avoid hearing it again. "Robert has me so spoiled. If I'm going on a trip, I tell Robert how many days and my suitcase is packed for me." We neared the airport as Max went on, "And the grounds-keeping staff…" Looking up, I wondered if I could form a noose out of the seatbelt shoulder straps? "They take the cars out and gas them up every morning and then hand wash…" We arrived at the airport gates and I rolled the window down. As the guard leaned out of the booth Max leaned over, "Hi, I'm Max Lexington, and this is my driver, Mark." The female guard smiled slightly and waved us in. The plane was supposed to land at 9 p.m. The car's clock said 8:45. We pulled up to the huge, rolling gate that separated the parking lot from the runway. The car's thermometer displayed a frigid nine degrees. I had forty-five minutes to wait with the boasting billionaire and nowhere to go. On the nearby highway in the surrounding disintegrating neighborhood I could see busses stopping to disgorge an odd bag lady or two. The busses' bright lights looked inviting at the moment, and I wondered how close one would eventually get to where my car was parked at the mansion. At least two miles, I calculated, which meant I'd freeze to death after I got off the bus. Then, as if to prove there was a God, Max changed course from "the grateful talk" to…women! "I saw Mary Roberts pulling out of her street this morning. Now her husband left her very comfortable when he died and she can't be but what, 55? Not 60 yet. They only had one child so she's free to go anywhere, just drop and leave any time."

Oh my gawd! I thought, Max's been scoping out chicks! Or at least what he considered chicks.

"Now is a 50 or 55 year old gonna be accepted? I don't know," Max went on. "I mean she's lived in the Pointes for probably thirty years, they belonged to the Yacht club I think. I saw her at Manutas' Christmas party, was it two years ago? I think you drove us, and she waited to approach me but she puts her hand on my arm when we're alone and says 'Max how are you? We have got to get out to lunch sometime and catch up!' Can you believe she said that? I mean why would she say that to me?"

I replied, "Maybe she's hungry."

"Ha, ha, ha, ha, oh Maaaark, yeah maybe." Max switched to another woman. "Now remember I told you about that Sophia in Bay Harbor, that Italian woman, she was a looker, boy. And the way she took her time taking off my coat at her party, her husband's in the other room, I'm telling you, and she says, 'Oh Max, I'm sooo glad you could make it, is Elizabeth still sick?' and then Maaark, I kid you not, she sits me across from her at dinner and she's got a lot up top if you know what I mean and she watches me and smiles at me the whole dinner." The surreal revelations continued. "I mean this is one classy looking lady and he's doing well, I mean he's not as far along as I might be in *his* business but he's doing okay. Now I don't think she's fifty yet and they never had any kids. I wonder if that's caused any problems between them in the past? I don't know that I saw them speak two words that night. Maybe I'm misreading but why would she say it *that* way when she took my coat?"

Listening to Max's thoughts on flirting, while making me somewhat uneasy, was one hundred and twelve times better than hearing about all the perks that his wealth brought. We watched a private jet taxi out and position itself for the rush down the runway. Nine-thirty rolled around and I watched a promising set of landing lights piercing the blackness as another private jet made its final descent. If that was it, we'd be allowed onto the runway in about ten more minutes. Max wasn't quite through.

"But Maaark, at the end of the day the simple truth of the matter is that what good is having everything if you don't have anybody to share it with? Now it's no secret that I'm playing the back nine but who really *knows* how long that's gonna be? And where does it say, whether it's five years or fifteen, that I shouldn't spend them happy, doing what I wanna do. And if that means traveling with someone or being with someone who enjoys the things that I enjoy how can that be wrong?"

My gosh, I thought, still not quite believing my ears, this man can sell! He had me eighty percent convinced that a man with a yacht and jets and a billion dollars wasn't happy. Was I supposed to say anything? A joke from my repertoire didn't seem appropriate in the silence that followed. As a marriage counselor, I was probably the most ill-qualified man on the planet, so telling him to stick it out wasn't going to fly.

In the movie "Annie Hall," Woody Allen is attending dinner at Diane Keaton's parents' house and is cornered in another room by her older brother. The brother confides in Woody that often, when he's driving down a highway at night, he stares at the headlights of the oncoming traffic. He goes on to morbidly describe how he wonders what it would be like to just flick the wheel and throw himself into the opposite lane and say goodbye to it all, ending his pain. Woody backs carefully out of the room but finds out after dinner that his car won't start. The strange brother immediately offers, much to Woody's chagrin, to drive both of them home. The next scene is that of a Porsche blasting down the highway with a petrified Woody Allen in the passenger seat staring at the line of oncoming headlights as well, wondering if each breath might be his last. At that very moment, as the security gate rolled to the side and we eased forward, I felt exactly like Woody Allen's character.

As we inched up to the plane, the pilots popped out with Elizabeth's luggage first. Bracing against the cold, I swung out and helped to load the car's trunk. Diving back into the idling car as Elizabeth's sister's luggage was off-loaded, I waited patiently with Max for his wife. One of her sisters was the first to step down off the plane onto the runway, followed by the other. It became immediately obvious why Elizabeth was obsessed with her weight and staying fit. The previous day's menu recitations that I listened to during her workouts now seemed more important as I watched sister number one, in her sixties and about eighty pounds overweight, amble toward her son's waiting car. Elizabeth, at only ten pounds overweight, was clearly the runway model of the family, and I resolved to redouble my efforts to keep her weight down with everything I had in my arsenal.

Max and Elizabeth had attended a local weight loss clinic sporadically over the past couple of years. For Grosse Pointers in the know, Dr. Bagger was worth the forty-five minute drive when a see-and-be-seen social event was coming up. A vitamin shot in the butt and a supply of something he vaguely called "weight loss vitamins" was just the ticket for losing a pound or two a day and fitting into that special dress or tux next month. Early in my sojourn, the Lexingtons spoke wistfully of the last time they visited Dr. Bagger. Max had dropped from 260 to 220 pounds. Proportionately, Elizabeth's loss had been equally impressive, taking her down from 133 to a waif-like 114 pounds.

With his eating and drinking spiraling out of control, Max was again becoming desperate as his weight tipped the scale one day at 268 pounds. Max impulsively called and saw Dr. Bagger the day after the disastrous weigh-in and two days later scheduled a Saturday afternoon workout.

Conversations with physician clients over the last several months resulted in the conclusion that a mere vitamin injection wouldn't accelerate weight loss. All of my doctors agreed that the thirty-day supply of "vitamins" were repackaged doses of phen-fen, a potent drug that had made recent headlines. Phen-fen was a dangerous combination of speed and an appetite suppressant suspected of causing serious heart damage.

As I strolled into the workout room that Saturday a trembling and dizzy billionaire was returning from yet another trip to an adjoining bathroom, claiming that while he was down ten pounds already, he couldn't stop peeing. Concerned that I might be calling an ambulance at any moment, I eased Max into a workout while asking as many questions as I could. Acutely aware that I was about six years of college short of a medical degree, I was nevertheless able to decide that this time the good Dr. Bagger had inserted a diuretic into the lethal mix. Not only was Max's pounding heart working overtime, his liver and kidneys were working double overtime as fluids were pumped out of his body. Fearing that a stroke might be imminent, I beseeched my shaky client to forgo that afternoon's dosage in lieu of my own new brand of "fat burners" that I would drop off immediately. To my relief he agreed, and I sped the two miles to my gym to make good on my promise.

I had carried the mild, natural and time-released form of speed for some time and had prescribed it with great success when a client had exhausted every other weight-loss option. I was extremely reluctant, however, to dish it out to a 70-year-old man and woman. I also felt that since they could easily afford consults with the best weight-loss physicians in the country, my college drop-out self shouldn't be prescribing *any* form of drug, no matter how holistic or safe. But it became obvious that the overweight billionaire was at the end of his rope and had fallen into the clutches of a money-grubbing Shylock who wasn't timid about playing Russian roulette with people's lives as long as he was paid $2,000 per visit.

A somewhat renewed attention to diet and a slightly increased dedication to his workouts were combined with a steady stream of my fat burners. Max's weight (after 20 glasses of water it was back to 268) began a gradual descent: 264, 262, 259. Every other weigh-in brought smiles and a rehash of the previous day's meals. At 252 we hit a plateau, and I began to pitch Max to visit a reputable physician and get a prescription for Androgel.

26

I HAVE A great deal of respect for some doctors and the drugs that are made available to them by the drug companies. Ten years ago, when I was still married, my wife and I would go out to dinner on a weekly basis with my in-laws. My mother-in-law was an extremely intelligent lady with a great deal of knowledge and opinions about almost everything. A dietician by training, she had a master's degree and was employed by the State of Michigan setting up menus for group homes and prisons. If you got up in the morning and decided to go out and get the paper, but found that the front door was locked from the inside and your ankle itched a little from the electronic tether, there was a good chance that my mother-in-law had already decided what you were going to have for breakfast, lunch and dinner and any snacks.

She and my father-in-law were gregarious, outgoing people with a great sense of humor. They belonged to numerous clubs and leagues and had many friends, but at 5 feet 5 inches tall and 220 pounds my mother-in-law loved to eat. I was 6 feet tall and weighed 225 pounds, and partly because of an ongoing caloric need from my weightlifting program, was able to proudly do some major damage at any restaurant. Although buffets were my favorite, I loved Italian food, and late one Wednesday night, after an immense meal, the four of us were polishing off huge plates of tiramisu at a nearby Italian place. The dinner itself had lasted nearly two hours as my mother-in-law and I went mano a mano. I would order two items off the menu, pretending that I was going to share with the wife, and my mother-in-law would order three, pretending that she intended to share also. Knives and forks flashing, chewing and gulping, we sat across from each other, eyeing each other's plates and casting wary eyes at our mate's plates for scraps. We were also ever watchful for the waitress to enter the vicinity so that we could order still more. This incredible woman was a pro, and it looked like I had finally met my match! The evening's contest ended only because the wait staff started going home. My in-laws generously insisted on paying, and we drove to their home. We were all tired and had to work in the morning and were saying goodbye in the living room when my mother-in-law raised her left arm in a doorway and began to stretch it out. She then demanded a shoulder rub from her husband "especially on the left side." My wife, tired, full and pregnant, kept tugging on my sleeve, exhorting me to leave. As a personal trainer with about 200 clients coming to our studio at the time, I would have found it very embarrassing to admit to each of them that I watched my mother-in-law croak in front of me and, without lifting a finger, just went home. I leaned down and whispered to my wife that diabetics often didn't feel any pain during heart attacks and that we weren't going anywhere but the hospital. Eyes bugging out, my wife sat down, and I began the hour-long process of cajoling and prodding a huge, exhausted, complaining woman back into the cold night and into my father-in-law's mini-van. After a short ride to William Beaumont Hospital, she was immediately admitted by a speedy staff, pumped full of lifesaving drugs and hooked on to monitors. Luckily, later tests showed no heart damage, and after a couple of angioplasties, the woman was back to all her old habits as though nothing had ever happened. Eye operations, kidney problems, back trauma and many other future health crises have all been corrected or medicated. Drugs and surgical procedures have brought this woman back from the brink of death many times with no obvious aftereffects!

Because of this woman's history, I have incredible respect and admiration for the medical profession, and in my mind, this helps to offset the many marriages in the Pointes and numerous other communities that I've seen broken up by doctors and their meddling ways.

Prior to Viagra, middle-aged executives with adequate erectile function hit on younger administrative assistants and other female co-workers with the same fervor, charm and persistence that they had exhibited for the last several hundred years. The end result was that many would leave their wives only to come crawling home after the initial excitement of the new chickie wore off. The maligned, embarrassed and furious wife, realizing that her prospects of another mate at her age were somewhat dim, usually took him back, resolving to keep a closer watch and to never let him forget his indiscretions, either.

Many aging workaholics in the Pointes are successful businessmen but, in their 50s and 60s, are starting to feel as though life is passing them by. With their clogging arteries, swelling prostate glands and softening muscles, they fear they have little to look forward to beyond grandchildren and retirement.

But Viagra has turned many of them back into high performance sex machines! With a young, energetic chickie riding him on top and doing all the work, the cheating husband only needs to relax and enjoy. It was similar to starring in his own porn film except that only a minimum of energy expenditure was expected by his co-star.

Why go back to the wife now (the Exec reasons)? It's time to use some of that accrued vacation time and travel! There are hundreds of cities he's never humped in before! Maybe he can even get this new one to sign a pre-nup, and the kids will learn to accept her. After all, there's only a five year difference between her and his oldest daughter; they must have a lot in common!

In the Pointes, keeping your secret Viagra supply at home is not an option. The wife is already suspicious and checks the medicine cabinet every few days to actually count the pills. The tablets at home are strictly for the times that wifey won't take no for an answer (which are hopefully few and far between if she's past menopause and shunning estrogen therapy). In addition, the nosey maid is always stumbling across odd things in little hidey-holes and reporting back to the *wife*, the one who pays her, determines her Christmas tip, and is of the same gender to boot.

Besides, when the opportunity is hot and your alibi is tight, stopping by the house for your "meds" can be a real deal-breaker. Keeping your Viagra at the office is a decided improvement. The office is often where the opportunity originated from in the first place. A locked desk drawer is safe, and can be one of the logical last stops before a business trip. But the best hiding place of all that *I've* ever heard of was a man's $176,000 S500 Mercedes. It seems as though these cars have a secret compartment built in under the driver's seat that can be terrific for hiding all kinds of incriminating items like secret apartment keys, spare cell phones, directions to clandestine meeting places and yes, even a man's Viagra.

A successful man may have had some novel business ideas. He worked hard and he reached the pinnacle, only to learn that there's *always* somebody above him, and always someone below him nipping at his heels. Dammit though, at least he can afford a car with a secret compartment!

Of course, I'm not at an echelon that demands a car with a secret compartment, but a female client has regaled me with indignant stories of finding this compartment with her best friend after an unusually thorough search of the husband's S500. I must admit that, even as a member of the male race, I no longer feel any obligation to guard this well-kept secret since the husband, who was co-incidentally a morning client at my gym, quit after being rebuffed by one of my female trainers. His not-so-subtle propos-itioning and attempted financial inducements notwithstanding, the ultimate turnoff to her was his incessant boasting about his economic power and the refinement and sophistication and pampering it afforded him. She knew full well that a palate numbed by two bottles of wine cannot discern between a $10 bottle and a $300 bottle, but the man kept trying anyway. My egotistical, powerful female trainer also found it somewhat pathetic and insulting to be hit on by an overweight, fragile CEO twice her age and half her strength. She rebuffed every advance.

As a man grows older, his level of testosterone—the hormone that makes young men aggressive, virile, and fearless—drops. Testosterone makes it easier to build muscle. When a young man has testosterone coursing through his veins he feels invincible in a fight, and a powerful motorcycle seems like a damn good idea. But in an older man, a faltering supply of natural testosterone can be partly responsible for his inability to lose bodyfat. A gradual loss of the muscle mass the man took for granted in his youth can rob him of his ability to burn fat for energy as well.

Androgel was invented and brought to market in recognition of the need for a safe and convenient testosterone therapy for men. It was packaged in the form of an ointment to be smeared on the man's chest after a morning shower. After a brief drying period, testosterone was then trickled in and absorbed through the skin gradually over the next 24 hours.

27

M AX LEXINGTON'S FLAGSHIP company was comprised of fifty huge retail stores evenly and strategically spread throughout the Detroit metro area (although none were actually located in the huge but impoverished and unprofitable city itself). In the mid 1980s Max and his eldest son Larry, the heir apparent and holder of a snazzy new master's degree in marketing, battled furiously over the direction of the company. Max instinctively knew that his bread and butter lay with the masses of average people. They could be worn down by a constant barrage of TV, radio and print ads that promised markdowns of seventy percent, no interest for years and other ridiculous come-ons that constantly skirted the edge of misleading advertising. Larry's proposed strategy was to take the chain upscale to capitalize on the growing wealth of the surrounding communities. Max, however, was happy catering to the middle class and while open to making gradual upgrades, refused to make any dramatic changes to his prize-winning formula. So in the mid 1980s Max purchased a five-store chain of a decidedly upscale retailer called Elegant Classics and installed the usurpient Larry as its president. Under Larry's highly educated hand, the five huge stores struggled for years to turn a profit.

In the mid 1990s it was decided that the youngest son Nathan, who had joined the family business, would be the spokesman for the chain. On camera for the first time, the budding media star was stiff; his delivery halting and poorly coached at best. The camera lens wasn't kind either, adding thirty pounds to his weight and causing him to project himself as a bloated-Elvis-in-a-suit without the charisma. But practice makes perfect, and after several years and many millions of dollars worth of TV ads, Elegant Classics had a more polished and natural TV pitchman. Nathan's dark hair, expensive suits and handsome Elvis-like look transformed the 37-year-old into a minor local celebrity. With a confidence born of appearing in a million living rooms twice nightly, Nathan also found himself enjoying the little congregations of females that gathered around him at parties and other events. As I drove Nathan and his wife Lu Ann, along with other family members, to events and dinners in long, white limos that I would rent, I found that his limit without smoking a cigarette was about ten miles. Aware of the strict no smoking policy of the owner of Pristine Limousines, Nathan would try to accommodate when he lit up anyway by rolling down the back window and blowing the smoke out. His furtive glances up front made me want to pull him out of the limo and slap him as I demonstrated how a rear view mirror works.

Nathan had, according to Max, been an all-star football player in college. As the legend went, the young man's blinding speed had made him a standout, but he gave it all up to concentrate on his studies in preparation for entering the family business one day. Now, as he neared forty years old, Nathan was growing ever more conscious of the toll that working, family duties and his sedentary lifestyle were taking on his health. Max suggested that Nathan begin a program at my little studio, and soon the TV commercial star called and made his first appointment. Thirty-five pounds overweight and with little upper body strength, Nathan didn't strike me as a former star athlete, and I began to suspect that despite the heroic tales from his father the truth lay somewhere in between. It was obvious that lifting weights was unfamiliar to him although he possessed some degree of hand-eye coordination. I started from square one, explaining about the involvement of each muscle group during each of the exercises we did. Although Nathan had a graceful running style and admitted to making the team because of the speed his father spoke of, he downplayed his role on his college team and sidestepped when I questioned why he quit.

As his workouts progressed and his weight dropped, the retailing scion began to take more of an interest in fellow gym members, with two female clients in particular peaking his curiosity. The first was Kim O'Brien, a pale blond, former auto show model with impossibly narrow hips and an equally impossibly huge chest. At 5 feet 7 inches tall and 111 pounds, the 35-year-old was too short to go on to runway modeling and somewhat mad at herself for wasting four years on a wedding-shy doctor. When she finally moved out of his house, the physician came to his senses and proposed, but by then Kim had fallen out of love with him and met a wealthy businessman on a ski trip. The man lived in Minnesota but Kim continued a long distance relationship with him while he got his divorce rolling. Kim joined my gym to add further tone to a near-perfect body and to stave off the aging process that even former models encounter. Braless and wearing spandex shorts and top, Kim drew the attention of every male client whose workout time coincided with hers, and Nathan was no exception. Kim, who lived within walking distance of the studio, announced at the end of a workout one day that she'd like to go get a tan at her salon two miles away but that the temperature was dropping dramatically on that March day. Nathan's workout was over and, in a moment of impulse that I'm still not proud of, I mischievously asked him if he was heading that way. Muttering, "I am now," with an eager smile, Nathan grabbed the keys to his Cadillac as he slid into his coat.

As they sped off together, I had a lingering period of remorse as I thought of Nathan's beautiful blond Lu Ann waiting at home with his children. With high cheekbones and a gorgeous smile, Lu Ann was still extremely beautiful even after bearing Nathan three heirs. Her exercise program consisted of running when possible, but unfortunately it wasn't working. Her hourglass figure was gradually descending into a pear-shape, and more than once I considered inviting her to join my clientele before it was too late. There was never a time that seemed remotely close to appropriate, however, and I continued to imagine from afar what an exquisite piece of sculpture I could mold her into given a little time.

Nathan was also distracted during his workouts by Janey Ladd, a 5 foot 3 inch substitute school teacher who, at 118 pounds, had arresting curves that stretched her spandex outfits to their limits. Janey began working out at my gym when her boyfriend, the heir of a computer leasing company, offered to pick up the tab. They lived together in the twenty-sixth floor penthouse of a nearby waterfront condo on the edge of the Pointes. Janey was certain that their three-year co-habitation was about to result in marriage and babies. At twenty-five years old, she was classically beautiful with long dark blond hair that wafted down the sides of her face. Janey's soft voice, ready smile and cute giggles belied a slightly wild side that pushed her toward a drink too many and some interesting late-night parties. The thought of settling down at the tender age of thirty was too much for her rich boyfriend, however, and he came home inexplicably late one night to announce that he thought that they should see other people for a while. More experienced friends cued a devastated Janey that this meant that *he* wanted to see other people because he already *was*.

With a little asking around and after checking some charge card receipts, Janey found his car at a strip club. His new love interest was dancing on his tabletop. With her head spinning and her world crushed, Janey moved out that night, in tears and shaking uncontrollably. To fill her evenings she worked out nightly at my gym, consoled by my female trainers and by concerned friends on her constantly ringing cell phone. As her weight dropped even further from a complete loss of appetite, Nathan grew ever more fixated with Janey. His frequent comments and questions to me went unanswered as I finally found a bit of moral character and warned her in advance to avoid this married man. It was obvious, even to the cold steel exercise machines in the gym, that the last thing Janey needed at this point was a disastrous rebound romance with a wedded father of three. Heeding my warning, Janey offered a polite "hello" whenever Nathan was present, but never anything more. Nathan soon realized that my sad, beautiful client was not interested and concentrated once again on remolding his body.

28

A FTER TWO YEARS, I knew more about Max's medical history than most of his doctors and was confident that the hormone replacement Androgel was the missing link in Max's health quest. Men with normal testosterone levels appeared to burn bodyfat more easily, and I was confident that raising Max's level would help him lose weight. After a month of prodding, Max made an appointment and two days later made an announcement.

"Maaaark, I saw Dr. Mason the other day and he put me on a cream that you apply to your skin after your shower. After a few weeks he said it'll raise my hormone levels back up to where they should be." Max went on, "Dr. Mason said if my tesserown is low I might even be gaining too much weight! Oh, and speaking of that there's a lady I know from tennis who says she saw you working out with Mrs. Lexington and me a year ago at Lochmoor when this room was torn apart. This lady is about a B+ now but she *could* be an A+ if she lost five or ten pounds. I told her about your gym and she said she's in the area all the time. I told her to call you and set something up."

Well, I thought, wasn't Dr. Mason an astute man! After only twenty years as Max's personal physician, this medical pioneer finally figured out that there may be a *reason* for his patient's weight problem. In his brilliance, this great healer had now prescribed a therapy that had probably been suggested by every medical journal and drug manufacturer's rep that he'd had contact with in the last three years. The fact that his patient had a recent near death experience with a quack was obviously not a factor with the tortoise-like diagnosis of Dr. Mason. Spending his career on the cutting edge of medicine, however, did not mean that he should perform a battery of tests or medical work-ups on his obese patients. It made far more sense to wait until their personal trainer or bodyguard/ driver figured out the problem and then go from there. I gathered that the client referral was supposed to be my thanks for my diagnosis.

I arrived at my studio the next day in the middle of the afternoon. One of my messages was from Summer Sevelas. I didn't recognize the name but could see that the phone number was from the Pointes. I called Summer, and she answered on the second ring.

"Hello," she said in a voice that sounded interrupted.

"Hi, this is Mark from Shores Personal Training and I received a message that you called."

"Hi Mark, just a minute." I heard a click and ten seconds later another click and she was back on. "Thanks, yes, I called because," she spoke slowly and thoughtfully, "I got your name from Max Lexington. I play tennis and walk and have a basement full of every kind of exercise equipment but I've been told that unless I have a trainer I could just be wasting my time." Summer continued, "So I thought that I'd pay you whatever you charge to come to the house and set up a program for me to follow or maybe I could come to your gym and we could get started there and I could keep it up here."

Boy, I thought, did we just get off on the right foot. No questions about early morning hours (which I hated), no grilling about my rates (which I felt were the most reasonable around), and no trying to find out what routine I had in mind over the phone (wouldn't know until I saw her anyway). Best of all, if she had a basement full of equipment already, I wouldn't have to schlep heavy pieces down rickety stairways or make do with a couple of large rubber bands and a cheap ab machine purchased from an infomercial.

"Okay, Summer, may I suggest that you throw a day and time

at me, and I'll meet you here at my gym. I'm always available after twelve and I have my appointment book in front of me."

"Aaah, I have tennis in the morning but that ends at 11:30, how about 12:00?"

"Twelve o'clock tomorrow is perfect. Do you know where we're located?"

"Oh yes, Max told me. I'll see you at noon."

It was the second Tuesday in April. The sun was pouring down into the parking lot as I pulled in at 11:52 a.m. Ambling into the gym, I was already pondering my lunch destination, considering something light and under 2000 calories so as not to encumber my 4 p.m. workout. Enter the gym and recheck the time…11:55, good, I thought, five minutes early. I sat behind the desk: 12:05, 12:10 and 12:15 all passed. Promptly at 12:17 p.m. a white Mercedes 4-door E-class pulled off Jefferson from the direction of the Pointes. I rolled my eyes and made a mental note not to schedule this one as my first appointment anymore.

There are many reasons that people exercise. For many women (and some men) a rush of endorphins—the "feel good" chemicals released in the limbic system of the brain to activate opiate receptors—makes them look forward to any aerobic activity. Exercising is also a way to expend more calories than you consume, which is the most common sense way of losing weight. In America's food-obsessed society, 64.5 percent of the nation is above their ideal body weight (or fat) and 30.5 percent of the nation is 30 percent above their ideal body weight, or obese. Yet few magazine covers feature fat people. Television shows and movies don't reflect the actual percentage of the populace that's fat. Healthy and attractive is usually associated with thin. No movie stars (other than Marlon Brando, and let's face it, he was thin early in his career) are fat.

As I get older, the main impetus behind my own workouts is to keep from getting fat and thus avoid all of obesity's health related illnesses. I learned long ago that my 5000-calorie-a-day intake wasn't compatible with my 33-inch waistline unless I lifted weights three times a week.

But when I was a teenager (14,15, 16 years old) I was obsessed with building up my upper arms until they were out of proportion with the rest of my body. An overbuilt upper arm represented strength, power, and athletic prowess. Most of all, I figured it would attract women! So in my spare time, I set about the business of building a large set of "guns" or upper arms. I became somewhat disenchanted in my quest when in the late 80s my hero, Arnold Schwarzenegger, admitted to using anabolic steroids to achieve his massive muscles. I immediately realized that it wasn't possible for me to achieve the kind of size and strength that would stagger the imagination unless I took drugs.

Hero-less, I was walking by a magazine rack one morning and a *Cosmopolitan* magazine caught my eye (actually...the cover did). This magazine claimed to have the results of a survey inside about women's desires. Men's physical attributes were ranked one through ten in the supposed order of their importance to women looking for a potential mate. Smugly, I scanned the top of the list for arm size...nothing. Perhaps they used the term "biceps." They did not. With a deflating feeling, my eyes wandered down the list to find that women ranked the size of a man's arms *seventh* in importance when they first "checked him out." How could this be possible? Skeptical and suspicious, I searched the article further for an explanation from the professor responsible for the survey. Her explanation was that massive arm size was far more important to a teenage male than it was to a twenty to thirty-year-old female. While the explanation made sense, I was crestfallen and began to read about response number one in the survey. According to the esteemed behavioral science professor, the male body part that women placed the most emphasis on was the buttocks! This rather unwelcome revelation meant that I had spent a good part of the last fifteen years of my life building an area of my body that impressed primarily (to my horror) teenage boys!

It became imperative to me that I begin a systematic independent verification of the survey results. I asked my girlfriend, and she said that it sounded "about right." I asked my female clients and they replied that the survey was accurate. I asked my twenty-five-year-old sister and she threatened to tell my parents and hung up. Further polling supported the survey. I also ascertained that women looked for gluteal roundness and firmness as well as abundant muscle development in the upper legs.

This meant that a considerable revamping of my exercise program was required. If I were to become the object of women's unleashed desire, I needed to forego my running program and concentrate instead on squats and leg presses. As my narcissistic obsession with building muscle below the waist grew, so did my obsession with women's legs and posteriors. My juvenile but comfortable average-American-male fascination with women's cleavage soon began to evolve. Now, when I surreptitiously evaluated a woman in workout dress or less, I began at her gluteus maximus (butt) and directed my gaze downward. Instead of looking for bounce and jiggle, I looked for the line that runs down the side of an athletic upper thigh, defining the separation of the front quadriceps and rear hamstring muscles. I would clandestinely gauge skin texture and tone, looking for telltale hints of cellulite. If clothing (or lack of it) permitted, I'd categorize the subject's tushy according to shape ("spherical" scoring the highest), height (lift is good, obscuring the back of the legs is bad), width (excessive width is very bad) and firmness. Ever mindful that spandex can mislead by enhancing shape and firmness, I had a separate set of criteria for glutes obscured by the stretchy material.

The raven-haired woman with the dark Giorgio Armani sunglasses stepped out of the white Mercedes and into my world on that bright Tuesday afternoon. She wore a long, black leather coat that flowed behind her, unfastened and teased by a light breeze. Shiny ruby red lips, sexy and slightly parted, framed hints of brilliant, perfectly aligned incisors and canines. A recent stint in the Caribbean had left her face, hands and—most noticeably—the smooth legs that appeared from behind her open coat with each step tanned and rich-looking. The upper section of her long legs jiggled with each tennis shoed footfall, and I guessed that she might be twenty to twenty-five pounds over her perfect weight. The darkened skin of her upper thighs, however, was forgiving as it stretched and flexed without a ripple to give her hippy walk an allure of its own. Her yellow tennis shorts disguised the pooch of her lower belly as my practiced eye sought it out. Only as I worked my way up did I notice the line of sun-kissed cleavage rising up from the matching cotton tennis top as it strove to cover her large breasts. Coach handbag in her left hand, she reached out with her right and opened the glass door outward, stepping through as she removed her sunglasses...all in one motion. In another motion, she swung her long hair to her right and redirected her purposeful stride to my desk as I arose to extend my hand. Glasses, handbag, a cell phone from out of nowhere and car keys were swiftly deposited on the desk.

"Hi Summer, Mark Steel." We shook hands as she shrugged out of the left side of her leather coat.

"Hello, Mark, nice to see you." She allowed the coat to slide off her right arm and sat down in one of the two chairs across from me. Draping the coat over the other chair, she claimed it as well. Her sleeveless arms were as tan as the rest of her, and she leaned forward slightly with her forearms lightly resting on the desk's edge as the long nails of her right hand absently fingered the cold metal band of her watch. Looking at her eyes and trying to avert my own from the rush of cleavage billowing out of her tennis top, I peripherally noted a fullness in her upper arms that hinted at natural breasts versus augmented.

"Mark, let me ask you a question," she began. In the twenty-five seconds that had elapsed since she'd walked in, this woman had taken over two chairs, half my desk and now had my undivided attention. "Is it possible," she intoned "for a woman to firm or reduce one area and yet not another?"

I'd only been asked this question by women about 6,000 times before. The translation for this question was, *"I know I've put on some weight over the last ten years. I can tell by the larger size clothes that I've had to buy but what the hell, some are really cute.*

But a lot of the weight gain has been in my boobs and my husband/boyfriend really likes them and so do I. Can you just take some of the fat off of my ass and belly and leave my boobs alone?"

I gave the woman my canned answer, which garnered her complete attention. "Whenever somebody gains weight they tend to gain it all over although some places on their body gain it at a faster rate than others. That's why some women are pear-shaped...they have more fat cells in the lower tummy, hips, thighs and glutes than in other areas." I continued on, "So when you lose weight you tend to lose it from all over (not what she wanted to hear) in about the same proportions that you put it on."

Her eyes began to glance away momentarily which meant that not only was I not saying what she wanted to hear, but she was losing interest in general. It was time to interrupt myself with a question. "Have you gained any weight in the last few years?" Her attention snapped back to me.

"Well, I seem to weigh just a couple of pounds more every year but my friends tell me that I carry it very well. It gives me even more of an hourglass figure and even my husband says that he likes me the way I am."

Smart man, I thought. No sense starting World War III with a woman who looked as though she could shop until your credit card caught fire and melted. This woman neither looked nor acted as though she'd ever heard of a Target or Wal-Mart. Everything about her screamed out Saks or Nordstrom. The wrong answer to "Honey, do I look fat to you?" could result in a *nasty* hit to the checking account. I had her attention back, so I decided to deliver the hopeful part.

"Some personal trainers, however, have started speculating that they are able to reduce one area more than another by not working the muscles under the area that you're satisfied with," I said. (Boy, was I smooth today). "Women are built differently than men. It's possible that women's muscles are interlaced with fat so that when you start working that muscle with resistance training that area becomes smaller relative to other areas of the body."

The unspoken translation for this was, *"I have been able to spot reduce on women sometimes, I can't say why for sure and, never having actually performed an autopsy on a female cadaver, have no way of knowing if this hearsay explanation that I've read about is true. The right answer, of course, is that women should achieve their ideal body weight by exercising more and eating less and, if they lose their boobs in the process and it bothers them, they should find a competent surgeon and get a boob job."*

The sun outside was rapidly heating the day as we wandered over to one of my treadmills. Summer's shorts were quite aptly named. A brief weigh-in prior to our stroll had indicated 158 pounds, which meant that at 5 feet 7 inches, I had about twenty to twenty-five to go, depending on how much muscle I decided to add. No cellulite yet, I again noted, which meant that I had good tight skin to work with. There was too much upper arm but still no sagging over the elbow which again meant that she was starting in plenty of time. There was definite excess over the bra strap that was easily visible underneath the thin cotton tennis top. But this bra strap might just be digging in deep under the enormous strain that her bra was surely encountering as it strained to hoist the substantial superstructure in front.

Once on the treadmill, a colored ring of elastic came from out of nowhere, and Summer reached back with both arms to corral the long hair into a ponytail. Trying to get a handle on her diet, I asked, "So, this morning I had oatmeal and two scrambled eggs for breakfast. What did you have?"

Without missing a beat, she replied, "I don't eat regular cereal because I can't tolerate milk products. I had a scone at Cuppocino's on Kercheval and a dark mocha coffee. When I'm at home I always start with my vitamins and some kind of juice, usually fresh squeezed orange but sometimes pineapple or grapefruit. Lunch might be a chicken Caesar if I'm meeting a girlfriend at 'The Hill' or if I'm shopping at Somerset I've been absolutely hooked on P.F.Changs. Have you ever been there? Well, Mark, I must tell you that if you don't mind the wait they're the best. I don't eat meat so

I only order from the chicken entrees. I get the rice with it but I never eat all of it because I've read that too much starch adds weight. Is that true?"

"Well," I hedged, "the liver does find it rather easy to turn carbohydrates into fat."

Summer talked about her favorite restaurants and what she usually ordered there. She talked about a close friend's diet and confided in me about her friend's lack of marital relations with her young but sick husband. After five minutes on the treadmill conversing, I already felt as though I'd known her for a week. We stopped and went to the leg press machine where I performed a quick demonstration. Summer pushed through a quick warm-up set and then stopped at fifteen repetitions. We had a minute to wait and she asked, "So, Mark, how long have you been working for Max?"

I replied, "Uh, two years next month."

"Do you work for him full-time?"

"Gosh no, in fact less and less as this place gets busier."

"You know," she exclaimed, "I saw you with him a year ago at Lochmoor. I was playing tennis and there were three of you on your way to the weight room. Was that his wife with you?"

"Uh, yes it was. Are you ready for another set with maybe a bit more weight?"

Her legs powered through another set on my machine. "How did you meet him?" she asked.

"He just answered one of my little newspaper ads," I said. She talked for a moment about tennis and how long he'd been playing. A little bit of disappointment crept out when she mentioned her inability to lose weight from playing regularly.

We did a third set with a bit more weight. She assured me that her legs were strong and she could handle even more, but by the end of the set she said "Oh, good, I can feel that starting to burn."

We stopped at fifteen again and she looked thoughtful. "How old would you say Mrs. Lexington is? I mean is she a lot younger?"

I didn't want to brush off Summer outright, but I felt as though this was the question that was starting to cross the confidentiality line. I also didn't want to be rude to a friend of Mr. Lexington. On the other hand, I reasoned, they couldn't be real close friends if Summer was asking me about his wife's age. Faking a slightly puzzled look, I replied, "Oh, I'd guess they're about the same age."

My inquisitor hopped on my answer quickly.

"Well, are you *her* trainer as well?"

"Uh, sure."

"So...Mark, what you're telling me is that you've been working out with her for two years and you don't know her age?"

I needed to buy some time. "Are you ready for a last set of leg presses?"

With a hint of a smug smile, Summer immediately began pushing through the last fifteen. The plates lightly and rhythmically touched as she gracefully willed them up and down on their fixed path. She finished and swung her legs out of the seat, standing up in front of me. Her bosom heaved perceptibly with the aftermath of her expenditures. Her ponytail had become slightly askew from touching on the headrest and she sensed it, removing the band and shaking her head until her hair flowed.

"I'm sorry, I didn't mean to put you on the spot." (She said it with no sign of sorrow on her face.) "How about you, are you married?"

"No, not anymore." *Great.* This was not exactly going to be a welcome change of subject. Suddenly, I was very comforted by the wide array of machines that surrounded us, counting on them as subject-changing allies if the inquisition continued. I offered a bottled water from the refrigerator in the corner and she declined. Got to keep this woman moving before she starts with more questions, I thought.

"I'd like to do some leg curls next, if we could. We already hit the front of the legs with the first machine so it makes sense to work the backs of the legs today too."

There were two types of leg curl machines in my little studio. The first was a cushioned seat affair that the user sits in upright and quite comfortably while the trainer adjusts the seat back. Weight plates are then added or subtracted to adjust the effort that will be necessary. Finally, the trainer snaps in a padded thigh cushion that stops the user from coming off the seat during the exercise. All things considered, the machine is a very civilized and spongy way to tone the back of a client's upper legs.

I didn't direct Summer to that machine, however. My other leg curl machine has less heavily padded cushions. The user must lay down on their tummy and contract their legs while a steel bar, covered by a stiff sponge and a piece of vinyl, tries to force them straight again. The main cushion, or pad that the user lies on is bent at a severe angle so that the user's head is close to the floor, and their butt sticks up in the air somewhat. This angle is supposed to prevent lower back injuries when the leg muscles are under a heavy load. Of course, this downward angling also encourages the blood to rush to the user's head, while lying on their tummy and chest also makes breathing a little tougher. This machine, however, did have one distinction over the other. It allowed for a fuller contraction of the rear leg muscles and necessitated some involvement of the muscles of the buttocks. And on this first visit, I could see that Summer's buttocks needed as much involvement as possible.

Finishing up with the day's leg portion, I moved her to an upper body and back exercise. If she wanted to make further improvements in her tennis game, then increased strength and flexibility would be an advantage that her opponents wouldn't possess.

There were four ways for potential clients in the Pointes to find out about my workout studio. The most common was when a friend of theirs who already attended started talking about the place because they lost weight rapidly or made some other change that they wouldn't have thought possible. This type of client still demonstrated some temerity when they first walked in, possibly because they may not have been the type of person to walk into a gym in the first place. The advantages to me were that they knew what to expect, they always kept that first appointment and they already knew what they wanted to change. This first type of beginner also knew what I charged and could easily afford it.

The second way a potential client responded was from driving by and punching the phone number displayed in my front windows into their cell phone. Their call was usually routed to Michelle, my manager. Michelle would then patiently answer all of their questions and explain, in her sweet little voice, about how caring and non-threatening our facility was. Given enough phone time, Michelle would always end up with a name and phone number in our appointment book, highlighted and scheduled for the hour with the fewest current clients. This type of client was always apprised of the cost but occasionally misunderstood, and usually insisted on Michelle at first as their trainer. Their appearance rate for the first session was also spotty as they began to have second thoughts after making the appointment.

New client method number three was a small offering of brochures in a clear plastic carrier affixed to the outside wall near the front door. Whether we were closed or open seemed to have no influence as the client parked their car and tiptoed up to grab a brochure. The brochure talked about how, why and when and displayed a couple of posed pictures of friendly-looking trainers. The brochure also listed our current prices to aid the potential client in deciding on the affordability of the commitment.

Number four simply dictated having the client walk in unannounced and unscheduled to check us out! Many were merely looking for a facility where they could work out on their own. If Michelle had spare time, they were encouraged to sit and listen to her spiel. As haphazard as this was, it resulted in a new client more than half the time and usually ended in a prepayment for future workouts.

Occasionally, I would field the call from a drive-by and answer their questions. Invariably they'd ask the cost, often at the onset of the conversation. I preferred this because I felt as though it was quite cheap and would rather talk about their past exercise endeavors and what course I would propose for the future. But once in a while,

a ten-minute conversation would ensue while they pumped me for
free information. They would then ask the cost at the end as if
listening to a proposal from an over-eager employee or one of their
child's friends.

Summer, with her workout over, sat down at my desk and
produced a checkbook. "This is exactly what I was looking for,"
she exulted. "I want to start coming four or five days a week and
I'd like you to come to the house once or twice a week. I'll pay
double what everyone else pays if I can work with just you each
time here and whatever you charge to come to the house. How
much do you want for the next two weeks?"

I hesitated. This was a trainer's dream client seated in front of
me. Money was no object, and other obligations would not stand
in her way. Business travel would not produce any interruptions.
During the workout, she had pointed to some of my equipment
and said, "I have one of these in my basement" or, "I have one of
those." Other than not eating meat or dairy, she would adjust her
diet to anything I suggested…even her fifteen-minute travel time
was not a constraint. Her Lakeshore Drive route had few lights
and relatively little traffic.

This woman was willing to give 110 percent but she was going
to demand 120 percent from me. She was requesting that I ignore
any of my other loyal clients when she was present. I would have
to focus my full attention on being a coach and teacher…on playing
the role of diet counselor and cheerleader…on being both mentor
and sculptor, with Summer as my breathtaking piece of only
partially formed (for now) clay.

Another part of me was outraged. This woman just assumed
that a smile and a checkbook were all she needed to get her way.
She obviously expected me to forsake or reschedule any faithful,
consistent client that intruded on her hour. I could see that this
Grosse Pointe Princess was demanding and accustomed to being
the center of the universe and would accept nothing less. I was
indignant at her assumption that I would re-arrange my entire world
to accommodate her. I now knew for a fact that she wasn't a very

close acquaintance of Max so it didn't matter one whit if I turned down her selfish little proposal!

She finished writing the check and pushed it across the desk saying, "I hope this is enough to get me started." With disdain I looked down at the pathetic little piece of paper. A molecule of curiosity had me wondering what Her Highness thought would buy me for an hour a day for two weeks. The check was for one thousand dollars.

"What time tomorrow would you like me to be here?" I asked. "And let me give you my cell phone number in case you need to change anything."

Nine o'clock the next morning found me in Max and Elizabeth's exercise room. The new prescription had already helped me pull a couple of pounds off of the frustrated billionaire and he was noticeably stronger as well. Max was huffing on his treadmill and Elizabeth was on hers.

"Say Maaaark, did that lady from Lochmoor ever call you? She said she was going to."

"Oh yes, sir," I replied. "She called, made an appointment, we worked out, she paid, and we're scheduled again for today."

"Oh, reeeaally? Do you know that she spotted us a year ago, in fact, it was over a year ago, wasn't it, Elizabeth, when we were over there working out with you? She plays tennis in a league. I believe her husband and his family have golfed there for yeeeaaaars."

Prior to the morning's weigh-in, Max had admitted to some overindulgence the night before ("I had a few pops") while Elizabeth rolled her eyes in agreement.

"Whooo boy, it's coming out of me now," Max exclaimed, and the sweat on his scalp confirmed it. "What saying do you have, Mark? About unfortunately not drinking...?"

Later on in the morning's workout after Elizabeth had left..."So what do you think about her? Maybe a B or B-plus? She might need to lose about ten to be an A."

"Yeah, maybe ten to fifteen," I agreed. "But she was focused.

She put a lot of energy into our workout yesterday."

Great, I thought. Not only is Summer going to hold me personally responsible for every quarter pound, but Max is going to be monitoring the situation. I was going to be under intense scrutiny. There would be no vacation until I passed an open-book exam. I felt like a lagging student with a final exam looming ahead.

Summer was late again that Wednesday, claiming that the woman who did such amazing work waxing her eyebrows had been running behind. To make it worse, she spent an extra five minutes on the treadmill, stating that she really felt it from yesterday and needed a couple of extra minutes to "stretch out."

Mercifully enough, the day's subject wasn't Max. It was how women who had given birth had more trouble getting back into shape than women without any children.

"How many do you have?" I asked politely.

"Oh, just one," she replied. "But haven't you noticed that childbirth seems to widen a woman's hips permanently and nothing she does reduces them again. I mean, look here," (she thumped a spandex covered hip bone with the palm of her closed fist) "this is bone right here, there's no fat on top of here. But I didn't have these before I had my son."

"How old is your son?"

"He's nineteen, but I mean that my hormones changed right after I had him. He can eat anything he wants and so could I when I was a teenager. Couldn't you?"

"Actually, I still can because resistance training gives me control of my metabolism."

With my statement she threw herself into the next set with a redoubled concentration that caused her to block out everything, even my counting, until I had to grab the bar, urging her to stop and rest.

She talked more about her son, bragging about his tennis playing ability and his potential for an outstanding physique if he would just begin working out regularly.

She began to explain about his real father but that it didn't matter because her husband Chuck had treated him as his own son since day one.

"It's not that we didn't try to have children of our own because we did. We've been to every doctor specializing in this since we got married. And Chuck's okay with just having Evan but sometimes I think that maybe his family would be more accepting of me if we had one more that was naturally his."

She then launched into intimate medical details about their mutual fertility, and I just kept counting and directing. By the end of her second workout, I had the distinct impression that I had known Summer for at least two months instead of two days.

29

CARDINAL FIAT LEANED forward with a sigh, both elbows propped on his desk, hands spread and covering his chin and cheeks, with eyes blinking slowly through splayed fingers. The enormous mahogany desk was immaculate save for a small statue of Jesus, hands clasped across the front of his porcelain robe, eyes directed at the heavens. A set of fat, glossy black pens sat in their holder, all three trimmed in real gold. The gleaming desk top was also marred, at second glance, by two sheets of paper and an envelope which had been gently slit apart with the solid gold paper knife. The knife had been a gift from an Italian ship building magnate. It was purported to have been cast from the melted down remains of a chalice, badly damaged from Allied bombs during the war and recovered by a penniless street urchin as the orphaned boy picked through rubble looking for a meal. Five large teak file cabinets lined the east wall of the study, the open drawer of one of them reserved only for correspondence containing direct orders from the Vatican in Rome. The rich, brown carpeting that had muted Father Pete's every footfall when he approached with the morning's mail reflected little of the indirect lighting that glowed faintly from around the intricately carved wood trim along the tops of each wall. Little additional light could be attributed to the windows in back of the tightly closed draperies behind the Cardinal's desk. In fact, the only noticeable source was the plate sized beam sent down to the middle of the desk by an ornate gold reading lamp shipped some years ago by a collector from South Africa. Even the lights of the long glass showcase lining the west wall, its shelves groaning with museum-quality gifts and artifacts obtained during the Cardinal's travels, were off today. An exact rendition of the Last Supper, painstakingly done in oil, stood alone on the wall near one door of the large study. Near the door of the study's huge bathroom hung another painting of the Ascension, a constant reminder to His Eminence of his own inevitable final journey. But the opulence of his surroundings was not going to be appreciated this morning as the holy man reread the papal directive that was already burned into his brain. The whisperings about some of the priests that had succumbed to the temptations of the flesh were well known, especially to the Cardinal. But the darkest and faintest whisperings, the ones that must have originated from the devil himself, were never accompanied by a shred of actual evidence. A few accounts sounded like nothing more than the dream-like imaginings of confused young men. Others sounded like vengeful tales from the mouths of vindictive male teenagers, told haltingly to sobbing parents as an explanation for sexual confusion or actions for which they refused to take personal responsibility. And there was little doubt that some of the horrific accusations had their basis in simple greed, thought up by opportunists after hearing about hush money settlements from other dioceses.

Nagging questions had surfaced in the past. Why would a diocese settle at all if there was no validity whatsoever to the accusations? It was nothing more than a tribute to unscrupulous lawyers if the accusations were groundless. A licensed attorney himself, His Eminence, in spite of his agreement with the attempts at equitability found throughout the law, was well aware that the judicial system had faults. The resultant negative publicity from trying a case such as this could do harm to the church body even if an innocent priest prevailed.

And yet the tone of the Pope's directive was quite clear. The Cardinal was to discreetly contact the pastor of each and every church through an emissary. Said designate was to inquire thoroughly about any and all accusations brought to the pastor's attention by any means or method. Each accusation was to be documented in full on a single sheet of paper for the perusal of the Cardinal alone. Until they could be hand delivered they were never to leave the designate's side; nor was their very existence to be discussed with anyone…ever. It was hoped that by taking a more pro-active approach with each accusation, no matter how seemingly trivial, that publicity-generating litigation could not only be nipped in the bud, but financial compensation could be dispensed with quietly and more cost effectively. Counseling, to both victim and accused, could be administered more effectively as well if done before the flames of frustration and anger, fanned by greedy attorneys, consumed all in their path.

The 70-year-old Cardinal, already burdened by a thousand responsibilities, sighed again, more heavily this time, at the thought of the man hours and money required to fulfill the terms set out in these two double-spaced pages. In a budget already stretched thin by controversial church closings in less fortunate neighborhoods and the waning donations resulting from a stock market free fall, there was no money for this investigation.

Even the refurbishing of the Cardinal's own cathedral, a magnificently rebuilt house of worship that trumpeted the indefatigable faithfulness of his flock, had fallen behind schedule due to budgetary constraints. Much detail work had been left unfinished, unnoticeable to the average visitor but obvious to the Cardinal.

Even his own private apartment and office—at 3,000 square feet, the size of a big ranch house—was lacking in some of its final appointments. Two crates of custom-made furniture still rested in crates in a Black Forest warehouse, their shipment delayed until payment could be promised. Heating costs for the several hundred glass and stone edifices attended each Sunday by the faithful were threatening to spiral out of control, exacerbated by an especially cold and unforgiving winter. Health care costs for a rapidly aging family of priests and nuns were outrageous, a by-product of medical advances that kept them on the Lord's earth longer than ever during their less productive years.

"You look troubled, Your Eminence," Father Pete's soft tone startled the Cardinal slightly, and he brought his hands down, folded his arms across his chest, and leaned back in his finely leathered office chair.

Standing apprehensively in front of the giant desk, Cardinal Fiat's right hand man looked as though he was waiting for an invitation. With still another sigh, the spiritual figure behind the desk gestured to the center of the three armchairs in front of him.

As Father Pete quickly situated himself, the Cardinal thought for a moment before replying. "It's the same old story, my son. We have accomplished many things in this diocese over the last twenty-five years. We have many good works in progress. We have many deserving projects in the planning stages. But we also receive a hundred requests per year for our participation in more, and we assist in some funding of emergency needs from parishioners on a daily basis too." He spoke with a hint of frustration in his voice. "Portions of our collections are allocated for international deeds as well…for people who starve because of war or drought or pestilence. Some funds from us also reach the Vatican itself, to be dispersed as they see fit."

Father Pete interjected hopefully, "I am confident that next month's dinner will give us a sufficient enough response to bid out the contract for new windows in all six buildings. The savings from this improvement will be reflected immediately in next year's gas bills."

The Cardinal smiled wanly. "I'm afraid that any funds pledged at that gathering and quite possibly the one after that, are already spoken for in this letter."

To Father Pete's quizzical look his boss merely replied, "All in good time, my son. I will first need the opportunity to pray for guidance in this matter, and then I will lay out the requirements to you."

Father Pete erased any further emotion from his countenance, making a mental note to look in the file for two double-spaced pages at a later date.

"I have received several answers in the mail to our invitations already," Father Pete reported, "and it looks as though attendance will be around seventy percent."

"Then I have only to hope that God will provide me with the words necessary to elicit their generosity once again."

Father Pete nodded in agreement and changed the subject to mapping out the week's travel itinerary, office appointments and phone schedule.

30

Summer's third workout that week was as intense as the first two, with the determined Grosse Pointer focusing on each exercise as though preparing for an assault on Mt. Everest. She claimed that she was walking every morning as well, and a weigh-in showed that she was down two pounds to 156.

Halfway through the workout, the subject turned from her son Evan's adoption by her husband Chuck to her own adoption years earlier. I was all ears as she described her adoptive mother's intelligence and the willingness to question authority that had gotten her booted out of the small town's church. Summer spoke with admiration about her adoptive mother's extensive knowledge of holistic medicine and quizzed me a bit between sets (yes, I knew that dandelion root made you pee more). But Summer couldn't seem to talk about the people that raised her from infancy without bringing me up to date on her efforts to find her natural parents. That they didn't care to be found was quite clear as she described one paper roadblock after another that had stymied all of her inquiries. The private investigator that she had retained eventually reported back that the road ended where it began. Any further information about the Virginia adoption ended with a Virginia judge who merely stated that no additional details would be forthcoming. Summer's speculation during her workout that day was multi-faceted and endless...was she Italian and Irish or perhaps French and Italian? She tanned too easily to be pure British or Irish. Her chiseled features negated the possibility of

Nordic heritage, and while some smattering of a Middle Eastern culture was a remote possibility, the Virginia of 1962 wasn't exactly known as a bastion of Arab immigrants. Summer had many practical reasons for wanting to meet and question her natural parents. Was there a history of breast cancer on her mother's side? Need she worry about early onset Alzheimer's or other mental diseases? Knowledge of cardiac problems or diabetes in older relatives might allow Summer to take preventative measures now. Then there was the question that had been nagging at her ever since grade school...the one question that she would have preferred be answered before all others. Summer would have given anything she owned to know if she had any brothers or sister, whole or half...it burned inside her every time she saw a family together.

Who was her real father? She asked me like I was withholding information. Was he residing in Virginia because he was an elected official in Washington D.C. in 1962? Was he a ranking officer in the navy or just an enlisted man? Was he still alive? Did he serve in Vietnam? And most of all, did he ever think about his little girl?

Summer waltzed out the door after the workout ended. She was happy about the two pounds, and all that was confessed was forgotten. Feeling emotionally blitzkrieged, I staggered out to find lunch. My week with this woman felt like a year had passed in a torrent of surmising and informational overload.

The next week's weigh-in revealed another two-pound loss. The week after showed us still another two, and week four arrived with a three-pound loss. Questions about Max continued to arise at a rate commensurate with the pounds shed. Week four's probing questions varied widely in topic matter from Max's European travel habits to his favorite restaurants. Trying desperately to be tight-lipped without obviously lying, I sometimes varied my answer from my usual "I dunno" and "not sure" by offering up something vague such as the name of the Italian restaurant that Max frequented for lunch. I decided that if Summer's fascination turned into stalking, the most unpleasant consequence may be merely a change in Max's luncheon locale.

Week five ended not only with a triumphant weigh-in of 147 (and a pleased and grateful Summer wearing ever more form-revealing workout gear), but a schedule change for the following week. She would now demand my full attention during my busiest times at night due to a weeklong tennis tournament. As her overpayments and dramatic changes continued unabated, I saw no reason to deny her and scheduled her for every night at 6 p.m., which was the same time that Nathan Lexington often reserved for his appearances at my studio. Thinking ahead to that time period over the weekend, I felt a brief pang of sympathy for Max's semi-famous offspring. It wouldn't be long after the initial introduction, perhaps a half-hour, maybe a bit more, until Nathan would be fending off a growing blizzard of questions about Max. This typhoon of redirected inquiries would not be sidestepped by Nathan as I'd been able to often do. "I don't know," would not be accepted as an answer by the beautiful inquisitor when posed to a favorite son and business associate of Max.

On Monday the hour grew near. Nathan showed up early, finished warming up on a treadmill and we were one-quarter finished with his workout when Summer arrived (late as usual). Summer never just walked into a room. She "made an entrance," and today was no exception. Although the day was cool, she wore a short tennis skirt. Pink-trimmed shoes and socks matched the outfit perfectly as did the pink cloth wristbands. Moving deftly with the quick, confident steps that always gave the impression that she was rushed but in control, Summer took over the near end of the desk with keys, cell phone, Walkman, purse and sunglasses. A brief glance around, and it was off to the bathroom with the purse for a make-up check and touch-up.

Some men are very transparent when they girl watch. Their eyes bulge as they follow their subject without blinking. Oblivious to whoever else may be watching, their mouths hang open and their heads switch to "auto-rotate." They aren't concerned if they're causing discomfort to the subject because they're too socially stupid to even entertain the possibility. Many of these Neanderthals take it one step further when, at some point, they "wooo!" or hoot, or "owww!" half-believing that the maiden will acknowledge him, leave her life and run away with a smelly shop-rat in his pickup. Girl-watching is trickier when the girlfriend or spouse is present. A proper "check" begins with keeping the mouth tightly shut. The adroit "checker" will then look past the subject and either ahead or behind, as if raptly interested in something else. Married men who master this sometimes decide they are ready for the next step…mutual checking. The married man points out the subject to his wife and follows with a comment such as "she's proud of 'em," or "who's she trying to impress?" or even "if that were any shorter she get arrested for bending over." Max was a master of this technique, and Elizabeth seemed to enjoy participating in the jibes.

Max's son Nathan, however, was the unrivaled master of discreet girl-watching. As Summer walked in, everyone in the studio acknowledged her arrival in a different manner. Whether it was a turn of the head, a glance, a raise of the eyebrow, a smile or sometimes a grimace, *everyone* had a reaction to the Grosse Pointe Princess. Everyone, that is, except Nathan. When I examined him for a reaction to her appearance, he was engrossed in a spot on his sweat pants. When she pranced out from her make-up evaluation to choose a treadmill, Nathan completely failed to notice, concentrating instead on the last few reps of some dumbell curls. As she loped on the treadmill, even the traffic on the main road in front of the studio seemed to pause as it passed, but Nathan struck up a conversation with an elderly female client.

Down to a walk again on the treadmill, Summer's cell phone rang and she answered, her face lighting up with a warm, "Suzanne, how *are* you?" Nathan was on his own cell phone, his back to the treadmills, gesticulating as he talked.

Summer hung up first, and sought me out, ready to begin. Her dark locks flowed down as she stretched, using a routine that was part yoga, part tennis diva. We began on a leg press machine on the opposite end of the studio from where Nathan was dispensing phone advice to an underling.

Fifteen minutes later, and Summer was back on her cell phone, moving and stretching in a corner of the studio. Nathan and I were completing his last set of tricep pressdowns, and a full half-hour had passed without the TV pitchman ever hinting that anything but his workouts could ever compete for his full attention. I looked over to Summer's corner to see whether her pow-wow with her esthetician had ended when I heard a whisper in my left ear.

"What the hell is that?"

I smirked and rolled my gaze sideways ever so subtly. The man to my left had gone for over thirty minutes without giving the faintest indication that he knew of Summer's existence. His eye had never flickered, had never strayed and his face remained an unbreachable mask of impassiveness. I had been watching like a starving hawk, ready to pounce with an introduction to her, only to feel like a tawdry voyeur while Nathan completely ignored her. But now waves of vindication engulfed me. I wanted to jump up and down yelling, *"I knew you couldn't pass up this one, I knew it!"* But I resisted the impulse. Instead I waited twenty seconds and said, "Pretty good, huh? And I'm not done with her yet."

Man! I thought, *This guy is the best there is.* I wanted to bow in front of Nathan with my arms outstretched in praise. This happily married man was the most subtle, most subversive, most clandestine girl-watcher I'd ever met! I'd been waiting in twisted knots of expectation only to be fooled by the master of feigned indifference. Finished with my hat-tipping, I watched Summer hang up and float over to us.

"Summer, this is Nathan. Nathan, this is Summer. She plays tennis with your father."

"Hello Nathan, a pleasure to meet you. What is your last name?"

"Lexington."

Her almond-shaped eyes opened perceptibly wider, relays clicked, circuits connected, and conclusions were printed out rapid-fire.

"Oh, yes, I know your father, Max. We've spoken on the courts at Lochmoor. Do you play? I haven't seen you there."

"Oh no," Nathan answered. "I've golfed there but I don't play tennis."

Summer began circling her prey, and yet at the same time began making him feel like the only man in the world.

"From the width of your shoulders I would have guessed football before golf. Do you work with your father?"

"No, not really, I work over at Elegant Classics."

At this point I wasn't yet sure if she recognized him. Surely she owned a TV set. She probably owned twenty. I knew she stayed awake after 10 p.m. She *must* have seen Nathan between one hundred fifty and seven hundred times on one of her screens.

"Oh really, you knooww, I've had my eye on a B. Dikkus ensemble for some time. Do you have any units in stock?"

"Ahh, I don't know for sure, but I think we have one left. If you're in the area you could stop by and just have the receptionist buzz me down from the offices."

"Thank you. I will do that."

During the next two weeks, as May approached, Summer's workouts continued with a vengeance. Nathan Lexington's workouts did not, however, as golf season made its demands on his free time.

Summer made good on her promise to appear at Elegant Classics but was rebuffed by an incompetent receptionist who mistook her for an opportunistic manufacturer's rep. She allowed me to listen to several frantic voice messages on her cell phone from Nathan as he repeatedly apologized and explained. He attempted to make amends by leaving a number at his office that went "directly to me." It might have, in fact, been a direct line to him, but according to a puzzled Summer…he never answered it. I wasn't nearly as puzzled. I'd noticed that Nathan hadn't exactly volunteered his cell phone number either (it might have been awkward if Lu Ann was in the vicinity) and I knew it to be on 24/7 in case Poppa called.

In my gyms and among my circle of friends, I'm not known for my impressions or voices other than to distinguish characters in a joke. Of course, I do Gomer Pyle, Bill Clinton, Don Adams ("Get Smart"), Marilyn Monroe, Richard Simmons and a damn good Mike Tyson, but other than a dozen or so of these basics, mimicking people is not my specialty. Maxwell Lexington, with a low nasally voice that could be picked out by Helen Keller at the Super Bowl, was too tempting to pass up. He also had a tendency to draw out his A's and his O's, which, when exaggerated a bit, would bring out the smirks in my audience, even if it were only Natasha. Like anyone else, Max had favorite phrases and sayings that peppered his verbalized thoughts and conversations. A truly outstanding Maxwell Lexington impressionist would be expected to have mastered each of these and to know when to interject them into a conversation. There was no manual for this. There was no school, no vocal coach...I was totally on my own. But I did the homework. I identified and catalogued phrases, elongated my A's and O's until my daughter snickered in amusement, and got low and nasally. When I felt ready for the public, I tried it on Natasha. She applauded but reminded me that she'd only spoken to him twice. I performed in front of Summer who said, "That's very close," and then asked if he'd talked to me about her. While dropping off some fat burners at the castle, I took the plunge and tried my impression on Robert the house manager. Widening his eyes in bemusement, he said that it was *amazing*! Robert's positive critique was encouraging. I was ready for stardom! I would wow audiences nationwide.

There were no audiences to wow, though, because Max didn't do much public speaking. The slightly reclusive billionaire had never made a movie as far as I knew, and his son Nathan was the television star of the family. I was never emboldened enough to try my skill on any of Max's offspring, and although Elizabeth had a sense of humor, a prank phone call to her seemed inappropriate. Impromptu Max impersonations for the family also seemed like a sure route to getting fired without any letter of recommendation.

I was unable to supervise Nathan's last workout at my studio. My daughter had a lead in her church Easter play and I decided to douse myself with holy water and attend. My girlfriend Natasha was working Nathan out for me when the gym's phone rang. She answered it and heard "Yeah, hi, this is Max Lexington, is this Nataaaasha?"

Natasha rolled her eyes and pursed her lips. She suppressed her impulse to yell out, "I know diss ees you Mark!" and instead said, "Uh, yah."

The voice said, "Nice to hear you again, is everything well?"

"Uh, yah." She replied again, every fiber of her being aching to call the bluff, or better yet respond with an uncanny Max impression of her own.

"Good, good. Say listen babe, I've been trying to reach my son Naaathan but he must have his cell phone off or the battery must be dead or something. I called Lu Ann at his house and she said she thought he might be working out. Is he there?"

The voice's explanation sounded logical enough to Natasha. But why didn't the voice ask for Mark first? Why was such an involved explanation offered? The temptation to end this hoax was becoming overwhelming. Natasha had reached the go/no go point. A straight answer might produce peals of laughter or an "I gotcha" at the least. Calling the bluff, however, would result in lengthy explanations to Max and apologies to her boyfriend, or outrage and outright termination of his part-time job if she were wrong. Natasha wracked her brain. Didn't he say he had considered quitting anyway? Perhaps new promises had been made by Max that she wasn't privy to yet? It was best just to answer and get it over with.

"Yas, he is, I vill get him for you."

Natasha handed the phone to Nathan…There was no laughter, no giggling or looks of derision sent her way. Her boyfriend's employment with Max would also continue…at least for now.

My next workout at the mansion was to be with Max alone. We spoke as usual about the previous evening's overimbibement. Then, from out of the blue, "Hey, how are that Summer's workouts coming? Whenever I'm playing now she runs right up to me and says 'Hey Max, how are you sweetie!' Can you believe she's that way? I mean this girl's a looker, isn't she?"

After the bombardment of questions at my studio, I didn't feel as though I was overstepping when I answered. "We just broke through the 140 barrier yesterday when I weighed her in at 139 pounds for a total loss of 19 pounds."

The perspiring CEO replied, "Oh, I caan see thaat, Maaark. I mean, she was the complete package *before* she started with you but now, whoo booy! You should see my partners' faces when she comes up to me now, Maaark, it's as if she's known me for yeeaars or something. She'll bounce right up to me, she doesn't care *who's* watching. Why do ya think that is? I mean, let's face it, she's maybe thirty-five and I'm playing the back nine, so what else could it be? I mean, she's gotta know all about who I am. She certainly wouldn't be this friendly if I were a plumber, would she?"

Great, I thought. Now I'm the host of the dating game. I thought I'd try a subtle subject change first.

"Have you noticed, sir, that because of all the inches she's lost off her legs that she now has that line that comes up the side from the knee to the hip? That's the line that women get when they've been working out and losing just fat. 'Course she's probably gained three or four pounds of muscle which actually means that she's lost *more* than 19 pounds of fat overall." I might have been looking for a little pat on the back that day but the main purpose of my bragging was to inspire my 257-pound charge to continue with his program. If I pointed out repeatedly that it obviously worked well on someone that he knew personally, he might be more inspired and consistent about his own diet and exercise program, including the drinking that buffeted his iron-like liver.

"Well, she certainly hasn't lost anything up top if you get my drift. Those have got to be all hers. I can tell when she runs for a ball. She wears her tops so that you can see she's proud of 'em too! I mean, why would she dress like that when she knows I'm gonna be on the next court that morning if she weren't trying to *say* something?"

My subject switch had been fruitless.

Two weeks later, Summer was lying on my leg press machine

contemplating the ceiling tiles. Fifteen minutes ago, we had just set a new record low when she weighed in at 136 pounds. Her firm, shapely legs were slightly tensed, even as she rested. As she stood on the scale that afternoon and steadied herself, she subconsciously flexed her upper arms, which had taken an entirely new shape in the past three months. I had observed earlier that instead of the back of her arm shaking when she ran her hand through her luxuriant hair, it remained firm and steady. The skin rippled with a hint of new muscles whenever she straightened it back out. The tops of her arms were beginning to pinch in instead of bow out before they joined at the end of her shoulder's perfect curvature. Also, with her arm over her head, I could begin to make out the three distinctive sections of her shoulder underneath the taut skin. Just below, Summer's collarbones were re-emerging from the fat that had engulfed them, and I began to wonder how gold or diamond necklaces would look as they cascaded over her collar-bones and down her chest. Even her neck had thinned, bringing back her regal appearance. Now, as she lay on the leg machine, reveling in her trans-formation and eager to continue, she used me as her sounding board yet again.

"I mean, it's been since last fall that I've seen Cindy and Mark, she was shocked! She was practically yelling when she recognized me! I'd never met the friend she was shopping with but Cindy dropped her packages right on the woman's foot and started running over to me. Frankly, I was kind of embarrassed for her…you know, she needs to start doing something herself, since her divorce all she does is sit at her desk at work. I know I look a lot different but if you could have seen the look of utter *shock* when she realized it was me! I keep getting more and more *reaction* out of people I know when they haven't seen me for awhile."

I nodded in agreement and asked for another set of presses.

As soon as she finished, she looked in another direction. I knew a different subject (and a transition to it) was looming.

"Of course I'm very grateful to you and all but the one I *really* have to thank for this is our friend Max. He's the one who turned

me on to you. I tried everything else and even thought Pilates was
the answer until a month went by and nothing happened. But if it
wasn't for Max's referral that day I'd still weigh the same or more!
The inches I've lost make it seem as though I've lost way more
than twenty-two pounds. How is my friend anyway? Is he losing
any more? I haven't seen him for three weeks now, is he okay?"

I mentioned a detached retina in Max's eye that had required
periodic sessions of laser surgery as an outpatient, but added that
it had responded beautifully. I had heard that he might try some
tennis again the next week and told her so.

She went on, "Well I suppose I could buy him something to
thank him. Of course I wouldn't have any way of knowing if I got
him something he already has. I'm sure a man like that already has
anything he needs and a card doesn't seem like enough."

"Maybe you could give him a thank you card but slip a crisp
new five or ten dollar bill into it," I offered.

"Very funny," she retorted as she smiled anyway.

We moved on to the next machine. After three months, I felt as
though I'd known her for about five years. I knew that she'd made
up her mind about something, and that I was about to find out what
she'd decided.

"Mark…" she began as she looked out the front windows, "How
do you think he'd take it if I told him I'd like to thank him for
referring me to you by taking him to lunch? Whenever we see
each other at the club we never have more than a minute to talk.
Either I'm getting in and he's leaving or the other way around.
Once when we did finish at the same time his tennis partners were
hanging around so close. I didn't want to put him on the spot. I just
think…that he would be the most interesting man to talk to. He
would make a fascinating friend, don't you think?"

"He's an interesting guy, all right," I agreed.

"I mean, even Chuck said that he's always admired and
respected Max. I don't think he'd mind if the two of us were seen
together. I'd tell him anyway. What do you think? Would he say
yes?"

"Lunch might work. I'd rather the two of you didn't pick a place with a bread basket, though."

"Are you saying I still look fat?" She smiled at me.

"No, no, I'm just saying that we've come a long way but I'm not finished with the project yet, and white bread isn't exactly your friend."

"Okay, hypothetical then. Should I let Max, if he says yes, pick the place? Or should *I* pick it. Should I suggest someplace *inside* the Pointes where somebody will surely recognize us and make him uncomfortable or should I make reservations somewhere farther from here…but then he might feel strange being in the car with me if it took a while to get there!"

"If it's just lunch with a friend. I don't see how it matters where," I replied.

"Oh, but Mark, people here talk. I mean they'll be just as pleasant as can be to your face but then minutes later when they're gone your ears will be *burning*! Chuck's brother George is the worst. Did I ever tell you about him…?"

Two weeks later, I was en route late on a Friday afternoon to the Cathedral with Mr. and Mrs. Lexington settled into the back of the Mercedes S500. It had been a very warm mid-June, and both the front and rear air were set low. A huge afternoon service was to take place in the parking lot of the Cathedral and a couple of thousand were expected to attend. I approached from the usual direction and was about to make a right turn onto the access road to the Cathedral when I noticed a barricade and a police car barring my path. Apparently, the small town police chief had decided that an event of this magnitude was going to require some traffic control. I was sure that the manual he bought, "Screwing Up Traffic For Your Small Town's Event," had a chapter specifically for dealing with a whopping two or three thousand cars and busses. The manual probably advised the little Napoleon to shut down any logical access roads and route the traffic in as circuitous a manner as possible. If the chief's puppet, a sleepy Barney Fife character in a patrol car ahead, prevented us from turning at his intersection, we would be forced to cast about for an alternate method of entry. I estimated that traversing five extra miles of road would be necessary to plunge into the line of stop-and-go traffic as the masses tried to gain entry.

Fortunately, we had a well-practiced plan in place to circumvent the rules that the common folk were required to follow. To begin initiating the ritual, I parked well out of traffic and as close as possible to the barricade. Step one required that I place the car in park but leave it running so that all power accessories continued to function. Step two dictated that I exit the vehicle and approach the cop guarding the obstruction to explain who I was driving and why it was imperative that we pass. "Guest of Honor" was one of several phrases that seemed to help. About half the time I never needed to go beyond step two. The reasonable cop would acquiesce, and I would be allowed to squeeze by or move the barricade just enough to do so.

On this particular occasion, I drew a cop on his first full day back at work after a lobotomy. Step three necessitated my trudging back to the car and its right rear passenger window, which Max would dutifully roll down as I reported my lack of success. Step four entailed my opening the door and standing by it as Max lurched out of the car and approached the cop while wearing a $5,000 suit. Max always tried sugar first, smiling broadly and introducing himself with a hearty handshake. To my amazement, today required a step five as Max strongly encouraged the severely autistic guardian of the peace to summon his lieutenant to the scene. Max was a master at citing from the book of "Do you know who I am?" without ever actually saying it, and read a chapter to the lieutenant. The superior arrived quickly and immediately realized that the man standing in the roadway was the sole financial sponsor of the evening's event. He ordered the lazy impediment to our progress to get out of his patrol car and move the barricade himself.

We never got as far as step six, but I suspect that it would have involved the state police to some extent even if it meant an hour tacked on to our time of arrival. Modifications of this procedure could be used at clubs, restaurants, valets or anywhere else that we encountered a non-cooperator.

The police department's "help" at this particular event ended at the main road and, observing the absence of any more badges or guns, I bullied our way to a prime drop-off spot, ignoring the security force in their darling red uniforms. Max and Elizabeth were soon whisked through the teeming throngs to a place of honor down in the front. Afterwards, they and a small select group of front rowers were asked to follow the Bishops and Cardinals to a private "after party" for the big givers.

The chosen ones fell loosely into line and, putting on their best "contrite" countenances, shuffled into an anteroom (where the undergivers were never invited). A private meeting with Cardinal Fiat and a Bishop ensued. Two hours later, after forty volunteers had folded thousands of folding chairs and removed them from the lot, the group of twenty-five or so "contributors" filtered out of the main door. Filled with the spirit (and a bit of blessed wine) of whatever private words had been spoken, the smug looking couples smiled and bade each other good-bye with "lemme put my hand on your shoulder to show my sincerity" warmth.

The next week at the studio, Summer weighed in at a new record low of 133 for a total loss of 25 pounds. When I factored in a gain of four pounds of muscle, I calculated a loss of 29 pounds of fat in four months. The woman's transformation was so dramatic that she was becoming a walking billboard for me and my little studio among her many friends and acquaintances. Almost weekly, a new client signed up exclaiming, "I want to look just like Summer, although I know I'll never be as tall/beautiful/big breasted as her!"

With most of her former beauty and figure returned to her, the chic socialite began to find other things to obsess about.

"Mark, do you think I should get another injection in my upper lip, just to fill it out here…and here?"

"No, Summer, I think your lips are perfect."

"Well, I already made the appointment. How about my eyes then? The doctor that does my botox injections is actually a plastic surgeon, and he says that two hours on an outpatient basis will remove all of the puffiness from here and…here."

"Your eyes are perfectly shaped, Summer, and I don't think you should mess with them."

"No, he wouldn't change the *shape* at all. I love my cat-eye look too, but if I got these two little pockets of fat removed and the skin tightened I wouldn't look so *sleepy* all the time, don't you think?"

"Actually, Summer, I kind of *like* it when a woman looks ready for bed all the time."

"Mark, I'm serious. And while he's at it maybe I could have him do something about my neck here, see? When I lift here…and here, see how it tightens it up?"

Summer was probably the only person I'd ever met who was considering a major cosmetic procedure after having a minor one because she was "going to be there anyway."

Potential liposuction areas were presented for my input as I did my best to discourage surgeries until I was satisfied that I could make no further progress. From my point of view, it had taken about fifteen years from the cessation of her "entertainment" career for her figure to fall into a state of neglect. I would have liked more than the fifteen or so weeks allotted to me to finish my project before the cosmetic surgeons took over.

31

WHEN I LOOK back over a sometimes tumultuous existence, I can now pinpoint defining dates and specific events that occurred that eventually—for better or worse—changed the course and direction that I planned on taking in my life. Sometimes an unrealized good moment, such as a client signing up who would later give me a profitable stock tip, can take weeks or months to manifest itself. Sometimes a bad moment, such as the German-born and trained auto mechanic I once hired who would periodically set a customer's car on fire, thus ensuring that I had adequate experience with the legal system, would have delayed repercussions as well. Until July of 2001, I would merely react to positive or negative events as they unfolded without necessarily bothering to trace them back to their origins. My ability to recognize the potential birth of a negative event at least allows me the option of stifling it before precious time is wasted reacting to its growth and running around doing damage control. Even early recognition of a positive event is beneficial because I can then take full advantage as it unfolds, trying to direct its course as best I can.

I didn't adopt any of this philosophy, of course, until well after a specific moment that occurred in July. What is unusual though, is that I recognized that moment, the instant it happened, as being one of life-altering significance.

There is a riddle in Michigan. What do you call the two days of rain following five days of sunshine? The answer is: the weekend. It was drizzling ever so lightly on a Sunday morning when I decided to stop for gas en route to lunch with Natasha. As I began pumping, my cell phone rang. It seemed at bit more shrill than usual, and I looked down at the caller ID as I opened it. With curiosity, I noted that the number had a similar exchange to other numbers at the Lexington mansion but had never before appeared on my phone. Robert always called on his own designated line. The few calls that I received on weekends from the residence were from Mrs. Lexington canceling a workout for one last-minute reason or another. These calls were always from the main house number, which I always recognized and had memorized. But this number that appeared was a digit or two off. Could this be from the number from the private line that had never been offered to me? Its existence was alluded to once or twice during workouts, but I had never received a call from it and certainly never been supplied with it. So strong was my curiosity that my finger was drawn to push the talk button without my willing it to do so. Pressing the button as I drew the phone to my ear, I said, "Hi, this is Mark."

"Yeah, Maaark, this is Max Lexington. Listen, I'm sorry to bother you on a Sunday (nevertheless he was anyway) but I was wondering if I could pick your brain for a minute?"

Whoa, this was it. This was that moment that would forever alter my plans and my life. For better or worse, the moment was beginning at this instant…with this phone call…from this private line. Perhaps most exciting of all, I recognized that it was happening…as it happened!

Any intrusion would have to be overlooked. A forefinger in the air to Natasha was the only indication I could give that this call was worth taking and I implored her patience.

"Of course, sir, please go ahead."

"I was talking with our friend on Friday. Now, Maaark, you know her far better than I. You've worked out with her non-stop for months now. You see her almost every day. And you've done some remarkable things with her, I'll be the first to admit. She's young, she's a ten now, no question about it. And I'm seventy, I've got eight kids, and all I've done is say hello to her and maybe talk for a minute. I mean, that's what brought her to you...when she asked me who my trainer was and how to get in touch with him. And I've done *nothing* to send a message that I'm interested in anything else. But last Friday I was at Lochmoor because the weatherman said we might get rained out at the Yacht Club so we switched. Now she couldn't have known I would be there...oh, she might have noticed my car maybe but it wasn't the *only* silver one in the lot. Anyway she comes up to me and says, 'Max! How arrrre you?' Mark, man to man, buddy, I thought she was going to kiss me right there or something. I was polite. I said Summer, nice to see you. You look wuuuunderful! And Mark, let me tell you buddy she's come a long way with you. I mean, she was a looker before but now...Whoa boy!"

I couldn't believe Max and I were having this conversation. "Yes sir, she's come a long way," I said.

"But then Maaark, she said something that really puzzled me. And the truth of the matter is, I still don't know what she meant by it. She said Max, I want to thank you for sending me to Mark. Now Maaark, I *never* sent her to you. I *just* told her how to get in touch with you, that's all!"

"Well, Mr. Lexington, nobody knew she could look like she does now."

"That's true, so she thanks me and then says, I feel indebted to you. You *must* let me buy you lunch."

I almost collapsed in the parking lot. She talked about it. She said she was going to do it, but my God, she did it! This woman had guts.

"Let me tell you Mark, this girl has chutzpah! I mean, why would she just ask me that out of the blue that way? You know her better than I, what is her reasoning?"

Levity time! I thought, *and hurry!* "Maybe she's just hungry, sir."

"Hah! No Mark, that's not it! I mean, the way she approached me about it. She knows about Mrs. Lexington, for God's sake!"

Like a twig cast upon a river heading towards a waterfall, I felt myself being drawn forever past the point of no return. This conversation was me crossing the line from employee to friend/confidant, never to be able to return, and I knew it as I watched it happen. I felt a bit queasy as I was yanked out of my unsatisfactory, yet comfortable, employer/employee relationship and thrust into a role that I was sure somebody else...anybody but *me* anyway...should be filling.

"Well, I already know *exactly* what I'm going to do! Something has given this girl the wrong impression completely. And at the end of the day, I know deep down that she wouldn't be asking me out to lunch if I was just a plumber, don't you think?"

"Not too many plumbers are members at Lochmoor, so we may never know," I replied.

"That's true Maaark. But I couldn't even be seen with her outside of there. She's *half* my age, for God's sake! What do you think she sees in me?"

"Well, besides that business of yours that I've heard is doing well, you *are* a pretty interesting guy."

"And Maaark, no question about it, she's very attractive and when she talks to a guy, she knows she's got his complete attention. She knows how to make a guy feel like he's the only man in the room. She's got the looks and she's not stupid, either. No buddy, I know *exactly* what I have to do, I'll just avoid her, that's all."

It was my turn. I would be allowed just a few words. "I'm sure whatever decision you make will be the right one, sir."

Max thanked me for listening and apologized for taking up so much of my time on a Sunday. My cell phone indicated that we had talked about fifteen minutes. I had been walking around the gas station parking lot for the majority of this unprecedented conversation and now got back in the car with an impatient Natasha.

"Oh my gawd," I said. "I think I've just crossed the line big time. I've just gone from employee only to employee slash confidant and I *really* don't feel too comfortable about it."

"Das it pay za zame or better zan juzt employee?" Natasha asked helpfully.

"Actually, I don't believe that conversation paid anything at all," I replied. "But hopefully it's just a one time thing."

The rest of Sunday and Monday went by without me hearing from Max. On Tuesday I worked out in the morning with Elizabeth, but the business tycoon was absent and "busy." Sensing that my line crossing had left me temporarily unemployed with him, I vowed to increase my hours at the studio as it continued to gain in popularity.

Even Summer canceled her workout that Tuesday, however, vowing to contact me later in the afternoon to confirm a tentative move to four o'clock. At 3:45 p.m. she called from her cell phone to apologize and reschedule for the next day.

I received a call from a slightly embarrassed and worried Elizabeth Lexington at seven o'clock that evening asking if Max had called me for a "designated driver" ride or, if not, did I know of his whereabouts?

Summer called one hour prior to her appointment on Wednesday, speaking quietly and in a muffled voice as she explained that she had been stricken with a stomach ailment and simply couldn't muster the energy to budge from her bed.

She managed to make her Thursday appointment and popped into the gym only fifteen minutes late, which meant that *she* probably considered herself to be miraculously right on time.

Summer impatiently watched me waste time as I made sure another client avoided injury on a machine. She sighed and harumphed as I set up an appointment with a new client on the phone. As I hung up, the princess beckoned me to her treadmill where she warmed up.

She had not missed four days in a row since beginning at the studio, and I was prepared to discuss the day's routine and the inadvisability of trying to "make up" for any lost workouts. I leaned forward to listen to her apology for being lax and to map out my strategy for the remainder of the week.

"Have you heard from Max?" she whispered.

That's just great, I thought. I had devoted months now to my living sculpture project, juggling schedules and pondering new workout tactics and strategies for her even when I wasn't at the gym. The peak time for presenting Summer to the world was just days away and the question that was first and foremost on *her* mind was the status of her upcoming lunch date, which I now knew to be doubtful at best.

"Not since Sunday," I replied.

Her jaw dropped in amazement. "You haven't heard from him since Sunday? Were you over there?"

"No, he called me," I answered warily, steeling myself for the barrage of questions that was sure to follow.

"Did he talk about working out?"

"Uh, no, he didn't."

"Well, Mark, did he talk about me?"

"What kind of season do you think the Lions will have without Barry Sanders as their running back anymore?"

"Mark, this is important. I need to know what he said to you about me. Did he tell you that I asked him out to lunch?"

"Because if their opponents know that there's no running game anymore then they're probably going to blitz on every play, especially with the injuries to the offensive line."

"Don't be a jerk, I know you hate football."

Saying that I hated football was a bit strong. I used to watch it a little. A more appropriate statement would be to say that I was heavily disinterested in the sport. Of course, I could name the top five recognized contenders in each boxing division from heavyweight on down and recant the highlights of their careers. No one gave me credit for that, however, in hockey-crazed Grosse Pointe.

"Okay, just tell me this. Did he...indicate one way or another what he thought about meeting me for lunch somewhere?"

"Let's just say," I hesitated, knowing Summer would never let up, "that I don't think you need to block out any time soon on your lunch schedule."

"Oh really?" Summer's eyes opened in a "we'll just see about that" expression.

I didn't hear from either of the Lexingtons for the rest of the week, which wasn't necessarily unusual. A visit from Robert that Saturday for fat burners told me that my new phone confidant was still thinking of me...or at least he was still thinking of his waistline.

As Robert was tallying up the pill packages he said, "Oh, by the way, both he and her are wondering if you could be there Monday morning for a workout?"

I said that of course I could. I privately doubted that both would make it and was beginning to get a little vexed at the haphazardness of their commitment.

A man is praying to God one morning. He says, "God, I hope you're listening. I think I'm about to lose my job, and I'm already a little behind on my car payments. I was wondering, God, if you might maybe let me win the lottery?" A week later the same man is praying again, "Okay God, they took my car away and I was right, I lost my job. My wife is very mad and I can't make the mortgage payments on my house. I'd be okay if you'd just let me win the lottery. What do you say God, please?" A month later, the disgusted man is praying again, "Oh God, why didn't you help me? My house is gone, I have no job, my wife left me, I'm living on the streets. I've never won anything before. Would it be so bad if you'd let me win the lottery?" This time there's a hush as dark clouds roll in and a voice booms out from the heavens and says, "Sam, meet me halfway, buy a ticket!"

After arriving at the mansion on Monday morning, I waited a few minutes for the billionaire and his wife to come down. Finding the scale in its usual closet, I hauled it out and placed in on the floor. Mrs. Lexington began the ritual by stepping on the scale. As the digits appeared under the glass screen her shoulders sagged in disappointment. She was two pounds up. Maxwell Lexington, clearing his throat and a little unsteady from the previous night's libations, took his turn on the small electronic machine of truth.

He shook his large head in disgust as the little scale reported back that he was five pounds up.

"Maaark, this is terrible. Tell me, what can we do to make these workouts work better?"

Inwardly, my jaw dropped. Outwardly, I kept it closed because doing so made it easier to bite down on my tongue. I thought, *"Sam, buy a ticket!"*

It had been at least a week and a half since the very busy Mr. Lexington had been anywhere near his elaborate home gym.

I checked my notes. Elizabeth had been averaging two workouts per week, or eight per month. Max, while he had been faithfully scheduling at least two per week, had only been averaging one session every week and a half or about three per month. I was often regaled with stories of new restaurants that the couple had tried and catered parties where they "nibbled." The businessman's drinking had increased to a nightly requirement. Max's growing determination to single-handedly ensure that the Crown Royal distillery was never tempted to discontinue its flagship product was wreaking havoc on his liver's ability to convert fat. It didn't look like the "weight loss fairy" was going to be visiting Max anytime soon. Not only was my resume going to carry a two hundred and sixty pound blemish on it but I was going to reap the blame as a "trainer in absentia." Fed up at last by my accuser's statement, I resolved at that moment to bail out as their trainer after over two years of mind boggling frustration. As I began to total my final bill, I started to flesh out the spin that I'd put on the whole situation if confronted with my failure. I could steadfastly maintain that I stopped a 260-pound billionaire from becoming a 300-pound one. I could protest loudly that a crazed tailor had padded all of his suits and he actually weighed 180. A friend had a program on his computer that digitally manipulated photos…If I took pictures of Max and asked for a favor…

Too depressed to deliver any more pep talks, I stuck to small talk and updates on my summer boating plans. I asked Max if the eighty-two-foot yacht was coming up from Florida at all, and he

said no. He mused aloud that it was a pity, too, because we were
having gorgeous weather and he missed having a boat at the Yacht
Club for evenings or weekends. I hadn't made any suggestions for
him to ignore in over a month, so I pointed out that he already
owned a perfectly good fifty-foot yacht that he wasn't using up
north. I explained that it would only take about eighteen hours of
actual running time to bring it down to the Grosse Pointe Yacht
Club. Max put on his best "I'm all ears" face before he tossed it
onto the refuse pile along with all of my other suggestions.

That afternoon at the studio, Summer seemed to be bursting
with more than her typical "have you heard from Max?"
questionnaires. Acting pensive and yet inquisitive, the brunette
salon princess started to take her deep "I've got a question for
you" breath but couldn't seem to bring herself to actually pose
one. I ignored her hesitations until the studio was nearly empty
and she could contain herself no longer. She finished a set of leg
presses and lay back on the machine, feet still raised and planted
on the platform.

"Mark," she began, "do you suppose that Max would accept
my lunch invitation if I asked him to meet me someplace discreet
and we then drove together to an even more discreet destination?"

"No, Summer," I answered. "While I might call it bold or even
brazen I don't think it would improve your chances of a 'yes' at
all."

"Well, let's say that you guessed wrong and that we met and
drove together at least twenty-five miles away and were sitting
side-by-side eating lunch and he reached under the table cloth and
started caressing my hand as we talked."

"I'd say that your imagination is taking over your sense of logic
because I can't visualize that ever happening."

"Mark, I know we're just speaking hypothetically here but
please just humor me. I don't know anybody else who is as close
to him as you are. He speaks very highly of you and says that you
wear a lot of hats for him. I don't know for sure why I'm so
fascinated by him. Maybe it's more…I'm intrigued by the…*power*

that he exudes. Not just the power that his money gives him but the fact that because of what he built and who he is people will move mountains for him when he asks." She paused, but just long enough for another twenty second set on the machine. "So just play along...please. I just want to know how I should react if he started kissing me at lunch and then wanted to take me somewhere else. Maybe take me to some other favorite bars or somewhere or if he just wanted to spend hours with me in his car kissing me and touching my hair or my face or my leg."

I'd met mentally ill people before. I was fully aware that they may act outwardly normal ninety-nine percent of the time until they had an "episode." Summer could be a bit flamboyant at times, with some eccentricities that might be called irritating. I also knew that feigning a psychosomatic condition is occasionally nothing more than a ploy to grab attention. Summer, however, had my utmost attention, often five days a week, as I sought to complete the most radical transformation that I'd ever attempted at this studio. I was a bit crestfallen as I realized that four months of work would be for naught as my subject slipped further and further into the abyss of insanity right before my eyes. I imagined Summer in a straight jacket and took some solace in the fact that I could still work out her legs if the court required her to wear it at all times.

I wondered if the psychotropic drugs prescribed by her clinic's director would have an adverse effect on her metabolism. If they kept her nails short so she wouldn't harm herself, perhaps I could convince her attendants to release her restraints long enough for us to use a cable machine or do some chest presses. I didn't know if it would be weeks or months until she began barking and chasing other clients around the gym, so I resolved to get as much accomplished in whatever time we had left.

Two days later, I was working out with just Max, and he asked me if I'd heard from "our friend Summer" lately. I said that I had seen her every day that week and that she had entered the tennis tournament at the Yacht Club at the last possible moment and was looking forward to it.

"You know, Maaark, I'm sponsoring that tournament, from the breakfast before it through the dinner banquet. I'm even putting up the guarantee for the special appearance by the pro."

"Yes sir, she told me. It sounded so good I was tempted to buy a racket, take a lesson and enter!"

"Haahh, that's funny Mark. But her workouts are going okay?"

"Oh, yes. She had a little lapse last week. But she's back at it this week harder than ever."

"Good, that's good, buddy. She sure has got what it takes…" Max seemed to talk much more freely about Summer when Elizabeth wasn't around. He wanted to know if she'd said anything more about her interest in him, and I said she had asked about him.

On Thursday afternoon, Summer was scheduled yet again, mentioning that she intended to take the next day off to be prepared for Saturday's tournament. I had decided that instead of weathering a blizzard of "what ifs" and other imaginary scenarios and dates I would burst her bubble early and hard. She started early, summoning me to her treadmill within her first minute. "Have you heard from our friend?" she queried.

"I was there yesterday."

"Did he ask about the tournament Saturday?"

"I mentioned that you planned on playing in it"

"Has Max mentioned anything about lunch?'

"Summer, I'm afraid it's never going to happen."

A look of victorious smugness came over her face. "What if I were to tell you that it already did?"

"I would advise you to have your car checked for exhaust leaks because I don't think you brain is getting enough oxygen when you drive."

"Mark, everything happened exactly the way I described it!" She was gushing like a school girl, and I was actually starting to believe her.

"Summer, you said that whole scenario was hypothetical."

"Well I couldn't tell you *then*. I didn't know what you'd say to him."

"That all happened last Tuesday, didn't it?"

"Mark, we went everywhere. We had lunch in a dark corner of the restaurant at the Ritz Carlton. We tried to go the Renaissance Club in Detroit but it was closed and we'd both had a lot of wine by then so we wandered around lost inside just trying to find it."

"Who was driving?"

"Oh, he was, of course. I've told you I barely drink so I was in no shape to drive. I barely knew where we were half the time!"

"You didn't have the flu on Wednesday. You were hungover!"

"What do you expect? We went to two other places after that. I even said once, 'Honey, are you okay to drive?' after we almost got in an accident!"

"You think that maybe an accident would have resulted in a bit of negative publicity on the front page of the *Detroit News*?"

"Believe me, that was the *last* thing on our minds. He didn't drop me off at my car until seven-forty-five and I have no idea how I got home. Did you know that he didn't get home until eight o'clock?"

"You mean you've talked to him since then?" I asked.

"Oh Mark," she said, giving me her best "you poor naïve boy" look. "He's called my cell several times since then."

I wondered why she had been paying special attention to it when I saw her lately, as though every call could be from the President. I had a brief surreal moment as a visual of the seventy-year-old billionaire kissing and cuddling with his young lunch companion flashed across my countenance.

"Mrs. Lexington called me at about seven that night looking for him."

"Really? Well I'm not surprised," Summer said. "He follows such a set pattern and has practically every move scheduled by Bertha. All of the kids were calling around when he didn't come home at five. Elizabeth was frantic, I heard, and probably started calling each one of them by five-oh-five!"

"Summer, are you sure you're not making this up, or perhaps it's just an extension of your hypotheticals?"

"I am a little intrigued by the fact that he didn't tell you. Maybe it's because you work out Mrs. Lexington too and he wasn't sure if you would react badly and spill the beans. You know, I felt *so* comfortable being with him. It felt surprisingly natural. I mean, it felt a little weird when he first leaned over at the Ritz and kissed me! But I think he looked around first to see if anybody was looking. It was kind of comical at first when we first walked in because he made a big point out of telling the hostess that he was interviewing me for a position with his company and we needed a quiet, out-of-the-way spot where we could eat and talk. I wonder what she thought later after he had a few and moved his chair next to mine!"

I had had a few questions answered even though some of the answers made me feel rather uncomfortable. I moved to the next one on the list.

"So if you were together about eight hours, and a lot of that was in public, weren't either of you concerned about running into somebody that you knew?"

"We were pretty far away," she replied, "from our usual haunts in the Pointes. I think the Ritz is about twenty miles or so, and when we were at those bars in Detroit we felt safe because Grosse Pointers *don't* go to Detroit unless they have a reason! But frankly, after the first couple of hours it didn't matter to us anymore because we were too tipsy to care! Oh, Mark, I haven't been able to see him since Tuesday because he said the family is watching him like hawks. I guess they're trying to make sure that somebody is either with him every minute or they at least know where he is! I can't wait to see him this Saturday at the tournament. It would be nice to sneak away somewhere at the Club for even a few minutes. Do you think that will be possible?"

"Considering that the whole thing is *named* after him no, no I don't. I would think they would notice if he were *missing*." We managed to finish her workout, but she continued to prattle on like a teenage girl returning from her first real date.

On Sunday morning, I was moving a little slow. Saturday night had been a late one, with pay-per-view boxing and Natasha keeping me up well past midnight. A grueling Saturday workout had me wondering if, at age 45, it was wise to be lifting even heavier weights than I encountered in my thirties. Although feeling groggy that morning, I made a mental notation of having just completed my sixth year in a row without a cold, and my fifteenth without any flu symptoms. Something strange had taken over my immune system in the last decade, and I could only attribute this "über-system" to my weight training addiction.

Something familiar, however, was taking over the caller ID slot on my cell phone as it rang that morning. I was used to Summer's number appearing often as she rearranged or postponed a workout depending on the state of her hair, nails or bikini line. I was not used to it appearing on a Sunday morning, though, and was forced to answer just out of curiosity.

"Hi, it's Mark," I answered, as generically as I could.

"Mark, this is Summer. Listen, are you working out with Max today?"

"Uh no. Not until tomorrow morning."

"Well, remember the tennis tournament yesterday?"

"Of course I do. You mentioned it more than once on Thursday."

"Mark, I went, and of course he was there with Elizabeth. She hates tennis. Everybody knows that. He's tried to encourage her to play, but she won't even take a lesson! But ever since our lunch that day she won't let him out of her sight! And I think I told you that if she's got something planned then one of her daughters comes over to watch him. They say they're just there to visit with their dad but I know what they're doing. Anyway I went to the Yacht Club and I could tell right away that something was wrong. He wouldn't even look my way…wouldn't even acknowledge that I was there! I knew right away there had been a change, and I was right! After I was done playing, I was talking to the visiting pro and as Max started to walk past I excused myself and went toward him to say hi. He signaled me off to one side and never smiled and his eyes, Mark, his eyes looked *so* cold! He said, 'Summer, I'm sorry. It's over. I've got to break this off.' Mark, we only went out one time! But he kept talking about the next time, and where it would be, every time he called me! All I ever wanted was his friendship and now I'm not even going to have that! You've got to talk to him tomorrow. *Please* find out for me what changed his mind?"

I listened for another ten minutes and tried not to make any promises, considering that I wasn't even supposed to know about their little tête-à-tête that Tuesday. Summer confessed to me that she told Max on Friday that I knew about some of the details about Tuesday, though not all. *That should make Monday morning quite pleasant and not a bit uncomfortable,* I thought sarcastically.

On Monday morning, I actually had a millisecond of butterflies in my stomach as I trudged down the long hallway to the workout room. I was the first one there and walked from wall to wall, clicking on the supernova of lights that surrounded the room. The brightness made the area seem like one big interrogation room as I waited for Max to pick his way down the circular staircase. To my surprise and relief, Elizabeth came down first. She had not been scheduled for that morning, but I was extremely glad to see her, knowing that even Max would have difficulty talking about breaking it off with Summer in front of his wife. The workout went smoothly enough until it was over, and Max announced that he'd walk me out to the garage. Upon reaching the entrance door, I saw my chance for a clean getaway disappear when Max stepped out into the garage with me. His Mercedes stared up at me, shiny and wide-eyed, as he began out of the blue in a low voice.

"Listen Buddy, I saw her Saturday and I told her it's over. I think we both know what she wants and I'm not going to get caught by her. Did she say anything to you?"

"Yes sir. She said she values your friendship, and now she's disappointed because she won't even have that."

"I see, I see. Well, the truth of the matter is that I *like* her and I wish her the best, I really do. But at the end of the day I say to myself, Max, what is it that this girl wants? And the answer is that it's got to be the money!" He glanced nervously inside the door.

"Anyway, thanks for listening, buddy, we'll see you on Wednesday morning."

Summer's afternoon workout was a deluge of questions about the morning workout's mood, replete with sub-questions about the tenor of the interaction between Max and Elizabeth. Was it stilted? Summer wanted to know everything. Did she seem aloof or cold towards him? Had he been drinking the night before? Did either one rebuke the other over any subject in a sharper manner than normal? I was beginning to feel like an unpaid spy and sidestepped with monosyllabic answers and "I dunnos." I watched Summer pull away after her workout was over with no small degree of relief.

My cell phone rang at eight-forty Tuesday morning with another Grosse Pointe number. I answered it.

"Hey buddy, I'm sorry to bother you this early." It was Max calling from his car phone as he drove into work.

"Good morning sir. How are you?"

"Good, good. Listen Maaark. Did you talk to our friend yesterday?"

"Oh, yes. We worked out in the afternoon."

"Did you tell her what we talked about in the garage?"

"Well, no sir. I didn't. I really didn't think it was my place to disclose anything that was said."

"Of course, of course. Well you're absolutely right. If I have anything to say to her I should just tell her myself. It's just that I keep going over, again and again, what it is that she would have to *gain* from me. I mean, if she thinks it's going to be blackmail then I'll tell her fine, we'll all just sit down, Elizabeth and the kids and her husband...I think it's Chuck...and I'll just explain what happened and apologize. That'll be the end of it."

"I don't think she needs the money, sir."

"No, you're right. I've done some asking and Chuck makes a fine living. He's well thought of too by anybody that deals with him. So what is it then?"

"I couldn't say," I replied. Max mused aloud for a considerable time and then promised to at least call Summer with an explanation. I hung up as Natasha padded up sleepily.

"Who vas dat?" she asked.

"That was Max," I answered. "He needed some dating advice."

"Vor haff an hour? Vat did zat pay?" she asked.

"Uh, actually, nothing. Since he called me 'buddy,' I guess it was for free."

I worked out with a distraught and professedly confused Summer on that Monday afternoon. After enduring unanswerable questions such as "How could he just turn it off like that?" I looked forward with near-giddy anticipation to the end of her appointment. My "consolation/hand-holding after the break up" session was finally over as her cell phone rang. Looking perturbed, she absently waved good-bye and drove off in her white Mercedes.

My afternoon continued on in a state of near bliss compared to the way it began.

At quarter-to-six my cell phone rang. It was Summer, in a decidedly more upbeat but very emphatic tone. "Mark. I'm finishing up lunch with a mutual friend of ours, and even he admits that he's had *too* many CRs and should *not* be driving. Could you please come over here immediately and get him home? We're at the Jefferson Beach Grill."

I mumbled something about being very busy with clients at the moment and asked if she was sure. She replied, "Yes, please come now!"

After a pause and a little crackling static, a slurring billionaire spoke into my ear. "Ahh, yeah, Maaark. This is Mr. Lexington. Our lovely friend here thinks that it might be best if I didn't try to make it home by myself. Could you…could you, buddy come over and give me a lift? I would truly appreciate it."

Before I could engage the reasoning center of my brain, I heard my mouth say, "Yes, of course." I looked around. The little studio was humming, with four of us working out at least two clients each at the same time. I approached Michelle, already wild-eyed and busy, and explained that I had an emergency and begged her to take one of my clients. She reluctantly agreed, and I gave a partial explanation to the client. Repeating the same procedure with another hustling trainer and my remaining client, I dashed to my car six minutes after hanging up with Max.

32

THE ENTRANCE DRIVE to the Jefferson Beach Grill was only about half a mile from my studio. The grill was actually a very large restaurant divided into several sections. The menu leaned more toward seafood but sought to please everyone. The food was quite good, and even I found it to be reasonably priced. The main enclosed dining section was off to one side of the restaurant and at the rear. Floor-to-ceiling windows comprised the entire back wall and offered a view of the huge rear deck dining area. The rear deck's plastic tables and chairs abutted its little "Tiki bar" and overlooked a wide canal of the surrounding Jefferson Beach Marina. Opposite the main room was a less used and more dimly lit dining room with upscale booths and tables. A band area at the far end presided over a large dance floor. Floor to ceiling windows in this section were tinted and let in far less light than those in the main room but still afforded a diner an excellent view of the outside deck. Overlooking this more intimate section was a huge bar that could seat two hundred partying patrons. Standing room only on weekend nights, the large bar area had a glass frontage that looked down on the front parking lot, where an arriving patron could assess attendance by merely looking up. In its totality, the Beach Grill was a modern, clean, well run local hot spot. It advertised itself, however, as waterfront dining and therein lie the only problem I had with it. It was located about a quarter of a mile in off the main road so that it was invisible to anyone driving by. Lake St. Clair was situated approximately one half mile behind the Beach Grill, which made any view of actual moving water or waves impossible. A long driveway required a patron to pass a series of huge dilapidated structures used for the winter storage of boats. The only access to the dining facility by water involved wending one's way up marina canals past rented boat wells to an extremely limited docking space behind the restaurant. The Beach Grills location always gave me the impression that someone had shoved aside a bunch of old boats and dropped the place right in the middle of a shipyard.

Ignoring the valet sign, I parked my car in the front lot and strode quickly through the front doors. Paying no attention to the cute young hostess, I entered the main dining area. One by one, I scanned each table for Summer and Max. Checking the tall booths lining the front wall necessitated my walking by each one and looking askance at its occupants. With phase one of my search complete, I passed the hostess again and crossed over to the dimly lit section. A "closed" sign stood outside its glass doors but I pulled one open and continued seeking out the couple. The section was empty save for the fourth booth from the door, where I found Max and Summer nestled in the back, on the same side of the table.

"Maaark! Sit down, sit down!" Max exclaimed, and I hesitantly slipped into the other side. "I was just telling our beautiful friend here why it couldn't work between us." Summer's sheepish smile made it unclear as to whether or not she believed him. "I mean, just look at her. She's gorgeous and smart and she knows how to make me laugh."

He was slurring his words regularly as he ordered another Crown Royal from a waitress who snuck up on us in the darkened section. The bread basket was empty, and I wondered about the other verboten items they consumed during the last three hours or so. Sensing my overall uneasiness, Summer asked me to order something to eat, but I politely declined. I could see that we weren't leaving immediately, and, feeling like the third wheel on a date, excused myself to an empty booth where I occupied the time with phone calls, checking periodically on my business as it tried to cripple along without me. Max, dressed in an immaculate business suit, and Summer, still dressed in her workout gear, cut a sharply contrasting pair as he guzzled fresh CR's and she sipped sparingly on a glass of wine. Finally, after one and a half hours and several false starts, the bill was paid and the expectant waitress was under-tipped.

It was two miles from Beach Grill to the mansion and just beginning to get dark. Summer followed in her Mercedes and ducked down a side street to park, idling, as I drove Max in his car into his main garage. The automatic door closed behind me as I dashed across the expansive front acreage and hopped a low stone wall to cross Jefferson (or technically, Lakeshore Drive). Summer waited across the road as I jogged to her car, and we started on the short trip back to my car at the Grill.

"Well, well?" she gushed.

"I can see that it's over," I said. Summer chattered on about what she saw in Max and what his intentions may be for her. Back at the Grill, I scrambled to get back to my car, admitting to the excited woman that Max seemed to find her irresistible and wouldn't break up with her again. Anxious to return to my neglected business, I roared out of the parking lot even as the victorious Summer called my cell yet again to ponder her next move aloud.

Max wasn't able to break up with Summer again, at least not until the next morning. My cell phone rang at about eight-forty. It was the repentant billionaire.

"Hey Maaark. It's the pest again. Thanks again buddy for last night."

"You're welcome, sir," I answered.

"I've already called her. I told her it's over."

"Oh, I see," I replied. "How is she taking it?"

"Oh, she's understandably upset. But in the cold light of day I have no other choice! What does she expect me to do? Give up half of everything I own? Give up my house and move out?" After another twenty minutes of unpaid counseling later, I heard a beep in the earpiece and checked the cell phone's caller ID. It was Summer's phone number. Max wrapped it up vowing never to see her again, just as Summer began beeping in for a second time. I bade the determined, resolute man good-bye and clicked over to her.

"Mark, that son of a bitch! Has he called you yet?"

"We spoke."

"Did that asshole tell you what he said to me this morning? After last night! Did he tell you?"

"Pretty much," I said. Her voice quavered as she related details of the conversation anyway. I live on a peninsula that wasn't allotted a sufficient amount of cell phone towers so, on a sunny day (and today qualified), I was forced to amble about on my driveway to maintain a constant cell phone connection. Experience had taught me that a dropped call would not provide any relief because Max or Summer would simply hit "redial" and reconnect for another round. It was already obvious at this point that Max's guilt and remorse surged whenever he was sober, and he was able to tell Summer that their affiliation was over. But ending their relationship did nothing to soothe the unhappiness that he had felt for some time now, and when Max was unhappy, he needed a drink to mask the unhappiness, or at least blunt it a bit. But a drink or two seemed to give him the inclination to contact Summer to apologize for the way he treated her, and the process began again.

If Summer didn't answer her cell phone, then a phone call to mine was next, and I was given the unpaid assignment, no matter what occupied me at the moment, of tracking her down and encouraging her to return his call. Completion of this task meant that I was able to go on about my business for several hours until I received the call from Beach Grill. My role as trainer and bodyguard rapidly deteriorated into that of "phone receptionist" and designated driver. Over the next week, I was repeatedly forced to ignore a client during one of the duo's calls or, worse still, it was demanded that I dash out to the rescue, naively believing that each time would be the last. Sucked into the vortex of this convulsive mating ritual, my attempts to quit or decline were met with ever more plaintive pleas and increasingly profuse thank you's. I soon learned to charge Max weekly at my regular driving rate but knew deep down that it wouldn't begin to compensate for the neglect of my business. The unpaid phone time accumulated, though, during this strange dance of pleasure and guilt, of sinning and atonement, and Max's calls grew ever more vehement. He spent hours listing reams of reasons that the drunken courtship couldn't continue, analyzing everything from Summer's dancing to her involvement with the beer distributor. My cell phone bill topped $600 a month as the exhausted batteries tried to keep up. Natasha kept a running tab of my phone hours and soon concluded that I had enough for an extensive European vacation if I could conjure up a way to bill for them. The breakups came as fast and furiously as the reconciliations in the next two weeks, with Summer raging and swearing about Max to me on my phone after each one.

Instead of having a part-time employment affiliation with an erratic but interesting hyper-successful CEO of the best known retail chain in the state, I had been sucked into the maelstrom of a conflicted alcoholic's desires. There were rules to the insanity, but they changed constantly. To minimize suspicion, Max tried to return home before dark, as if *that* represented some sort of a witching hour. Elizabeth was not fooled for a nanosecond, and I, as his co-conspirator, was punished in the only way possible…her workouts ground to a screeching halt.

Promises were never made to Summer but compliments flew like shrapnel from a grenade. Any plans beyond the next ten minutes were uncertain. I was only to be summoned by mid-encounter or later, when the sufficiently soused retail mogul no longer felt any embarrassment.

The only reason I was able to keep my cool in this typhoon of insanity is that I was certain that sooner or later something had to give. Either my charge would finally crack and seek help, or Summer would change her phone numbers and get out of Dodge for a while until everything cooled off.

Max, chagrined (when he was sober) at his own behavior, made the first move.

It is a longstanding fact that one of the ways for a man to forget about a woman is to ship out to sea. There, the wind, the waves, the monotony and the shear amount of accumulated distance place a protective chasm between the man and the temptations of the woman. It gives the sailor time to think. It gives him time to either bury her memory deep or to make soul-searched decisions on whether or not he genuinely desires to spend eternity with his beloved.

Max called me on a Tuesday afternoon and asked me to meet him at a huge indoor showroom owned by Colony Marine. With my own boating time cut drastically due to my participation in Max and Summer's dating holocaust, I jumped at the chance to look at some previously-owned yachts.

Colony Marines "showroom" was actually an enormous storage facility that housed a number of thirty-five to fifty-five foot Sea Ray boats. While primarily used, versus new, these boats had been mechanically inspected, repaired, cleaned, waxed and detailed. The boats sat, side by side on the smooth concrete floor, chocked upright and appearing even larger in the diffused light of the warehouse. I had arrived a few minutes early as usual and was a bit surprised to see Elizabeth Lexington's Jaguar pull up behind my Corvette. A non-swimmer in spite of the mansion's two pools, Elizabeth's lack of enthusiasm for the open water was apparent anytime the subject was broached. Colony Marine was located off of Jefferson and right next door to Jefferson Beach Marina and the "Grill" I'd been frequenting so often lately. Resisting the impulse to throw myself prostrate at her feet and blubber out apologies and confessions, I greeted the diminutive lady as naturally as I could given the proximity of the "location of our sinning." My attempt at small talk was cut mercifully short when I spied Max's Mercedes pulling in.

Aided by ladders, the salesman and the three of us clambered aboard a grand total of two boats. On board the second one, a fifty-footer, Max commented to Elizabeth that it was nearly identical to their boat up north. We had been perusing the vast showroom's inventory for a solid five minutes or so when Max grunted his way down to the floor and, with the salesman in tow, began to stride toward the front offices. Unsure of Max's next move and up to that point never having piloted a Sea Ray larger than forty-four feet, I stayed behind to familiarize myself with the three-year-old yacht. The specifications sheet said the price was $650,000 as I sat in the captain's chair imagining the 35,000-pound boat under way. Snapped out of my reverie by an employee turning off lights, I scrambled down the ladder and hustled toward the front. Max had just sat down in a chair in front of the sales manager's desk and was asking him if the boat could be in the water and ready to go by this time tomorrow. The sales manager was trying his best to explain the multitude of mechanical and safety checks that would have to be performed. The least mechanical and most disinterested future Sea Ray owner in the area nodded distractedly and asked a second time if they would have everything done in one day. The sales manager picked up the phone, trying to act nonchalant as he elicited promises from busy mechanics and yard men. The manager hung up and assured the impatient billionaire that it would be in the water by five o'clock the next day. Max stood up and said, "Okay then, that'll be fine." Turning around and pointing through the window of the glass enclosure at me, Max said, "That's Maaark Steeeel, he's my driver and he's going to be my captain. Make sure he has your card and I want you to call him if there's any problems."

Maxwell Lexington then walked out of the office. He had just spent approximately $600,000 without negotiation, without a sea trial or professional inspection, and certainly without signing paperwork of any kind.

"You can handle that boat okay, right buddy?" Max asked as he walked by me.

"Of course I can," I said as I wondered what he would have done if I'd said no.

The next day was a Wednesday. At mid-afternoon, I began checking the boat yard's hoists to see if the Sea Ray was in yet. At three o'clock it wasn't. By four o'clock it was. I called Max to inform him that the boat was in the water and didn't appear to have any leaks. The huge nylon hoist straps were still around the boat's hull though, and it didn't look as though we would be sailing it any time soon. Max said that he would meet me at the boat at five o'clock anyway and asked me to contact Summer so that he could show it to her. A larger boat can be a small home on the water, but with a few twists. Large batteries will allow the lights to work, the engines to start, pumps to pump and toilets to flush. Fresh water had to be pumped on board into the one hundred gallon reservoir. If there was no electrical hook-up at the dock, the three air conditioning units on board weren't going to work unless the boat's generator was running. It would have been easy for an experienced Sea Ray technician to demonstrate the boat's electrical systems and any little nuances that I should know about, but there was no time to plan for it. I fired up the generator and began to cool the boat down in the eighty-five degree heat. Max arrived at quarter to five and Summer pulled up ten minutes later. Max had already been quenching his thirst and I steadied him as he lurched onto the Sea Ray. Summer grasped my hand to step onto this (for her) unfamiliar mode of transportation.

The aft deck of the little yacht, even under the large green canvas that stretched over the thick aluminum poles across the top, was sweltering in the afternoon heat. I'd had time to unzip a few plastic windows, but heat still radiated from the seating and decks in unseen muggy waves. A duck of the head and six padded steps down from the main deck took the boater or his guest into the carpeted, dimly lit coolness of the main salon.

A long, leather sofa filled part of one wall and the back of the salon. Two small, round marble tables in front of them held a small plastic floral display but were each big enough for one diner to eat at. The huge hi-definition television sat in its cabinet on the other side with its accompaniment of VCR, CD decks, and major stereo components. A twelve-bottle wine cooler was tucked off to one side of the sofa. The kitchen (or galley) had every amenity including a stove, refrigerator, freezer, microwave and dishwasher. A combination washer/dryer nestled at the far end of the lower cupboards. Heavily laminated blond wood covered everything, including the door that hid the built-in trash compactor. A Bose stereo system wafted love songs in the coolness from a syrupy Detroit radio station's play list.

Max and Summer descended into this amenity-proliferate coolness for her "tour" of Max's latest acquisition. He pointed to the stereo controls, said something about the CD player and pulled her to him awkwardly in an embrace that haltingly evolved into a series of kisses. My discomfort rose almost immediately to the level of salmonella poisoning as I stood on the top step waiting for orders. Turning away and stepping back onto the baking deck, I resolved to give myself an assignment that didn't involve the two lovebirds below. Venturing another peek into the darkened boat interior, I watched their backs as they retreated farther forward to where the master stateroom and its pedestal-type berth (bed) filled the room. The door closed behind them, and I began my assessment of the situation.

Max had purchased a floating hotel room for $600,000 and twenty-four hours later, it was in service just outside the showroom where we had met his wife. His car and Summer's were parked askew about thirty feet from the boat. They were unlocked, but without the keys I wasn't going to be able to move them to a more discreet location. I certainly wasn't about to interrupt them in whatever (I fought back a wave of nausea) might be going on to ask for sets of keys. A mechanic from the marina pulled up to offer insights into any operational questions that I had, but I was forced (with a wink and a jerk of the head to below-deck) to tell him that it was a really bad time at the moment. We stayed on dry ground and discussed the repairs that ought to be performed before the boat was completely safe to be on the water. After the yard's mechanic left, paranoia began to set in. Max was now overdue at his home by at least a half hour. Mrs. Lexington now had a definite place to look for her errant husband…or at least a starting point for her army of offspring if she so ordered. A long rollaway security gate required a magnetic entry card but was automatically opening every three minutes or so as boat owners or employees exited the marina. Max and Summer's cars were readily visible from the gate. Not wanting to be in the untenable position of refusing entry to a furious emissary of Mrs. Lexington, I hopped back onto the boat. When Elizabeth or her foot soldiers showed up and spotted Max's car, I was quite sure they wouldn't rest until they gained entry. I couldn't quite picture myself repelling a boarding party of rampaging daughters, so I decided to draw a "line in the sand" beyond which I would not allow them to cross.

The doorway that led down to the salon was quite narrow. If I closed and locked it, however, I feared that Max and Summer would panic when they were ready to exit. I shuddered at the thought of what they were attempting to do down below and pushed it out of my mind. Apprising the width of the doorway, I decided that "Mark, The Human Blockade" would be the best recourse when I made my final stand. During the confrontation, I calculated, the concussion bombs of outrage from the daughters would probably be enough to bring the impetuous billionaire out of his floating love nest to relieve me of my duty and carry on the battle. A half hour went by and there was no sign of either scouts or an advancing army. At seven o'clock, two hours into my perspiring watch, Max and Summer emerged, sweaty and smiling.

"Hey buddy, the air isn't working in the front bedroom," Max stated.

I had turned on the forward air soon after starting up the boat's electrical generator, but the control panel in the forward stateroom was a digital touch pad. Max's ineptitude with anything electronic was legendary among the mansion's staff, and I imagined (and then as quickly turned off the visual portion) the fumbling around that probably occurred as the room heated up. Opening the stateroom door would have allowed ice-cold air from the salon to tumble in but I was sure they had been too preoccupied to think of that.

"I'll fix it immediately sir," I answered.

Still concerned that several of Max's daughters would round the corner any minute and descend on us like wailing banshees, I cautiously mentioned that it was seven o'clock, and Max might want to check in. Max rechecked his own watch and, with a hasty good-bye to Summer, accepted my hand in climbing down from the Sea Ray. The tardy conqueror loaded himself into his Mercedes and drove off, leaving me alone with Summer. It had quickly been agreed that she would wait for a minute before leaving. *As if that would throw any suspicious observers off the trail,* I thought. I cringed as I waited for the expected details to spew out, getting prepared to ball up into a fetal position and go to my "happy place" if it got *too* detailed.

I wasn't bothered, necessarily, by the prospect of a July/December romance. I wasn't revolted, either, by the image of a much older man in less than top physical condition making love, despite whatever limitations he may have, to a woman with a body that even a twenty-five year old man would now find very desirable. The fact that both were married and that I knew Max's wife very well was terrible, but in my years at the gyms I had been confronted with worse.

The essence of what repulsed me about this relationship between the two was far more personal. Over the last two years I had reveled in Max's presence and kow-towed to his whims because he began to represent the business mentor that I never had. He was perhaps even a bit of a parental authority as well after many years of self-employment and following my own drumbeat. It was for these reasons that I felt entrusted with his care, responsible for his well being and frustrated as he played cat and mouse with a DUI charge and the terrible newspaper headlines one would bring.

Summer, during the last four months, had not only paid me well but had confided her deepest thoughts to me, as though a sister had found a long lost brother. In spite of her demands on my time and her assumption that she was the center of my universe, I had developed a certain fondness for her.

Whenever I saw Max and Summer together, it evoked strong emotions that I was witnessing an incestuous relationship of sorts and didn't know how to stop it.

A coy smile and a few well placed "hmmm's" was all the input that I received from Summer regarding her "tour" of the yacht.

The next day, however, had Summer scheduled at one o'clock at the studio. Only one hour late, Summer rushed into my gym in a state of excitement. "Did he call you yet? He said he wants to take the boat out tomorrow! He said around twelve."

"Uh, no he didn't."

"He wanted you to find a first mate for tomorrow too. I can't believe he didn't call you yet!"

Why should he call so soon? I thought. *It would be best if I were told at the last possible second.* On Tuesday when he handed me a fuel credit card he had said, "It's all yours, Maaark, the bat, the ball, and the glove!"

A first mate on the boat would need to have many responsibilities. The ideal candidate would be a former waitress or bartender who was an avid boater as well. She would be as adept at casting off dock lines as she was at mixing drinks and supplying them to guests on a moving boat. Her skills would have to range all the way up to being able to steer the boat without hitting anything while the captain checked charts or engines or simply took a quick break. A little bit of cooking ability as well as some knowledge of local catering suppliers would be useful in the event of extended trips or on-board guests. Social skills would be a definite plus as we tried to make guests feel as "at home" as possible. Political correctness aside, physical appearance was a plus. It simply wouldn't do to have quivering guests screaming and afraid to come on board because the first mate looked like a gargoyle.

Even if all of the above requirements were met, the candidate would have to be available on short notice (as little as one hour on some days), incredibly prompt and able to be absent from friends or family for an hour or a day, depending on the owner's inclination.

If what Summer said was true, I had less than twenty-four hours to find, interview and hire this person.

"So, Mark, what did you think about yesterday?"

"I was thinking that maybe we weren't in the most discreet location available."

"I know, but let me ask you a question. What do you think was happening after we went in that front bedroom?"

"Summer, on a boat, it's not a bedroom, it's a stateroom…or a berth if it's small, and it's not a kitchen, it's a galley."

"Okay. But what did you think we were doing?"

I was starting to go to my happy place, but I decided to sidestep if I could. "And you don't go in back of the boat, you go aft. And it's not a bathroom. It's called a head, and a front bedroom is the forward stateroom."

"Mark, the second we got alone in that room, he was so passionate!"

I considered plugging my ears with my fingers and loudly chanting "na, na, na, na, na, na" at that point but there were other clients nearby.

"And Mark, I started to lift his shirt off over his head without unbuttoning it, I mean I loosened his tie and everything first, but I forgot his cufflinks!"

I didn't want to know this. I needed to think of something else before I lost my lunch.

"But Mark, he was laughing too! I mean, there he was with his shirt over his head, and I couldn't figure out how to put it down. I mean it was *stuck*!"

As I held my stomach with one hand and grimaced, Summer mistook my gestures as "stop it, I'm laughing so hard I might throw up" and continued on.

"But eventually we got everything straightened out and he was so gentle with me and let me tell you, he knew what he was doing."

I briefly considered faking a stroke but knew that to be convincing I'd have to collapse in a heap on the floor.

"One thing though."

No, no! I thought, *This is way more than I can deal with!*

"We had a little trouble getting it in even though I was ready, if you know what I mean. Do you think there's something he could take to become….uh….more fully aroused? Don't get me wrong, he was still able to…complete it…more than once, but…"

My head was reeling from informational overload. I ran across the gym to warmly greet a client that I didn't particularly care for. From there I ran into the bathroom. Every time the gym's phone rang I'd answer it. Finally, in frustration, Summer began to discuss the snacks she would bring for Friday's voyage.

At eleven the next morning I arrived at the temporary boat well assigned by the marina. The marina was well aware of our intention of docking for the remainder of the season at the Yacht Club but wanted to correct any and all mechanical problems at one of its own wells first.

As tactfully as possible, I explained that the mechanic would need to pack up for now and meet me again at a later date. A cleaning crew was scrubbing down the entire boat and informed me that they hoped to finish by two o'clock. I gently said that their plans would not fit in with ours and sent two irate ladies packing. At 11:45, I turned on the generator and fired up the engines. Max arrived, waved good-bye to the departing mechanic and ladies, climbed on board, and hid below. Today's brilliant secret plan called for picking up Summer at another marina's gas dock where she had stashed her car. First mate-less, I pulled the boat out of the well in a light wind without smashing into any of the busy marina's heavy boat traffic. As I performed the work of two, Max and I arrived forty-five minutes late at the gas dock. It coincided perfectly with Summer-time, and we only waited an additional fifteen minutes for our guest while Max had "refreshments" down below.

It was an absolutely cloudless, gorgeous day and my charges began enjoying it to the fullest by staying secluded down below. Max had mentioned "The Old Club" as a destination, and I set our course for a lazy one-hour cruise. The Old Club was located at the tip of Harsens Island, a large inhabited island at the north end of Lake St. Clair. The Old Club was members only, a bit stodgy and a frequent dinner destination for Max and Elizabeth when their eighty-two foot yacht was "up" for the summer. The Old Club was also located at the mouth of the St. Clair River as the river began its thirty-mile journey to Lake Huron. It was guarded by a breaker wall of huge boulders that provided excellent dockage; even for yachts of over one-hundred feet in length. Although I'd never been there in my own loud, nasty, disruptive offshore boat, I knew that the deep waters of the Old Club's harbor would be a safe, simple destination for today, crewless or otherwise.

Upon entering the South Channel of the St. Clair River, I throttled down even further. I began to wait for verification from Max that the Old Club was indeed our stopping point. Just as I was preparing to pass the club and turn around up river in a waterborne holding pattern, Summer emerged in her bikini with Max soon following in shorts and T-shirt. I pointed out our proximity to the club, and as he pointed out details to Summer, I could see his mind racing with a thousand memories. Memories of trips with the wife, no doubt, and the old friends he had there that would soon be gossiping. Memories of family trips to the club could not be far behind, and I could see the hesitation mixed with guilt at the prospect of bringing his new "friend" to this old haunt.

"Maaark, it's a beautiful day and I'm not ready to eat just yet, are you, Summer? Do you think you can find the River Crab restaurant?"

I'd heard of it. I had even passed it several times in my boat travels. I had my chart book and my cell phone. I was punched in on a beautiful day. "Of course, Mr. Lexington," I answered. I pointed the Sea Ray north once again. The couple stayed topside for an hour or so, lounging on the back sunpads.

After deeming both her front and back to have absorbed sufficient tanning rays, Summer got up and poured more drinks for herself and Max. Together they approached the captain's chair where I sat, happily guiding the fifty-footer through moderately busy boat traffic in the wide river. Any guilty thoughts I had about the family members back in the Pointes that might be looking for us were overridden by my contentment with my new command. Following a few topics of light and polite conversation with their sole crewmember, Max and Summer began to exchange shoulder touches and knowing looks with each other. Two minutes later, they disappeared below again! In between light guilt spasms, I felt a slight welling of admiration for the seventy-year-old stud muffin but quickly suppressed it.

The weather remained perfect and beautiful. The eighty-five degree temperatures that were being endured by Michigan residents farther inland were not a factor on the broad, cool river. I guesstimated that we were experiencing seventy-six or seventy-seven degrees at most. Using a little imagination, I supposed myself to be the only one on the boat on this gorgeous day. Knowing well that it was a toy I would never have bought, I reminded myself that I was getting *paid* to enjoy the ride upriver on this perfect day. I felt the tension flow away from my neck and shoulders. Smiling almost perpetually from the captain's chair of my yacht, I told myself that this situation wasn't so bad. In fact, it was a good thing. This weird romance would soon burn itself out as Max finally went back to his wife and apologized for worrying her. Summer would soon realize the impossibility of their age difference and have an affair with someone nearer her own age. Life was very good for the moment.

Nature began to call at about the same time that I reached an unusually wide and temporarily trafficless section of the river. Unless pirates had dropped off a first mate while I was appreciating the afternoon, I needed to stop the boat for a minute. Throttling down to a float, I checked fore and aft one last time. There were no boats for at least a half mile. The Sea Ray bobbed complacently as I ducked down the stairs toward the head off the main salon.

I paused and squinted for a second as my eyes adjusted to the dimmer light below. A motion off to my right caught my eye, and my eyelids flew open as I stared into a huge set of eyes as they bugged out to stare back at me! The eyes belonged to a naked Summer as she lie on the leather sofa on her back! She was partially covered by Max as he straddled her during some sort of a top entry. In complete horror, I realized that they were right in the middle of it, and that I was watching! Even worse was the shock on Summer's face as she watched me watch! *Well, I belong here dammit,* I thought, *and you two don't!* They had a whole master stateroom for this sort of thing, and they couldn't even make the extra twenty-foot trip to its door!

Wheeling around one hundred and eighty degrees, I re-ducked and flew up the short staircase, flinging myself back onto the safety of my command deck. Rubbing my eyes couldn't help erase what I had just seen as I fought a strong urge to draw my knees up to my chest and search for a "happy place." The Sea Ray's engines rumbled gently beneath my feet in their efforts to calm and reassure me as I slowly began to throttle them up again. Life was horrible! I wondered what I was doing out here today when I could have been doing a thousand other decent, respectable things. I felt a brief emotional after-shudder at the thought of one or the other of my passengers coming topside to ask if everything was okay.

Twenty minutes later, the weather, the muffled rumbles of the engines and the splashing of the waves that the Sea Ray created as it plowed ahead had me calm again.

Repeating the slowing down procedure, I waited until the speed gauge indicated a complete halt. I crept down the stairs one at a time allowing my eyes more time than before to adjust. *The way my luck was running, another unexpected intrusion might prompt them to ask for my help in getting dressed,* I thought. I angled my line of sight, reconnoitering one small piece of the couch at a time. Only after checking galley surfaces and any salon carpeting (where the two might still be trysting), could I proceed. The front stateroom door was closed, and the coast seemed clear. I dashed to the salon's head to quickly complete my mission.

Twenty minutes later, I was rapidly nearing the riverside docks of Charlie's River Crab. As he rejoined me with glass in hand, it was obvious that Max had been fortifying himself with double Crown Royals. I noted that he seemed surprisingly in command of his faculties. He also had an air of contentment about him that I hadn't noticed in months. Summer emerged minutes after Max and looked at me smugly as she poured a small glass of wine. I averted my eyes and concentrated on docking the boat safely in the choppy afternoon waters of the river.

As the boat heaved with the lake freighter waves, I fought an impulse to declare the docking area unsafe for disembarking. I wanted to insist that we find a safer harbor further up in the city of Port Huron. Max seemed agile enough though, as I weighed the safety risks of maneuvering the tipsy billionaire onto land. Emptying my pockets and stowing my gun in a safe place, I hopped onto the dock, secured the boat and extended my arm. If Max missed the dock as he stepped down, he would plunge into the slow moving but wavy river waters. I calculated that his bright white tennis shirt would give me at least two tries to dive in, find him and fish him out onto the west bank. The depth finder showed eight feet of water in the boat well, but the temperature of the August river waters told me that I had well over a minute under water if necessary. My fears were assuaged somewhat when Max gratefully accepted my hand and together we timed the heaving of the boat until he stepped quickly down to the dock. Keeping an eye on Max as he stood on the trembling planking, I helped Summer onto the boards as well. They graciously (although half-heartedly) invited me to dine with them, but I declined. Max encouraged me to at least find the hostess and order a meal to eat aboard the boat I insisted on staying with.

Hungry enough by now to accept a peanut butter and ant sandwich if that's all they had, I devoured my salad and a delicious swordfish steak while bobbing on my yacht.

33

AFTER CHECKING THE engines and performing some clean up below, I settled in on my cell phone to report and gloat about my location to Natasha. I read until the waning light prompted me to check on my boss and his date back in the waterfront restaurant. My waitress had added my dinner onto Max's bill per his instructions but the wealthy man was in no hurry to leave. Most yachts have a generous amount of electronic navigational equipment, and this one was no exception. An excellent radar system could show me the location of every buoy, boat and seagull within a mile or more on its illuminated screen. My depth finder could both warn me of shallow water and read its temperature as well as flash the boat's speed.

The sun sank rapidly, and the shadows lengthened. Still another gizmo's time of usefulness was fast approaching. The Sea Ray had an electronic chart plotter. Its job was to receive GPS signals from satellites and display my exact location on a well-lit screen as I threaded our way back home. Buoys, islands, shallow rocky areas and destination points with the most direct routes to them all appeared in nautical map form on a bright screen. The chart plotter made nocturnal navigation, no matter how moonless and dark the night may be, a safe no-brainer. The chart plotter was a marvelous marriage of space age technology with practicality. For night boating, it was a godsend. Except that this Sea Ray's chart plotter was *broken*. In the haste to correct any mechanical problems that might prevent or necessitate an early end to our voyage, the chart plotter had been ignored.

Night boating, with its unlit shapes and moving shadows, was never my favorite pastime. Drunken speedboat owners were a hazard as they blasted across the water, either homebound or speeding recklessly toward the next bar. I knew from experience that familiar daytime landmarks would take on clever disguises at night in their efforts to be unrecognizable. Water towers and smokestacks that could be viewed from miles away in the sunlight were now gray dots among dark clouds. A distant light may be a plane, the back of a boat, or somebody's porch light. Still, with all of these conspiracies looming in the darkness, I knew that my boat's beautiful white hull would remain intact as long as I remained alert, attentive and proceeded at a sensible speed.

"Maaark," Max said as I hauled him aboard, "We took a little longer than we planned at dinner and the latest we should be back is seven o'clock. What time is it buddy?"

"It's seven thirty, Mr. Lexington."

"Okay, and what's your best guess as to what time we can be back?"

"At fifteen miles an hour it would take a little over three hours to do the fifty miles."

"Which means?"

"About ten-thirty…eleven when we tie up."

"Okay, then. Let's open it up for the ride back. I know we were down below earlier and anything faster than you were doing would have been too bumpy. But we'll sit on the back on the ride home and you get us there fast, all right my friend?"

I could see that a "safety first" speech wasn't going to go over too big at that moment. An eager-to-help restaurant patron assisted in casting off the lines, and I roared down the river. I pushed the throttles farther and farther forward, cutting a wide swath of foaming water behind the surging yacht. At twenty-nine miles an hour I passed freighters, pleasure cruisers and fishing boats at anchor. Nightfall caught us one hour down the river in a "no wake" zone as I slowed the Sea Ray to five miles an hour. I could see Max's agitation grow at the slower pace as he increased his consumption rate of Crown Royals. With each of Max's trips to the head and every refill of his glass, I observed his increasing unsteadiness. The moonless night grew darker as we left the "no wake" zone, and I picked up the pace. Visions of Summer's husband, Max's wife and the entire extended family and the police...all waiting at the marina's dock...flashed through my brain. As I strained to peer through the curtain of ink in front of me, I tried to keep one eye on Max in back, ready to shut down the boat immediately if he fell off the back. I knew that it simply wouldn't do to show up at the marina without him on board and that explaining his disappearance to just the Coast Guard alone would take all night.

The billionaire finally grew too tired to continue drinking and he and Summer settled onto the aft deck's couch and cuddled.

Threading my way through boat traffic outside of the marina, I pulled the Sea Ray into its well at 9:45. Strongly encouraging Max not to attempt to disembark until I got back, I drove an impatient Summer to her "hidden car." Racing back to the Sea Ray, I found a very drunk CEO fumbling around on board for his keys and shoes. I didn't have a "chase car" driver available, so I stuffed the staggering man into my Corvette and hustled him to the mansion gates. I punched in the code and watched the gates begin to swing out of the way. I saw that the giant home was unusually dark. As I pulled and pried the excessively soused and tired man out of my car, I took deep breaths to ready myself for the long push up the front steps. When we reached the top at exactly 10 p.m., a mere three hours late, I pushed the front door's intercom button. Somewhere in an upper hallway, a faint light clicked on, and I prepared to be greeted at the front door by the mistress of the house. A glance at Max showed that he was still standing (but not for long). Another light clicked on as Mrs. Lexington approached.

Sometimes a desperate situation requires action. Sometimes an impending confrontation can be mitigated by a show of remorse.

Occasionally, the unbearable tension created by a terrible transgression can be defused by a little levity. I decided that my warm, close relationship with Mrs. Lexington dictated the third option. As Elizabeth, clad in a thick robe, opened the front door, I helped Max across the threshold and into the huge foyer. As he stood facing his wife, bleary eyed and swaying slightly back and forth, I said, "Here he is, safe but not sound!"

Elizabeth's cold stare froze my lips, nose and ears. *I was wrong,* I thought, *this was not a time for levity,* as my other extremities began to lose feeling. Deciding to let Max handle the explanations, I backed out through the front door with an apologetic-looking good-bye grimace to the angry woman.

Back at the boat, it took nearly two hours to shut down and button up. I was at home in bed by 1 a.m.

I was not oblivious to my role in Max's Friday transgressions. While not exactly covering up for him, I was enabling the man to medicate with Crown Royals until he was numb enough to shelve his guilt for a few hours. With no way of knowing if other employees of his had "covered up" other flings over the years, I could only do my job or quit, in which case I was quite confident that he would quickly replace me and continue revisiting his fantasies with Summer. I increasingly saw my role as that of an armed babysitter, keeping Max out of danger and, if I could, out of the newspapers.

I received two phone calls from Max on Saturday morning. Wide awake and quite lucid, he carefully filled me in on the details of our story. We had met at the marina to take the boat out for a quick run. We were at the gas dock when "lo and behold" he had spotted two old business rivals gassing up a smaller boat. Max convinced them to accompany us to River Crab. At the restaurant there was much imbibing and even more reminiscing. We were back at the dock by seven or seven thirty, but neither compadre was in any condition by then to drive home. In a fit of humanitarianism, Max had me chauffeur each man to his doorstep, and only then did he allow himself to be taken home. I winced at Max's recitation of the story. It had more holes in it than a fishing net. The mere thought of the impatient billionaire spending three hours playing taxi instead of being the first to get dropped off was out of character, at best. At worst, it was an indication that, at any moment, I was going to be asked by Mrs. Lexington or other family members for an independent verification of our whereabouts.

Unfortunately, my fabricator-in-chief was arguably the worst liar in the contiguous United States. His far-fetched explanation would not be believed by his wife, his daughters or anybody else possessing more than a third-grader's understanding of human nature. The wisest move for me, as his unwitting alibi and co-conspirator, would be to avoid all contact with Max's family. I would, beginning immediately, ignore any unrecognized numbers on my cell phone. I would be diligent about not placing myself alone in a situation where a family member could engage me in an interrogation. With my guard thus heightened, I received a second call from Max an hour later.

"Yeah, Maaark. This is Mr. Lexington again. Listen, buddy, a couple of the kids want to take the boat out today with Mrs. Lexington and me. Do you think you could come up with a first mate by four o'clock? We thought we might head up to River Crab again."

"Uh, sure, I'll have the boat ready by three."

"Good, good, Robert will meet you there with towels and supplies, you know, plates and cups and things."

"Fine, sir, I'll be there by one o'clock."

I hung up amazed. Max, in his infinite wisdom, was proposing that we return to the scene of the crime as quickly as possible. Of course, just returning to it wasn't enough. We needed to bring an entire team of detectives and interrogation specialists with us as well. Bertha and Joe, Nathan and Lu Ann, and another daughter/heiress and her opportunistic husband would round out the forensic team quite nicely. I couldn't help but look forward to spending the afternoon and evening with a suspicious and wounded looking Elizabeth Lexington. I would no doubt be put at ease as I sat in the captain's chair while her eyes bored into the back of my skull. I desperately needed some type of first mate, and I needed one quickly.

My girlfriend Natasha was not my first choice. She would not, in fact, have been in the running at all if my back weren't against the wall. Blond and beautiful, Natasha packed 140 pounds of boobs and muscle into a square-shouldered five-foot-nine-inch, deeply tanned frame. Years of heavy weight training had given her long stride the confidence and power of a male athlete and a sassy, pissy attitude that she would have possessed even without the licensed .38 that I made her carry.

Her sarcastic, wicked sense of humor and uncanny ability to mimic anyone perfectly behind their back made spending time with her interesting and amusing. If one crossed a gorgeous, sexy runway model with a Doberman and then a more biting version of Joan Rivers, they would end up with my girlfriend. Even if it were possible, I wouldn't have changed a thing. A crushing grip and brutally deceptive upper body strength made her the perfect choice for my own boat when I needed an anchor pulled or a dock line secured, but her hostessing skills were a little rusty.

Although I was very comfortable with it, Natasha's personality wasn't perfectly suited to her Saturday role as first mate aboard the Sea Ray. I had begged for her help knowing full well that her "fetch it yourself" demeanor would result in less than stellar service for the pampered Lexington family. An hour into our voyage Natasha and our passengers reached an unspoken, albeit uneasy truce. As long as they didn't ask her to wait on them, she would remain at my side on the captain's deck...and would no longer scowl at them.

Max had begun the day's outing in a pre-medicated condition and frantically continued treatment with one glass after another as the afternoon wore on. The rest of the passengers reached for the medicine cabinet frequently, with only Mrs. Lexington nursing a single glass of wine for the entire two-and-a-half-hour ride.

Heavy pleasure boat traffic and a constant stream of rusty freighters kept the St. Clair River in a constant state of choppy agitation. The fifty-footer rose and fell dramatically as I managed to slip into the guest well along a rocky wall on my third attempt. Natasha threw her lines like a professional seaman after I chanced a leap to the dock over the surging waters. In spite of being tightly lashed between the dock pilings and opposite seawall, the Sea Ray continued to rise and fall in two foot jumps as one wave after another assaulted it broadside. Waiting for a respite in the violence, Natasha and I seized a five-second pause and helped Elizabeth leap to the dock. Apprehensive about the ability of the other inebriated guests to find solid ground safely, I grabbed the boat's pitching railing and swung back onto the deck. I half expected to see the remaining guests lurching about in various shades of green but found Lu Ann, Nathan and his spineless brother-in-law lounging on the back. Bertha, Joe and the other daughter were working over the inebriated family patriarch below, railing about the previous day's excuses not adding up. I heard Summer's name mentioned, followed afterward by a drunken denial. Minutes passed on the pitching craft, and Joe staggered up the steps to where I stood checking and tightening lines.

"Mark, do you remember what store Jim and Bill from yesterday worked at?"

"Yeah, Joe, I do," I said and told him.

"And it was just the four of you?"

"Yeah, Joe. I always check for stowaways before we take off, and I didn't see anybody else."

I hadn't eaten for awhile and was feeling a little belligerent. Joe wasn't too drunk to sense it and backed down, muttering, "Jim's been in my shop before, I know him." Joe the barberman wasn't too intimidating in his grand inquisitor role, and Nathan didn't seem eager to jump in. Max lumbered and lurched up the steps with Bertha and her sister close behind. I dashed to the fore deck and timed my leap perfectly, landing gently on the dock to supervise Max's journey as he grappled handholds and railings. Once ensconced on the fore deck, Max hung on for dear life as the boat bucked and jumped. During a two-second lull, Max swung a leg over the railing as two successive waves crashed vindictively into the hull. Max hung on tightly but pitched to and fro as the Sea Ray, like a bucking horse, tried to throw him off. Bertha, still behind Max and clinging onto the railing as well, snapped out, "Dammit Mark, this is too dangerous!" I would have placated the nasty woman by calming the waters with outstretched arms if I thought it would work, but I chose instead to keep both eyes on Max. The boat lunged toward me, and I grabbed a piece of his shirt. Natasha heaved on a line, and the Sea Ray inched closer to me. The waves took a brief time-out, and Max threw himself into my waiting clinch. Bertha reluctantly reached for my extended arm, and I tossed her onto the dock. Still glowering, she skulked past me, and I made a mental note to locate a cinder block during dinner. If she fell in trying to board for the journey home, I would toss her the block and tell the Coast Guard I mistook it for a life vest.

Natasha and I ordered a wonderful dinner and watched a glowing orb drop in the sky. The wind, the boat traffic and the waves all abated considerably, and the yacht began to settle down. My cell phone, which I had ignored during the trip up river, rang again with renewed vigor. It was Summer, hungry for details. I told her about the ambush below decks, but was unable to furnish much detail. Summer pried me for my assessment on the outing's mood. I told her that there was less tension during the Cuban missile crisis. She asked me to evaluate the interaction between Max and Elizabeth. I explained that the daughters had circled the wagons around their mother, and I was too busy piloting the boat to submit a questionnaire to either.

Dinner ended, and an hour and a half later the group began to troop out of the restaurant in twos. Re-boarding went smoothly, and we motored down the river into the dusk. Darkened factories and their smokestacks loomed over the banks and everybody planted themselves on the aft deck. Max became obsessed with hearing a Motown CD.

"Naaataaasha, see if you can play that CD with that singer and her two friends, will ya?"

Natasha looked at me quizzically. "I think he means the Motown CD," I said. "There's at least one cut on there of Diana Ross and the Supremes."

Natasha searched every cubbyhole on deck. She searched every cupboard below. She looked in every nook and cranny in the salon, as well as every compartment of the salon's CD player/changer. There was no mountain high enough and there was no valley low enough. The Motown CD was no longer on board.

"Vee kan't zeem to locate it, Mr. Lexington."

"Are you sure? Because we played it yesterday."

I turned the proper answer over in my mind, *Your Mistress took all of her CDs back last night when she left.* No...that answer wouldn't do. *We're purposely keeping it hidden because we think it would be fun to hear you sing it and try to remember even five of the words, sir.* No....that might be misinterpreted as being a little insolent.

The undeniable fact was that Summer had been careful to remove every trace of her sojourn before the family decided to go yachting. Part of those traces were her binders of catalogued CDs.

"You know that CD, right Maaark? It's the one with that other fella singing that song about what's happening."

"Vat das he vant me to do, *sheet* heem von?" Natasha asked me.

I turned the stereo to the Oldies station and the rumbling about the missing CD died down. Two hours later, we were at the mouth of the river with only the smallish Lake St. Clair to traverse.

"Maaaark, how fast are we going?"

"Fourteen miles per hour, sir."

"What time is it?"

"It's ten o'clock."

"I've gotta get home, Dad," said Bertha.

"Us too, Dad. Lu Ann and I were supposed to be back an hour ago!" chimed in Nathan.

"Maaark, let's open 'er up, buddy!"

I throttled the engines up, and the Sea Ray roared into the night.

At twenty-eight miles an hour we only had eight miles to go, which meant I'd throttle down to enter the marina in about twenty minutes. Beckoning us on in the clear night sky, a well-lit tower near the marina made navigation easy. Four miles out, the radar screen showed at least twenty "blips" around us.

"How much longer Maaaark?"

"About ten minutes to Colony Bay, sir."

"Fine, open 'er up!"

Two miles out, the radar screen showed one hundred and twenty blips. A swarm of boats with their night running lights on flitted across our course like gnats. Hundreds more were anchored in flotillas closer to shore. Some were beginning to cross our bow, while I changed course constantly to avoid others. A thousand boats now appeared on my radar screen, each one seemingly determined to block our way.

The city was having its annual Venetian Festival, and the turnout to watch two dozen festively illuminated private boats was a record-breaking one.

A forty-foot Sea Ray crossed my bow, and I throttled down to twenty miles an hour. Our yacht was closing in fast on three more boats directly in our path, and I reduced the speed to fifteen miles an hour.

"Watch it! Watch it!" Max yelled. A small boat sped across our stern at sixty miles per hour. Natasha had been following it on radar for over a minute, and I had gotten a visual twenty seconds ago. My back seat billionaire had just seen it and was getting panicky. Fervently hoping that he didn't work his way up front to help us navigate, I dropped our forward speed to eleven and continued threading my way between dozens of boats, both moving and anchored.

"How much longer, Dad?" Bertha asked loudly enough for me to hear.

Slowing down to five, I put the fifty-foot yacht in a sixty-foot gap as I sidled to port. Spotting an opening to the marina, I squeezed past a forty-two foot Mainship and eased into the calmer waters of the marina. Bullying my way around in reverse, I managed to back into our well on the first try in spite of my anxious passengers standing up trying to block any view I had. Thanking me repeatedly, Max handed his car keys from Friday to Joe, who, at only four drinks above the legal limit, was deemed more fit to drive. In a caravan that was four cars strong, the yachters drove off, and Natasha and I worked until midnight, shutting down and tying up.

34

O N SUNDAY THE well at the Grosse Pointe Yacht Club was ready and I moved the Sea Ray a mile and a half into its new home.

Monday morning my cell phone rang at 8:30 a.m. "Yeah, Maaark, this is Mr. Lexington."

"Good morning sir, how are you?"

"Fine, fine, listen, Jack Sullivan, the manager of the Yacht Club called me. He said that well is ready for the Sea Ray."

"I'm already on it, sir."

"Good, good. Has *she* called you yet?"

"No, I haven't heard from her since Saturday." (At least Summer knew I liked to sleep until nine, and had a modicum of consideration.)

"It's over, you know. I called her this morning and told her."

"I'm sorry to hear that."

"I mean it this time. I know you don't think I do because I've said it before but this time I really am firm about my decision," Max went on. "When I really examine the whole thing, Maaark, it just doesn't make *sense*! I hear she's married to a great guy. He's well-respected, maybe not in my league but he's sharp! I keep asking myself, what *is* it she's after? And it must be the money! Maybe she and Chuck are in on this together. But I would *never, ever* give in if that's what they want! What's your take on that angle?"

"I think Chuck has enough money, sir."

253

Max droned on. At nine o'clock he pulled into his parking spot at corporate. After a half-hour of persuading me that the affair was over, Max bade me good-bye and hung up.

At nine-oh-one my cell rang again. It was Summer, crying and swearing.

"Did he talk to you yet? Than son-of-a-bitch! He did it again! That asshole called me this morning and as soon as he said hello I knew what he'd say next! Friday he swore, Mark, he swore he'd never do this again! And then as soon as he's in his car this morning he does it again! Well, when you talk to him again you can tell him I said 'Fuck you, Max, fuck you!' Just because Elizabeth and the daughters stepped over the line this weekend he shit on me again. He has no control over his kids at all and I hate him. I *hate* him!"

It was a sunny day, my cell phone's reception at the house was intermittent unless I walked around slowly on my front driveway. I listened to Summer's tirade for twenty minutes, and spent ten more trying to hang up. I walked back in and Natasha asked "Dass he pay you to tuck to heem *und* her, or just heem?"

"Well, neither, I guess," I replied. She was right. The phone hours from both sides were really starting to add up. My best estimate was that, between the two adversaries, I had spent over one hundred and fifty hours as their friend/psychiatrist/cry rag.

My cell's caller ID had alerted me often to an upcoming phone blitz/bitch session, but I eventually learned that avoidance was futile. If I ignored cell calls from Max, I received voice mail messages that grew increasingly urgent. On Tuesday I heard, "Maaark, this is Max, I'm in the car, call me if you can." And then, "Maaark, this is Mr. Lexington, I have a question to ask you. I'm at the office, please call me immediately." And then, "Maaark, okay, okay, I see I'm being a pest. Looook buddy, I know I've been bothering you a lot. I have something important that I need to tell you, please, please call me now."

When I called him back, he sounded distracted instead of relieved.

"Good morning sir, this is Mark."

"Yeah, Maaark, is everything okay?"

"Of course. I was in the shower," I lied.

"Listen, my friend. Did you get the Sea Ray into the well at the Yacht Club? Al at Colony Bay says that they need their space back."

"Two days ago, sir."

"Fine, that's fine. Listen, I haven't heard from our friend after I left a message, have you heard at all?"

"I think she's under the impression that you broke up with her…again." There, I had said it, or at least strongly inferred it. I could never directly pass judgement on his schizoid behavior, but a man who had spent his life reading between the lines should be able to understand my last jibe.

"I know, I know. Did she say anything to you?"

"She's pretty upset," The Master of Understatement replied.

"I see. Listen Maaark, how long have we known each other?"

"Two and a half years."

"Right, that's right. Look, all I'm asking is that you call her and have her call me back, I'll be in my car in five minutes. Would you do that for me, my friend?"

"I'll try right now." Clicking off, I dialed Summer's number.

"Hello? Hi sweetie. Did he tell you to call me? Did he tell you that he's called me like ten times this morning? I decided that I better have a long talk with my husband. I didn't want him hearing about it from one of the daughters. We went to breakfast and I told him about everything. Well, I didn't tell him about the sex part. But I said that Max and I have grown really close as friends and I have even been on his boat. With you captaining for us, of course. And you know what? He was okay with everything."

"Does Chuck own any guns?"

"Yes. But just for hunting. Oh, but he's not like that. Besides, I said I didn't tell him about what happened below."

"Below what? The waist?"

"Very funny. You know what I mean. I just told him that we'd developed a strong friendship but had mutually decided to back it down because of the way this area might perceive it."

"Are you going to call Max back?"

"I'll let him stew for awhile and then maybe. What do *you* think I should do?"

"So far, there's been no permanent damage to your marriage."

"You don't think I should call, do you?"

"You've said Chuck is a terrific guy."

"I know, I know. He is a sweet guy. But he never stood up to his family for me. And that still hurts."

"He *did* adopt your son?"

"You know he did. I told you that! And I love him for it. I really do. I don't know what intrigues me so much about our friend. I'm just drawn to him. And it's more now than just the power. His family knows about me now, you know! Bertha and one of the twins, Missy, have been asking questions. My friend told me."

"Do you think he'd ever stand up for you against all eight children?"

"I don't know, Mark, I really don't. Should I call him? What do you think?"

"I think Chuck is a fine man."

"You're right. You're right."

The next morning my cell rang at nine-oh-one. It was Summer.

"Hi, sweetie. Hey…I need you to do me a big favor. I'm ordering breakfast at the Pancake House. I'm getting everything to go. I've got you an omelet and crepes and juice. Max's playing tennis at the Yacht Club. Could you please, please go there and tell him we'll be waiting for him on the boat after he's done at eleven? And could you be a dear and open the boat up for us and make sure that the air is on? They said that Max's egg white only omelet is going to take a little longer but they'll do it!"

"I'm having my head examined this morning. Should I make an appointment for you too?"

"Very funny. Please, sweetie, could you just open the boat up and then tell him?"

I pulled in across from the Yacht Club's tennis courts at ten o'clock. Two groups of four men, all well past their prime years, were playing on separate courts. Feeling a trifle conspicuous, I walked over to Max's court and waited until he spotted me. I expected him to be embarrassed, but he wasn't and he walked over to me quickly.

An hour later, I was sitting on the back of the docked Sea Ray at that bastion of proprietary correctness, the Grosse Pointe Yacht Club.

One of the Club's most famous members walked nonchalantly down the docks toward me, greeting me warmly as he stepped aboard.

"Hey, buddy. How are you?"

"Good, Mr. Lexington, how was your game?"

"Fine. Fine." The king of willpower then stepped by me and down into the salon where the lady he had "called it quits" with "once and for all," bustled in the galley, laying out breakfast.

My crepes and omelet were excellent. After breakfast and what I deemed to be an appropriate amount of time, I peeked down into the salon. Max and Summer were preoccupied behind closed doors. One omelet was untouched until I peeled apart its container and demolished it. I reasoned that in the event of a sudden familial visit, I would eat any evidence that indicated more than one person was aboard. Back topsides, I stared out at the lake as Diana Ross promised me from below that no mountain was high enough to keep her from me. I used my cell to beg Michelle to cover for me at the studio while she reminded me that our afternoon business was beginning to wilt from my lack of attention. She suggested that we commission decals for the still nameless boat and dub it "Luv Shack." I told her that I'd run it by Max and get back with her.

Afternoon delight was over by one o'clock, and the pair emerged into the sunlight placing Armani sunglasses over squinting eyes. They cleverly agreed to stagger their individual departure times by ten minutes in order to fool any window-seat diners in the Yacht Club's restaurant. Max left first. As he disappeared around the main building, Summer pounced on me.

"Mark, guess what he said?"

"The eggs were cold?"

"No, no, be serious. Guess what word he used while we were down there?"

"Oh, God," I said. "What word did he use?" I asked with a wince.

"He said he loves me! He used the L word. Can you believe it! I told him I loved him too! I'm soooo excited! He said that he could see how much I'd like to take care of him. He was *very* impressed by breakfast. He said his own family had never done anything like this for him before!"

I hoped to hell not, thinking of the front stateroom.

Later that afternoon, my cell phone clamored for my attention with Summer's number showing on the caller ID.

"Mark, I'm soo irritated. His kids are out of control. They're grown children, his youngest is thirty remember? He just called me and he said that his disappearance after tennis caused an *uproar*! And get this...his kids have scheduled a family meeting at Corporate Headquarters for six o'clock tomorrow. Mark, my God, they're going to do an intervention regarding us. Bertha has been gathering information on me! But she works for Max! *She* works for *him* and she's really crossed the line. He says he's very angry and they're all going to feel his wrath if they dare confront him with any of their information. He said he's ready for them. He said they're all *far* from perfect and he's going to remind them one by one. They've told Elizabeth everything they know and after all he's done for them they've all sided with their Mom! I know he's going to stand up for me, for us really, and that's something Chuck *never* did for me with *his* family!"

I found myself hoping, fervently, that Max's family was successful. I wondered at that point how they would respond to a pre-intervention pep talk from me. There were only eight of them, admittedly, going against their father, a powerfully persuasive force. They were all adults, however, and no doubt thoroughly convinced of their own righteousness. I was concerned about the motivation of some. In spite of their trust fund incomes of a quarter million a year apiece, there was the potential for a much larger pot of gold. A billion dollars, divided eight ways, was 125 million dollars apiece. But an untimely demise of their adored mother would leave an easily altered will to the sole discretion of their straying father. The grieving parent might marry the despised mistress and reconfigure the will out of spite *or* as the result of being manipulated by his new bride. The offsprings' silver spoons would be forever tarnished. A lot was at stake at this meeting…their standing in the community, the cohesiveness of the family, and most of all…the money.

It wasn't until 9:01 a.m. the day after that my cell phone rang with the results. "Mark, that son-of-a-bitch did it to me again! He promised he wouldn't, but that asshole! He broke it off this morning! He has taken every bit of trust that I ever had in him and thrown it away! And nothing, nothing he can do will ever win me back! Not this time."

"The meeting went badly?" I asked.

"No. He called me after and he sounded very tired and, you know, wrung out. He'd been drinking but that wasn't it. He said it lasted over two hours and all of the daughters had their fangs and claws out. They said I was the whore of the neighborhood and that he was making a total ass out of himself. They asked him how could he do this to their mother. All three of his sons didn't say much. They kept pretty quiet. But the daughters *totally* crossed the line and showed him *no* respect! They talked about my relationship with Mot Montgomery and said that I was about to do the same to him! They called me a whore and a stripper and said that he was blind if he couldn't see that it was just about the money!"

"So, it *did* go badly?"

"Oh, no. He fired right back at them. He talked about what he'd done for them. He reminded them who paid for their weddings, for their houses, and even where half of them were employed! He asked what gave them the right to tell him how to run his life when they have trouble, even with the money, running their own."

Each of the trust fund adults began to receive $250,000 a year at the age of thirty-five. It came from an irrevocable trust set up for their benefit by their father. Longevity ran in the family, making it safe to assume that their "average age of demise" would be at about age 85. Fifty years of annual checks would accrue to a total amount of 12.5 million over each son or daughter's entire lifespan. A princely sum, to be sure. It was a reassuring flow of cash, but paled in comparison to the possibility of receiving 125 million dollars in a lump sum. If, God forbid, their beloved father passed first, their saintly mother could no doubt be counted on to alter the will, giving each heir (and the church) their rightful portion. If, God forbid more, their adored mother were to pass on first, their esteemed father was now an unpredictable loose cannon. The will could be rewritten as many times as he pleased, with his new wife at his side as he wrote, making helpful suggestions.

His offspring must have been apoplectic at the thought of this new stranger in their midst. I realized that they didn't need any input from me. One hundred twenty-five million was 500 *years* of $250,000 checks! In fact, I was sure that Dale Carnegie himself could not have motivated them to a higher plane at that meeting.

Max began calling his determined mistress the day after he broke it off with her. With his alcohol consumption on the rise once again, I was enlisted frequently to ensure his safe arrival home from the office. The Mercedes only made it directly home on half of these pick-ups, however. The other half resulted in a rendezvous at the Beach Grill with his malleable mistress. Phone calls and promises of loyalty were all it took to bring the gullible woman back into his orbit. A night of drinks and promises usually resulted in a morning of regrets and reneging as the waffling billionaire swore his undying loyalty by night and wondered by morning if anyone as man-pleasing as Summer had ever worked as a "pro." The tortured woman would run back to Max every time, until I wondered if Max was pulling his scripts from a Charles Schultz comic strip. In one famous scenario, Lucy holds a football for Charlie Brown to kick, constantly reassuring the gullible boy that *this* time she won't pull it away at the last moment. Of course she does, and she seems to get a perverse delight from her actions in the next week's strip. She apologizes for the previous week, holds the football and does it all over again, much to Charlie Brown's chagrin at being fooled again.

Summer had been "Lucy'd" so many times by the vacillating billionaire that we developed a derisive dialog behind his back just to retain some sanity. I would call Summer on her cell phone. When she answered, I would summon my best Max Lexington impression and begin.

"Yeah, hi Summer, this is Max."

She would reply, "Well hello, my dear."

When it was my turn again I'd say, "Yeah, listen, Babe, it's over, never again. In the clear light of day, I realize that it's just not going to work between us."

She would answer impatiently, "Yeah, yeah, yeah, so where do you want to meet for lunch?"

I would retort, "No, I really, really mean it this time. I'm crazy nuts about you but let's face it, I'm playing the back nine, and you deserve…you'll find somebody else. It's over."

Summer would say, "Uh huh, sure Max, whatever you say sweetie. Hey how about if we meet in the church parking lot and have dinner at the Omni Hotel?"

I'd answer, "Okay, sure Babe. Can you be there by five o'clock?" At this point we would both laugh hysterically and then get to the real point of the call.

35

THERE WAS NO laughter on the morning of September eleventh, however. Natasha and I watched the planes strike the Towers on the news as many times as we could bear. Michelle's call from the gym informed us that we needn't be there as client after client called in to cancel. They were either staying put to watch television and cry or to drive directly home to be with loved ones. Max called my cell to advise me that he and Elizabeth would be driving to his vacation home up north. Even Summer readily scrapped her plans to be with Max and declared that she would be spending the day with Chuck. Natasha and I packed lunch into a cooler, drove to the Yacht Club and commandeered the Sea Ray for a one mile voyage to float, untethered, out in the lake to contemplate the undiscussable.

Several days later, prompted by an unsolicited phone conversation with Max's daughter Missy, Chuck called the famous man. During a long but respectful conversation, Chuck asked Max how many of his "anonymous" source's accusations were factual. Max explained that he and Chuck's wife had eaten lunch together a couple of times, but certainly nothing more. Max promised that even these innocent lunches would end, especially if they made Chuck uncomfortable in any way. Chuck thanked Max. He explained that he wouldn't have called but for the fact that he still loved his wife very much and didn't want any baseless rumors taking root. Max thanked Chuck. He appreciated the opportunity to set the record straight. After all, he told Chuck, a man with Max's exposure in the community could not afford to give even the appearance of impropriety.

The next day was a Thursday, and Thursday morning was still reserved for a tennis foursome. It was raining, but Lochmoor was able to accommodate Max and his co-players with an indoor court. Summer knew all of this because Max had mentioned it in a message to Summer's voicemail on his way to play. Summer had spent much of the prior evening listening to a CD from a blind Italian tenor named Andrea Bocelli. All that evening she found herself longing, while listening to one heart wrenching song after another, to share songs from her new find with her mature lover. In several of the most poignant cuts, Bocelli sang of the lover that his heart ached for...of the one that he was separated from. Photographs of surging seas were included next to the translations provided inside the cover. These pictures spoke to Summer of their time on the yacht together, mesmerized by the roiling waters behind the Sea Ray as we journeyed down rivers and across lakes.

By morning it became clear what Summer must do...she must share this insightful compilation of songs with her lover. One song in particular, *"Il Mistero Dell'Amore"* (The Mystery of Love), stood out from the others.

"I who sing at night to the sound of the sea," Bocelli sang. *"I who speak to the moon to understand the mystery of a love affair"*...This was perfect! *"Inside my life the music plays new poetry in memory of you."* Maybe she could gift wrap it! *"Vast oceans of freedom days of celebration I won't forget. The cold winter won't take you from my life. Desires, memories, what mystery in this love of mine."*

Yes, she would wrap it up as a gift, and leave it under the windshield wiper of the Mercedes as it sat waiting for him at the end of his tennis match. She could highlight cut number seven with a yellow marker. It would be Max's first introduction to Bocelli, this vibrant song about a lover celebrating a mysterious, exciting relationship.

Summer highlighted number seven on the outside of the "Tosca"

CD, signed it at the bottom, wrapped it simply and drove to Lochmoor. With time to spare she placed the special gift between the windshield and the wiper blade. The edge of the package protruded from under the hood on the driver's side, waiting to be discovered and then appreciated in the S500's CD player.

Max finished playing tennis, toweled off, said good-bye to his partner and walked, alone, out to the parking lot. The object of Summer's affection got into his car, started it up and without getting out again, drove home. After parking in the garage, Mr. Lexington went upstairs to take a shower and contemplate whether a half-day at the office would still be worth the drive in. As Max showered, the household's faithful manservant, Robert, freshly back from grocery shopping, pulled into the bay alongside Max's car in the Mercedes wagon. On his very first trip in, the ever-observant butler noticed a small package sticking out from under the hood of the silver luxury car in the next bay. Plucking it up with less than a thimbleful of curiosity, the alert house manager handed it to the first employer he encountered upon entering the kitchen.

"I found this stuck under the hood of Mr. Lexington's car," Robert absently told Elizabeth.

Mrs. Lexington's first inclination was to throw the thin package out. It looked like the free CD ROMs that always came in the mail. Elizabeth couldn't even imagine what those were for, but she knew they had something to do with the home computer that they didn't know how to use and never went near. This one was different though. This free sample was gift wrapped and reminded her of the little packages that some of the grandchildren exchanged at Christmas. Elizabeth tore off the wrapping for a quick inspection before tossing the item. It was an album for a CD player, and from an artist that she'd never heard of. Track number seven, "*Il Mistero Dell'Amore*" was highlighted under the plastic cover. How curious, she thought, as she dialed her daughter Bertha at the office.

"Has your father taken a sudden interest in Italian Opera that you know of?" inquired the lady of the house.

"No, Ma, not that I've heard," Bertha answered.

"Do you know what Il Mistero Dell'Amore means? Somebody has highlighted that one."

"No, Ma, I don't, but I'm coming over after work anyway, remember? We need to go over next month's calendar."

Four hours later, the pair was settled into the upstairs den, listening to the fine tenor speak to the moon about the mysteries of love affairs. Elizabeth, however, had no interest in speaking to the moon at the moment. In fact, the seventy-year old matriarch didn't think that love was very mysterious at all right now. As the two listened for clues, Bertha flipped over the cover and spotted "With all my Love, Summer" at the bottom in dark pen. The atmosphere in the house suddenly became very volatile, waiting for a spark of combustion to ignite it. A whole book of matches came home from the office in his Mercedes an hour later. The flash of the explosion could be seen from the street in the windows.

Working out with clients in my little studio a mile and a half away, I thought I heard a muffled roar above the din of the stereo.

To my mild surprise, Max called me the next day and asked me to prepare the boat for Sunday. My guests were the president of a mattress company and his wife, a daughter and her husband and the boss and Elizabeth. The mattress company president had actually owned the local company until the last recession, when Max had bought him out. As the company lay on the verge of bankruptcy, Max paid pennies on the dollar and now was the main supplier of mattresses to his thirty stores. The business tactic was called vertical expansion and added still another couple of million a year to the tycoon's coffers. With the unheard-of three-day-notice, I was able to enlist first mate services from Sherri Pine, my part-time trainer. Sherri looked strikingly like the actress Adrienne Barbeau from "Maude" except bustier. Sherri, with her cute little giggle, curvy figure and dark tan came across initially as shy. As she opened up, however, she projected a bit of a bad girl/party girl image combined with that of a competent registered nurse, which she was.

On Sunday the eight of us cast off from the Yacht Club, passing slowly by the Trailer Park King's 118-foot Yacht. In shorts and a dress T-shirt with a *real* pocket, I was feeling quite nautical and ready to enjoy the sun-kissed afternoon. Sherri was wearing a skintight white T-shirt, painted-on black pants and black deck shoes with no socks. Max was quite taken with her as she plied him with drinks and snacks on the boat's rear sundeck. But Sherri wouldn't rest until she had won the women passengers over as well, conversing with them fluently about their various medical conditions and medications. The trip was a short one down the nearby Detroit River to Sinbad's, a popular waterfront eatery. Sherri and I ate on board as Max and the others flagged the owner (whom Max knew) and received exemplary service. As we eased out of the well and back toward the river, six men disembarking at another well began to hoot and holler. The object of their attention was my voluptuous first mate, who smiled and waved from her aft deck position next to Max. In a move that surprised even me, the inebriated Max Lexington smacked Sherri's rump with an open palm and yelled, "Eat your heart out, fellas!"

Sherri was even more attentive to our guests on the short trip back as I reveled in my perfect choice of first mates. She smiled and cooed gamely as Max pulled her down onto his lap more than once with an arm around her waist. Back at the Yacht Club, we docked as dusk descended. Profuse thank yous resounded from everywhere as the guests departed, and I inwardly gloated as one by one they turned around to re-thank us in happy echoes. My perfect first mate helped me tie lines and zip up canvas as well as clean up and bag garbage. It had been a perfect day, and, thanks in part to Sherri, I had finally arrived in my part-time sea captain position.

Monday afternoon I received a call from Summer. She was livid but this time her wrath was directed at me. "What did you think you were doing?" Summer began.

"Uh, when?"

"You know damn well, when. When you hired that *slut* to make moves on Max. She's just white trash, you know!"

"Uh, I thought it went pretty well."

"Oh, yeah, it went well all right," Summer bitched on. "He couldn't *wait* to call me today and tell me how she was hitting on him. She was all over him, Goddamit, and you just let her! I thought we were friends. That was *not* smart, Mark. I can't believe you did that behind my back!"

My heart began to sink as I saw the ideal first mate being terminated after the first voyage. Later in the evening, when Sherri stopped in to work out, I explained how she had tried to seduce Max, according to his mistress.

"Oh, gross!" Sherri said, and walked away.

Two days later, a still angry Summer called my cell. "There's more problems because of your poor choices last Sunday. It seems as though Ron Weevil, the Trailer Park King, spotted what was going on and called Max today! He said that it looked bad. He said that it looked as though Max had a bunch of hookers on board."

"Actually," I parried, "one woman was Max's daughter and the two others were fifty-five and seventy-one years old. Real hookers are usually younger."

"You know what I mean, he told Max that he was embarrassed for him and that Max used to come across as much classier when the crew had uniforms."

I wondered if the mattress company president realized that the matronly mother of his children looked like a prostitute when she wore white, knee-length shorts. Her sun sensitivity had required her to wear a sweatshirt that day, but I supposed that underneath it all the Grosse Pointe lady was a real vixen.

My days in Summer's doghouse were short-lived, however. Twenty-four hours later, I was forced back to my unpaid phone liaison job. I was, unfortunately, the only possible messenger for Summer when she needed to reach Max at home. I was also the only pipeline that Max could use to reach Summer when she was at home on a "poor cell phone reception" day. The grateful billionaire had thanked me repeatedly one night for putting my life on hold whenever they asked and strongly hinted that he would soon find a way to show his appreciation. A friend regaled me with stories of another billionaire's loyal cook who proffered his resignation one day only to find that his name was indelibly entered into the rich man's will. I determined to soldier on until the boss had his personal life together and my services were no longer necessary.

Summer's frantic call came at 6:15 p.m. on a Thursday. "Mark, dammit, if you've been joking around it's not very goddam funny!"

"I'm sorry, I'm busy and can't joke around right now."

"I mean it Mark. You didn't leave a message on my voice mail just now?"

"I have *not* called you today."

"Well somebody sure has and if it wasn't you now I'm scared."

"What did they say?"

"It's some guy and he threatened me Mark, he threatened me!"

"Threatened you how, Summer?"

"I can't go home and I don't want to. I'm coming over there!" Ten minutes later the white Mercedes swung into my parking lot. Summer walked briskly across the parking lot, her head swiveling from side to side. I begged two trainers to take over my clients. The roll of their eyes said "yet another crisis" as they accepted the charts.

Shaking and trembling, with real tears visibly streaming down her cheeks from under her sunglasses, Summer held out her cell and punched a couple of numbers. Putting the phone to my ear I prepared myself for "one new message." It began, "Hello, whore. If you know what's good for you you'll stay away from Max Lexington. I won't warn you again, slut!"

Whoa, I thought. Gently, I put my hand on Summer's shoulder and moved her away from the front windows. I mentally counted the steps to where my Beretta and its extra rounds lay. For now, at least, Summer was following the caller's instructions. Max wasn't anywhere near the gym. A debate began to rage in my head. The police should be notified. A call to them would, of course, initiate an investigation. An investigation would require a great deal of explanation from Summer…and Mr. Lexington. At my studio, the woman was in no immediate danger. I decided to pass the buck. It was obvious that Summer was more than ready for me to call Max at his residence…we would let him decide the next move. There was one sure way to get through to Max at his home, no matter who answered. I dialed.

"Lexington residence, may I help you?"

"Hi Robert, this is Mark Steel returning Mr. Lexington's call."

"Yes, Mr. Steeeeel, he just woke up from a little nappy. I'll tell him you're on the phone." Ten seconds, twenty seconds, a half-minute went by.

"Hello?" A slightly groggy voice inquired.

"Yes sir, this is Mark. I'm sorry to bother you, but I'm standing next to a friend of ours and she's rather disturbed by a message on her voice mail. Are you able to speak with her?"

"Yes, yes, put her on!" The pair conversed for an animated minute or so, and Summer began to punch buttons on her cell phone. Holding her earpiece to the mouthpiece on my gym phone, she played the message to Max. Two minutes later, she played it again. During the next half-hour the distraught mistress repeated the process again and again while her lover listened. Finally, Summer hung up. Appearing calmer, she implored me to drive her to the Beach Grill to meet Max. Peeking wistfully at my still busy evening schedule, I hesitated, but agreed. I wondered what excuse the closely watched billionaire intended to give as he dashed to his Mercedes. Perhaps "Gotta go Babe, my mistress is getting death threats." Or maybe "Stay at home and keep the doors locked, dear, my girlfriend is scared, lonely, and she's only thirty-nine!"

It was a long night at the Grill as Summer's cell phone played the message over and over. After the Crown Royal flowed freely, the boss decided that his oldest daughter was the instigator somehow and would feel his wrath the next day. Finally, the man who made $3,000 every hour of every day sent his mistress home without a police escort, without a bodyguard and without even a key chain canister of pepperspray.

36

FALL WAS RAPIDLY introducing itself back to the Pointes, and the yacht had been ignored for two weeks until Max phoned me one Sunday morning. A glorious seventy-five degree day had been forecast, and he desired a trip to The Old Club with Mrs. Lexington. In the short time it took the three of us to get there, the destination changed and (surprise, surprise) I was instructed to take us up to River Crab. The trip up the south channel and St. Clair River was calm and uneventful, as was the couple's dinner after we arrived. I could see the pair's table from the Sea Ray. Max and Elizabeth appeared to be having a drinking contest as Max ordered glass after glass of "Double Crowns." Max won the contest hands down when Elizabeth stopped after one glass of wine. On the way back, the soused yacht owner lolled back, admiring and exulting in the spectacular sunset on the glistening lake waters. The boating-indifferent Mrs. Lexington sat at a table farther forward, opening and sorting a huge pile of mail she had brought. I ignored Summer's constant calls on my cell for compatibility updates, but if I'd answered I might have said that Max was being totally ignored. The yacht had barely slipped into its well and I only had one of the eight lines tied when Elizabeth gathered up her mail and bolted off of the boat. Tripping after the woman as she trotted down the docks, Max thanked me and called out a last instruction or two.

In the next several days, Summer frequently suggested a last rendezvous on the yacht before it was taken out of the water for winter. Max was in one of his "if there's no sex then it's not cheatin'" phases and continually sidestepped every invitation and suggestion for a week, knowing well the outcome if he accepted. The man who had spent the majority of his business life in the commander's chair detested being told what to do. He had marched to the beat of his own drum for so long that any other drumbeat was anathema to him. After two-and-a-half years, I finally realized that if someone demanded a specific behavior or action from the man (even if that someone was his mistress), he was inclined to do the opposite.

On a bright, clear morning in the tiny downtown of Grosse Pointe Park, Summer stepped out of Conga Coffee with her usual. She was suddenly confronted first by one, and then two screaming daughters. The pair of heiresses raged at the surprised temptress, using words that rhymed with war, scamp and mutt. They strongly urged her to "stay away from our father," and used words that rhymed with witch and punt. Summer fired back for a minute but finally dove into her Mercedes and reported the public chastisement to me to relay to the boss. That afternoon, while Max raged in Bertha's office only to be offered more repeated denials from his eldest daughter, Nathan stopped by. The youngest son finally cracked. He admitted to making the phone call and leaving the warning on Summer's voice mail. He had used a pay phone. He loved his father very much and didn't want him to make a mistake that he would later regret. Dad was hurting too many people and needed to stop seeing Summer immediately.

The next morning was a Thursday, and Max woke up mad and continued stewing and simmering until five o'clock. At 5:01 he called Summer and asked her to be at Beach Grill at 5:30. At 5:02 Summer called my cell and begged me to meet Max at the Yacht Club as soon as possible. At 5:12 I fired up the port diesel on the Sea Ray and at 5:13 the starboard. Minutes later, we were sliding out of the Yacht Club's harbor en route by water to the Beach Grill. Summer was waiting and practically leaped onto the stern as I crept up to the seawall. By the time we pulled back out into open water, the Crown Royal was flowing. Andrea Bocelli was booming out his joy on the stereo system, and the two lovers were reunited in the throes of ecstasy. First-mateless as usual, I set a slow, lazy course for the mouth of the Clinton River, a muddy tributary of Lake St. Clair. Only ten miles away as the crow flew, the river boasted of a waterfront restaurant called Crews Inn. After an hour, the pair came up for air, one hunger sated for the moment. Neither had eaten since lunch, though, and both were ravenous. Only two miles from the river's mouth by now, I explained my plan and promised dinner docking within a half hour. As expected, I received the okay.

As we worked our way up the river, Max asked me if we were still in Michigan waters. I replied that we were (smiling at the fact that Crews Inn was only one mile from my house by land). The new owners had hired a gifted, talented chef and my dinner on board was excellent. During dinner, Max and Summer discussed the brazenness of his children as he expressed the depths of his indignation and swore his loyalty to her. The return trip was dark but beautifully lit on the river as the reunited couple sat on the aft deck and urged me homeward. In spite of ingesting a generous amount of distilled beverage, Max seemed edgy at the lateness of the hour.

At 10:30 we docked at the rear of the Beach Grill. The restaurant was nearly empty. Not knowing how long we would be there, I was on shore attaching the second of three lines when my cell phone rang. It was a Grosse Pointe number. I hesitated. I answered, "Good evening, this is Mark speaking."

"Mark, this is Missy, Mr. Lexington's daughter. I know he's with you right now. I want to talk to him."

Whoa, I thought, as I looked warily around for occupied cars. I glanced into the Sea Ray. Bright lights were on in the salon. They looked to be winding it down with a last good-bye. I reviewed my answer options. Number one was: *"I'm in the shower and I'm not alone, may I call you back?"* Number two: *"Your surprise call has prompted a stroke, may I seek medical attention and then call you back?"* Number three: *"I haven't seen the man for days, if you could describe what he's wearing, I'll help you look."*

I chose number four. "Just a moment please."

I hopped back onto the yacht and peeked into the salon. My right eye twinged, and I blinked hard when I found them standing in the salon locked in an embrace. I retreated back up a step and placed my thumb over the phone's mouthpiece. Certain now that Missy couldn't hear me, I loudly repeated, "Just a moment please," and added, "I'll see if he's available."

Simultaneously, Max and Summer looked up from their clench. In a loud whisper, I looked at Max and asked, "It's Missy, on my cell. Would you care to talk to her?" Max eyes widened and some of the haziness subsided. Summer's face and neck grew pale under the tan. Bocelli sang in soft Italian and promised to watch over me in silence while I was sleeping. Max reached out for the phone, "Yes, yes, I'll take it." Now Summer's eyes widened and her arms dropped.

Max began, "Hello, Missy, hello?" I backed up the steps completely and Summer soon followed. Together, we sat and listened.

"Dammit, Missy stop telling me what I should do!…well of course I love her, but that's not the point!…yes, I love you too, honey, but this isn't how you show it, either!…liss…liss…listen to me! That's *none* of your business, do you hear me…that's none of your goddam business either…he does that because I *ask* him to."

I looked at Summer with an arched eyebrow…she looked back. That one was probably about me.

"Fine, fine, then. I just might do that. *Then* would all of you be happy?…what does it matter where I am right now?" Another half-hour ticked by as the argument continued on. At least he hadn't revealed our position, so I could settle back and stop searching for pairs of headlights.

As I drove Max home that night he managed to make it the entire two and a half miles without calling Summer once to break up with her. Colder days came quickly after that, and the yacht didn't see any more use by Max Lexington or his family.

Max began to go on a series of business trip/vacations after he nixed any deal with Warren Buffet and tried to refocus on his business enterprises. He always seemed to be accompanied on the trips by one of his three sons. When he came back home from one, his daughter Bertha always seemed to have another flight in the planning stages for Max and any son who stayed home on the previous one. While home, Max and Elizabeth attended sessions at a local former priest's office. Married for years after turning in his white collar, the counselor specialized in reconciling differences between married couples. Max informed Summer and I that he intended to give his marriage the "old college try." It seemed like an odd statement for the self-made billionaire to make when we remembered that he had never attended college.

It wasn't long before the master salesman had won over the experienced psychologist. Max convinced him that he was being ignored by his family after a lifetime of servitude to them and to God. The ex-priest finally agreed and assured Max that because of his long record of charitable giving and other good works that Max was already guaranteed his place in heaven. He should take his remaining years, the counselor advised, and find whatever it was that made him happy. Elizabeth threw up her hands and stopped attending the sessions.

One night in late fall after my gym was closed, Summer summoned me to the parking lot of the Beach Grill. She and Max had been talking in his car for some time, and he wanted to drive himself home. He had not imbibed for over two hours, and it was agreed to allow me to judge his competency. After speaking with him, I decided that he was only one sheet to the wind and may not even blow "impaired." The insistent executive kissed Summer good-bye, and we followed closely in her car. The game plan was to make sure that a police officer couldn't pull in directly behind our tipsy leader and directly assess his driving ability. As our tiny caravan started up, Summer's car phone rang. Motioning to me with a forefinger across her lips, she clicked on the car's speaker-phone.

"Where are you?" It was her husband, Chuck.

"Hi honey, I'm out with friends," she replied.

"Not what are you doing, I asked where you were!" Chuck repeated.

"I said I'm out with friends, okay? I'm following one right now to make sure they get home safe. Where are you?"

Chuck retorted, "I've been driving around all night looking for you after *you* wouldn't answer your phone!"

"My battery was dead so I left it charging in the car."

"Well you should've had your *goddamn pimp* bring you a new battery when he met you at Beach Grill!" Summer's eyes bulged, as did mine. For once, she was speechless. "Hello, are you still there?" Chuck asked.

"I don't have to sit here and take this!" Summer yelled, and hung up. "Jesus, Mark, he knows where I've been. He saw you pull up. He was there. He was watching me and Max before you got there. Oh shit!"

"That could have got real ugly, real fast," I offered.

"I would have noticed his car if he were close. He must have been far away," Summer was thinking out loud, "but how long was he watching? And how well could he see in? He's been talking to Missy. He's got too much information."

"Does he always call me your pimp?" I asked.

"Well…you and Chuck aren't in a very good place right now."

"But I've never even met him!"

"I don't think getting you two together would be a good idea for the moment, sweetie. That pimp thing is just something he calls you when he's mad."

Two days later, I was working happily with clients at the studio. My cell phone rang. I answered reluctantly. "Hi, sweetie." *It was my ho.* "Say, I need you to do me a big, big favor. Max met me at The Townsend after lunch and I got a room and we've been here all day. I'm okay to drive home but we had room service and Max's been drinking all afternoon. Can you please, please come and get him? I'm registered under my maiden name."

I looked myself over in one of the studio's mirrors. I was wearing a fairly new T-shirt and light blue, slightly worn jeans. As far as my gym's dress code went, I was outfitted perfectly. Even my tennis shoes were still reasonably white and less than a month old.

The Townsend Hotel was a large, fashionable, five star hotel in Birmingham, about twenty miles away. When Divas sang at venues in the Detroit area, they stayed at The Townsend. When ex-president Bush was in town, he stayed at The Townsend. Impeccable service, excellent food and posh surroundings made The Townsend the logical home away from home for many of the rich and famous. The media's cars and equipment trucks knew the way to The Townsend on their own, and could make the trek driverless if necessary. Max's family was turning up the heat in the Pointes, and his regular haunts were becoming infested with spies. I could think of no better place for the famous man to hide out, with the possible exception of the reporter's men's room at the *Detroit Free Press.*

Running home to change into anything remotely appropriate was impossible. My cell phone would begin ringing impatiently before I even picked out a belt. It was six-thirty. If I left immediately I could be there by seven o'clock.

In Birmingham, I found a street parking spot two blocks from my destination. My black leather bomber jacket may not have been suitable for The Townsend's dining room, but it kept out the thirty-five degree November chill. I jogged to the lobby and called Summer's cell phone. It rang three times and switched to voice mail. I left a message and sat down to wait. Feeling like an upper middle class vagrant in the luxurious surroundings, I people-watched until my cell rang a half hour later.

"Hi sweetie, sorry if you had to wait. I got your message and thanks for getting here so fast, but we got involved in round two, if you know what I mean."

Oh yuck, I thought, *that's more than I needed to know.*

"Can you come up and walk me down? I'm in room 638."

Two minutes later, I was outside the room. The door was ajar, and I "halloed" before slowly swinging it farther. A holocaust of dirty plates, glasses and towels strewn about greeted me as I entered. A hammered hotel guest was struggling with his tie in a mirror until Summer adeptly finished the task for him. Dinner in the hotel's dining room was deemed to be too risky on a Friday night, and for once, Summer was anxious to call it a night. Her shopping alibi was wearing thin, and she feared the imminent beginning of "check-up" calls from her husband. Max fumbled for a ten and asked me to have both cars brought up by the valet. I walked Summer to the lobby. While she paid the bill in cash, I discovered that the minimum valet charge was seven dollars per car. Finally ensconced in the two cars, Max had me call Summer as we drove, and he pitched her to meet us for dinner at a Ruth's Chris steakhouse. Summer, audibly apprehensive about the lateness of the hour, agreed only after much cajoling from my plastered passenger. It was 9 p.m. and the restaurant was emptying out. Max explained laboriously to the maitre'd that he and I were meeting a young lady there momentarily for a job interview and would like a table that was out of the way. The maitre'd's raised eyebrow and smirk told me that he bought the whole story...hook, line and sinker. We were seated by the kitchen in a nearly empty restaurant. Summer joined us minutes later and, in a state of obvious discomfort, ordered a glass of wine. Our host ordered a double Crown Royal and, as the first one came, another.

"Maaark, do you eat here a lot?" Max asked.

"No sir, this is my first time." (I preferred Capital Grille down the street).

"I'll tell you whaaat, then. Let me order for you. I've been here and I know my way around the menu. Do you like steak?" Summer forgot her timetable for a moment and smiled.

"Yes sir. Of course I do."

"Fine, that's fine then." When the waitress reappeared, Max ordered two forty-eight dollar aged steaks, cooked to our request.

I added a salad to my order as Max dove into the bread rolls.

At last, Summer could wait no longer. Excusing herself after two sips of her wine, she kissed our chewing chief discreetly on his cheek and practically hurdled a waiter on her way out the door.

Our steaks came after a short period, and the booze-filled billionaire began to slice away at his. Throwing back one medium rare piece after another, my companion's alcohol-influenced table manners began to slip. As I looked up from my own steak, I watched in fascination as steak juice dribbled in rivulets down Mr. Lexington's chin.

"That's a nice jacket, Maaaark. Is it new?"

"No sir. I've had it awhile."

"That's nice. Y' know, my friend, I've always believed that clothes say who you are. They're your first chance to make an impression on someone. Oh, sure, there's a time and a place for dressing casually but even then there's a certain style of dress that's acceptable." The steak juice had formed two distinct rivulets now, and were cascading in little miniature waterfalls onto his hundred dollar tie. "When I walk into a nice restaurant like this, I know I'll get better service when I'm dressed right for the occasion."

Note to self, I thought, *try a three-piece suit at the gym on Monday.* I was tempted to stem the tide of chin juice with my own napkin but thought better of it.

The lecture melded into one on how spoiled he was when his tailor came to the house to make adjustments to his expensive suits. I silently resolved that the next time Gianni Versace's long lost brother here got wasted at The Townsend Hotel, I'd let him find his own way home.

Summer was pretty sure that she'd made it home that Friday night in time to avoid suspicion. But she had not. On Monday morning, Chuck called Max Lexington's corporate office to request a face to face with his wife's aged lover. Max arranged to borrow a conference room at the mattress factory. The meeting was set for Wednesday afternoon at what I found to be the most ironic location possible.

37

"Your Eminence, Missy Lexington is on the phone again. Do you wish to take her call?" asked Father Pete, standing in the doorway, respectfully snapping Cardinal Fiat out of a deep reverie.

Fewer and fewer young, spiritual men had been heeding the calling. The Michigan priesthood's ranks, as in other states, were sorely in need. The holy man had been lost in thought, searching for the right words to inspire perhaps one potential soul at the biblical conference he was scheduled to address tomorrow.

The Cardinal sighed heavily. "Yes, yes I'll take it in here." He picked up the phone. "Hello Missy, how nice to hear from you again. How are you and how is your father?"

The woman was apologetic, "Your Eminence, I am so sorry to bother you again like this. I'm fine but my mother and the rest of us are having a *very* hard time with this test of God's."

"Have you been praying over it, as I asked?"

"We have prayed and prayed, but we are at our wits end with this situation. Dad didn't come home until eleven-thirty Friday night. We figured he was with his driver again and he said he was but we know they didn't spend the whole day together. Dad drove off somewhere from the office at lunchtime and didn't call in once. We know he was with *her* again and mother is just sick about it."

Another heavy sigh emanated from deep within the spiritual leader's lungs. What was it about these good men when it came to weaknesses of the flesh? Why couldn't they see the pain that it caused and use prayer and their own vast experiences to see that these were not opportunities but temptations sent by the devil? Until just one year ago, the Cardinal and Max Lexington had been very close, and the holy man had felt as though their friendship had broken new ground. Max's love of drinking was no secret, but he was careful to keep it in check around men of the cloth and besides, the pressures in the rich man's life were many. If drink were to be Max's only cross to bear, the man was better off than most. Apparently, though, it was not.

The Cardinal spoke, "I know that this is a very painful time for you, Missy. You felt such a closeness and an admiration for your father and all of his good works. Now you feel as though you are losing him, in a way, and you are not ready. As I mentioned the last time we spoke, sometimes the Lord tests us. You and the others can continue, through your prayers, to show your faith and your belief. God is listening even if, at this dark hour, you feel as though He is not. Your father, for all he has accomplished, and for all he has done for the church, is still just a man. What you have to realize is that he is being tested right now too. Tell me this, is he still attending masses?"

"Every Sunday, as far as I know, and sometimes during the week still. During some weeks last year, though, he used to go every day!"

"That's good. That means that he is still searching for answers, too. I know that this whole situation is causing great pain for your mother. I think your father knows that too, and he is asking God's forgiveness for hurting her. What you must remember is that it is God who has also given your mother so much, and now he is testing her also. Your task is to try to make this easier on her if you can. The public confrontation that you and your sister had with that woman will only lead to further embarrassment for your mother. Try to at least spare her that."

"May I call the husband again? He claimed that the woman and my father were just friends, but at least he seemed willing to listen."

"May I ask how you got the woman's home number? I assume that it was unlisted."

"My sister, Bertha, supervises all of the bill paying at our corporate headquarters. All of the cell phone bills are paid out of Corporate too. The woman's home phone and cell phone numbers show up on the bills for my father's phone. She calls him from her home and her cell three to four times a day. He's called her as many as twenty times in a day! He calls her every morning as soon as he gets in his car. If it's only for a minute he must be just getting her voicemail. He hangs up and a minute later calls again. Sometimes he'll talk to her for a half hour and then call his bodyguard or driver, or whatever that guy is, right away. We *know* something has been going on for a while."

"Do you think that your father would be angry if he knew that his daughters were monitoring his calls?"

"Yes, I suppose he'd be furious," Missy admitted.

"I think so too. Perhaps it would be best to stop. If you think that one more discreet call to the woman's husband would help, then I see no harm in discussing your concerns with the man. Try to see if they intend to seek marriage counseling individually or as a couple. Try to find out if they are currently involved with their own church, whatever their faith may be. If the woman can experience a greater spiritual fulfillment herself and she sees her marriage getting stronger, perhaps she will not seek out your father. Meanwhile, for my part, I will make a phone call. While it would not be appropriate for me to involve myself in this because of all that your father means to me and all that he has done for the church, I know someone who may be able to help."

"Thank you so much, Your Eminence."

38

CHUCK ARRIVED AT the mattress factory at exactly one o'clock in the afternoon. He was shown immediately to a small conference room where a secretary plied him with coffee and soft drinks, which he politely declined. Max Lexington soon stepped in from another door and offered his hand out in a surprisingly hospitable manner. As Chuck shook the business legend's hand, he tried to conceal his surprise. Up close, he appeared much older than Chuck remembered and even his Armani suits could not conceal the weight the man had put on. Excess skin hung underneath his jaw and obscured his chin line from his neck before disappearing behind his shirt collar.

No longer streaked with gray, a shock of white hair slicked back from the front covered the massive head. The intense, inquisitive eyes were still as blue as ever, but the face was ruddier and more jowly. The expensive suit could not hide the billionaire's slightly stooped posture or his slightly bow-legged walk. There was no question in Chuck's mind...the man who had his wife entranced and under his complete control showed every bit of his seventy-one years. Chuck's forty-fifth birthday had just passed with little fanfare from his wife of ten years because of this man? What hold could he have over her? It wasn't money. Summer had three charge cards in her wallet at all times, and each had a limit of at least twenty thousand. It wasn't gifts of jewelry either. Chuck had showered numerous trinkets on her in the early years, and now she seemed happiest when spending weeks picking out a new piece for herself. The dowel rods of her walk-in closet groaned with designer clothing, and the shoe racks were stacked in Imelda-like scenarios.

The demands on Chuck's time made by his ever-growing real estate business limited their vacations alone together to twice annually. Summer, however, was free to make arrangements with girlfriends at any time for either warm weather or shopping getaways. Chuck's frequent business trips were open to Summer at any time, and when she declined to accompany him, his calls to her from the motel rooms were numerous and seemed welcome. Summer's son, whom Chuck had adopted ten years ago, was in his first year away at college. Chuck recalled the high hopes he had, when he wrote the tuition check, of eventually inviting the young man to join the family business. It had, to the best of Chuck's recollection, been over a year now since the trio had traveled as a family unit.

Chuck had heard all about Max's corporate jet from Summer herself. At least he was sure, since she hadn't spent a full night away from home since the onset of this mess, that she hadn't flown on it yet.

"So what hold did this man have on her?" Chuck wondered. Had there been promises of vast sums of money? Maybe he was wooing her with grandiose travel plans? The respect of the tightly knit Grosse Pointe society that seemed to interest his wife at times would certainly be less attainable if she were at the epicenter of a "controversy." The respect that Max Lexington had earned, success by success, check by check, and event by event could never be transferred to a young wife in a new marriage born out of scandal and surely Max must realize this. Perhaps the man had simply had enough. Maybe he was tired of the status, of the limelight…of his every decision having far-reaching consequences.

Chuck began the meeting by briefly outlining his awareness of all of the older man's accomplishments. He had known of and been in awe of Max and his success for years and wasn't ashamed to tell him so. Until the younger man and his brothers had formed their own investment company, Chuck had made his living selling commercial real estate. Mr. Lexington, meanwhile, had always maintained a constant search for potential new locations for his stores. Their paths had thus nearly crossed on several occasions, but fate had never quite allowed them to formally meet until now.

Chuck had two distinct agendas for the afternoon's meeting. The first was to try and ascertain, from Max's point of view, what it was that drew Summer to him. The second was to elicit a promise from Max, man to man, that he would have no further contact with Chuck's wife. Bluntly but respectfully, he told Max so.

Chuck's question and subsequent request did not draw howls of outrage or indignation. There were, however, looks of hurt, anguish and shock at the thinly veiled accusations. Max brought out his best sales pitch and laid it on Chuck thicker than the front lawn at the billionaire's mansion.

"Chuck, I don't know where you're getting your information from, but it's simply *not* accurate! Yes, I've had lunch with Summer on a couple of different occasions, and she appears to be a fine, fine woman. But nothing, and I mean nothing, has occurred beyond lunch for Christ's sake. Chuck, I'm going to be seventy-two years old this year! And she's…what…going to be forty? My oldest daughter turns fifty this year! Now, I wish you'd tell me where you're hearing this stuff from so that the three of us can sit down and go over what they think they know!"

"I received a phone call, Max. I'd rather not say from who."

"Well Chuuuck, whoever it is, they're obviously saying things that are hurting and upsetting you. But whatever they're saying is simply *not* true! You're a young, good-looking guy. I hear that you do okay for yourself and your future is very bright. With my position in the community it simply wouldn't look right if I was seen with somebody your wife's age whether she was married or not. Now, over the years I've had employees come to talk to me about their wives. Maybe they were working too much, maybe the time that the kids demanded was getting in the way of their marriage, but I'll tell you what I tell them. Find someone to talk to that the both of you can agree on. Maybe a counselor that specializes in marriage, perhaps a priest that you've developed a rapport with over the years, but go see him together, and use him to help figure out why *you* feel as though you're growing apart. But Chuck, don't, *don't* look for someone outside to put the blame on! As for my part, I will break off any contact I have with her. If she calls me I won't answer. The last thing I want to do is give *anybody* the faintest impression that anything inappropriate is going on. I give you my word that I won't talk to her anymore! I simply won't."

The comedian/actor Eddie Murphy used to reenact a segment in which his girlfriend walked in on him and another woman having sex, "It wasn't me!" Eddie would declare.

"But I saw you!" she yells.

"I said, it wasn't me!" he tells her again, and eventually, with his increasingly emphatic denials, Eddie convinces her that she saw somebody else in the bed.

Chuck drove away from the meeting in a cloud of frustration. *"That lying son-of-a-bitch,"* he thought.

The next morning Max called my cell phone at 8:20 a.m. to say that he knew he'd told me before, but this time it was really over.

Half and hour later, Summer called to tell me that Max was a matriarchal impregnator (or something similar). Half an hour after Summer's call, my cell rang yet again. Missy was on the line. She proclaimed dramatically that her father was an alcoholic and increasingly incapable of controlling his impulses. She asked for my help in getting his drinking under control. I explained that I was an employee, that my job was to keep him safe, and that I had little influence over his actions. I promised, however, to look for an opportunity to encourage Mr. Lexington to seek help.

Twenty minutes after Missy hung up, I was called by yet another daughter. Our conversation was cut short by Summer's persistent "beeping in" on my "call waiting." I hung up with the second daughter so that Summer could remind me what an intestinal exit path Max was. My three hours of counseling sessions ended promptly at 11:30 when my cell phone's battery died.

A week later was the first week of December, and it was bitter cold. I had the S500 safely stashed between two boats in a shipyard not far from the Beach Grill. It was ten o'clock at night, and as I sat in the driver's seat of the Mercedes with the heat control set at seventy-six, I was very sad. I was sad because Andrea Bocelli was singing to me. Through the car's speakers, he was promising to be mine, to be a real angel who dreams…who can hold my hand and give me his soul. We would even fly to paradise if I would just stay here with him.

I could not turn his words off, either, or the sobbing in the back of the car would become more audible. Summer and the shnockered billionaire were entwined in the rear seat, and he was crying uncontrollably. Over the last four hours, goaded on by a dozen Crown Royals, Max's lamentations grew with an ever-increasing finality.

Uncomfortable and powerless to stop all of the carrying on, I set my mind to translating the Italian prose emanating from the car speakers. At last, after what seemed like an eternity of weeping and opera, the car's owner calmed down enough to instruct me to find Summer's Mercedes. After a last tearful good-bye replete with decidedly indiscreet hugs and kisses in mid parking lot, Max made his last half-journey to her car window for a final, final good-bye.

Even my emotionally calloused heart oozed hope that this may indeed be the absolute, last farewell. As I drove double-time towards the gates of the mansion, I counted the miles to go in tenths. I felt as though the mountains of resolutions tearfully proffered throughout this night actually had a chance of pushing their peak through the clouds this time. If Max could climb to the top of this mountain and stay there, it was only a matter of time before he would feel the sunny rays of common sense warning his mind. With the blubbering billionaire repeating, "I really loved her, you know," like a new mantra, I calculated nine-tenths to go. The outside temperature read fifteen degrees, and I had seven-tenths to go. With my nights free again, I might be able to go out on a date. Dinner perhaps, or maybe even a movie in a real theater would be a long dreamed-of fantasy that was now only four-tenths of a mile away. Three-tenths to go and the darkened castle loomed into the cold night sky. One-tenth of a mile to freedom and a job well done as I passed the mansion for a final boulevard turn into the entranceway. Two hundred feet, turn signal on, fifty feet…

"Keep going, keep going, don't turn, keep going!" Max had snapped out of his reverie of woe and had frantically changed his mind. I glanced wistfully at the beginning of the driveway as we glided past. My shoulders slumped a little, and I cancelled the turn signal indicator until Max came to life yet again. "We gotta call, *right now!*" he exclaimed and began to fumble with the numbers on the car phone's keypad. I flipped around on Lakeshore Drive a half mile down, reversing direction and heading back toward the mansion. I was hoping for yet another quick change of heart and orders to head for the gate once more, but my preoccupied passenger was intent on dialing a third wrong number. I finally dialed for him, and her voicemail came over the car's speakers loud and clear, apologizing for not taking our call. At the beep, Max said, "C'mon, now, pick-up…pick-up…it's me and we need to talk!"

I sailed by the house a little faster this time and as I did asked, "Where to sir?" Frustrated but showing more self control, Max replied, "Four blocks after Vernier, turn right." Haltingly giving directions as he successfully pressed the redial button on the car phone, Max received the same voicemail message. He yelled, "Stop it, it's me, just stop it!" and hung up.

Fourteen degrees (the dash informed me), and we turned into the parking lot of a small chapel attached to a much larger church. Max reminded me that he had paid to have the chapel built as he got out to stagger in. I let him go in alone and called Natasha to explain my where-abouts. Summer soon cut in, and ten minutes later parked next to the S500. As she entered the chapel, I braced myself against the seat back, waiting for the roof of the small chapel to collapse on the two in an act of divine retribution.

The next day, Max began a new habit of meeting Summer in

my gym's front parking lot. I cringed every time that Summer waltzed over to his waiting car, waiting for spouses and offspring to drive screaming into the lot, blocking any exits in a triumphant round of "gotcha."

On Friday of the next week, my evening was interrupted by the usual urgent "tippler transport" call. Max was in a booth at the Beach Grill, keeping his solemn oath to Chuck by snuggling up next to Summer as she sat next to him. After an hour, it was decided that I would drive them instead to an old bar in Detroit underneath an apartment that Max grew up in. Sixty years ago, the area had been middle class and prosperous, now it was in an impoverished urban decay zone, and even the panhandlers and crackheads scurried to be off the streets before nightfall.

The little bar was shoehorned in between several other dilapidated businesses on what used to be a proud main thoroughfare. Max directed me to a back alley where I parked in one of four muddy, icy spots behind the bar. A little square window cut into the top of the door had me anticipating that a "secret knock" would be required to gain entry. I activated the car's alarm system as Max led the way through the open back door into a dingy hallway. Belying the outside neighborhood, the well-used establishment was adequately lit and boasted a thirty-foot-long bar. Tabletop seating for about twenty-five patrons was scattered around two pool tables illuminated by hanging domes under a smoky haze. Eight snaggly-toothed patrons were dispersed throughout, nursing glasses of pre-Christmas cheer. The dress code seemed to dictate thick plaid cotton coats (provided they were worn threadbare enough), and Max's Armani suit, although it complimented Summer's Versace outfit, contrasted noticeably. As Max ordered a drink for himself and Summer, an incisor-challenged patron staggered up and said, "Hey, I think I know you!"

Max basked in the glow of recognition and said, "I'm Max Lexington, here, let me buy you a drink!" A wad of fifties and hundreds appeared in Max's hand as a large redheaded female bartender began to set glasses on the bar top. The rear door opened again, and a shifty-looking patron, clothed in a layered look of unwashed jackets and rags, made his way toward us. His vacant eyes honed in on the wad of cash in the boss' hand instantly, and a discolored half-grin broke through while he stared.

My own gaze switched back and forth from his yellowed eyes to his nervous twitching hands as he adjusted his rags. He greeted the bartender, but when she all but ignored him in return I sensed that no maitre'd was going to escort *him* to a table. Six feet away from Max, the less than fashionable intruder stopped and peered around, as though looking to join another party for dinner and drinks. His eyes darted back to Max's money wad as it was placed back in the billionaire's suit pants. Spinning around on a well-worn boot, the ragged clotheshorse retraced his steps to the back door, losing his shuffle and moving much faster than he had on the way in.

Sipping his drink and sitting at the bar on a stool, Max began to regale the bartender and another nearby couple with reminiscences about his days as a resident of the neighborhood. Another round of drinks was ordered, and I decided to check on the car. Sidling up to the back door's little window, I peeked out for an instant and then took a quick step back to evaluate what I saw. The Mercedes seemed untouched enough and had even been joined by another car parked next to it. My area of concern lie with a rusty, full-sized Buick parked fifty feet away down the rutted alley. A second stolen recon glance told me that two occupants shared the front. Exhaust vapor from the tailpipe indicated that the Buick was running. My biggest eye opener, though, was the scruffy passenger. The Buick's passenger was the same suspicious hombre that had checked us out not ten minutes prior. The driver looked to be bigger and wider than his passenger and was lighting a cigarette by the time I risked a third peek out the little window.

The new Mercedes had attracted some very unwelcome attention, but it was okay for now. Reaching inside my jacket, I found the butt of my Beretta and made sure the safety was off. I walked back down the hallway reviewing my options. Someone had selected an oldie on the jukebox and at Max's insistence, he and Summer left their drinks on the bar while they went to dance. I spilled the unattended drinks into a sink behind the bar and watched them "hoof it" to a fast one. Even in his partly fried state, the tycoon was a decent dancer and toothless smiles came out from everybody as the pair swung around.

After another minute, I decided to recheck our new escort vehicle in the alley. I surmised that they had been passing through earlier and the smaller one had been sent in to check for the owner of the Mercedes. The appearance of the wad of cash had been bad timing on Max's part and had obviously inspired the pair to stay. The two watchers were still there, and they were in the midst of an animated conversation. My first option was to phone the police. Unfortunately, we *were* in Detroit, and they might not respond to a cell call about a suspicious car until next Tuesday. Option two was to wait them out. I was concerned that Max and Summer would grow impatient, however, and his currently diminished powers of reason would make him insistent on chancing an exit.

Inside, Max and his date now settled down into a slow dance as the jukebox poured out a woeful tune. Option three was to phone an ex-cop buddy for a back-up car, and sneak my charges out the front door.

My friend was employed as a bodyguard for a wealthy family, however, and I vaguely remembered that he had mentioned working all weekend. To even contemplate option four was horrible. Walking out the back door with the couple in tow, I'd keep one hand in my jacket and draw on anybody who approached us if there was even a hint of a weapon. A firearms instructor had once told me that warning shots were okay, as long as I fired two to the chest and one to the head. This messy scenario, however, would have the newsmen scrutinizing Max's life for months, and a myriad of other things could go wrong as well.

I finally decided on option five. When Max and Summer were on the absolute edge of leaving, I'd tell them that we were blocked in but that I found the offending car's owner, and they were to stay put until I returned. Uneasy at leaving them unattended even briefly, I still felt that they were somewhat safe in the bar. My plan was to go out alone and pull quickly around the front. I had decided by now that the Buick's occupants were after Max's cash and not the car and would stay put if they didn't see him. Even if Max and Summer ignored my instructions, I would be in the front door before they could mosey near the back. Hustling them out the front at that point should be relatively easy, especially if I loudly explained that, "You don't want to go back there!"

I checked on the pair again. The driver of the idling Buick was increasingly agitated. Suddenly, he flicked the parking lights on and hunched over the dash while talking. I stared, puzzled, wondering what was on the dash that was so fascinating? It finally dawned on me that he was staring at the gas gauge and the getaway car was on the verge of running out! Slamming the steering wheel in frustration at his bad planning, the driver pulled on his headlights as well, put the Buick in drive and left!

I had a minimum of five, but probably ten more minutes until the vultures could resume their stakeout! A modified "option four" suddenly looked very attractive. A check on Max and Summer revealed that the song had ended, and their coats were on! Five minutes later, I was backing out into the alley with Fred Astaire and Ginger Rogers smiling and cuddling in the back seat.

We slid down the street, passing a gas station with a rusty Buick at one of the pumps!

39

SOMEWHERE IN WASHINGTON D.C., in a quiet neighborhood, lives a devout man. His living quarters and offices abut a large church's rectory, and the windows look out onto a small garden. He is a man of the cloth, but his role is not to lead the faithful in prayer. The man is at peace in a church, but his battlefields are corporate boardrooms and offices. He fights for the Lord not in the den of the lion, but in the dens of earthly mansions.

At only thirty-eight, Father Mike is still a young man, but in a cadre of persuasive men who are driven by their faith, he is by far the most persuasive of all. Father Mike's ability to convince others that his point of view is the only one possible was bestowed upon him at an early age, and he has honed it to a razor sharp skill that he uses to serve God. Had he chosen the private business route, Father Mike's cognitive powers and the ability to think on his feet would have made him a top corporate salesman. His vast knowledge of human nature gives him the uncanny ability to know what his opponent is going to say next…long before he says it. Respectful by nature, but brazen and brash when he had to be, the good Father is both articulate and impossible to say no to. He is, if it is the Lord's will, able to sell seawater to a marooned sailor. His real forte, however, and the one which gives him the greatest amount of satisfaction, is in saving the church millions of dollars every year in lost contributions.

Errant Catholic millionaires and billionaires could be annual contributors of huge sums of money, were of immense value to the church, and could not be allowed to stray without a fight. Whether disenchanted with current church dogma or distracted by other endeavors, these fabulously wealthy men sometimes needed an occasional spiritual tug to return them to the flock *before* they forgot how to tithe.

And so Father Mike sat in his office in Washington D.C., waiting for a phone call from a beleaguered Bishop or even a Cardinal. A suitcase lie packed next door at his residence. His secretary waited, the phone numbers of every airline at her fingertips, for the calls that always came. With a cross in one pocket and a cell phone ringer set on "hum" in the other, Father Mike was prepared to leave on five minutes notice.

The jet stream had bulged down far enough to bring below-freezing December temperatures to the nation's capital. It was two weeks before Christmas, and Father Mike's secretary had just fielded a call from the Archdiocese of Detroit. Cardinal Fiat had great concerns about a man who was not only a friend but a huge contributor to the church as well. Information coming to light was revealing that the married billionaire philanthropist was being estranged and isolated from his family. A secret liaison with a lady thirty-two years his wife's junior was at the core. A breakup of this magnitude could affect the family's financial contributions in the needy Detroit area for many years to come. Long term, a change in the wording of the wills could have even more devastating consequences.

His secretary's call had reached the holy man as he was about to walk into a seminar titled, "Taxes and Trusts." As he spoke with her, he thought, *This one can't wait*, and he turned around to walk back to his car. Another minute later and he was dialing as he drove, connecting with Father Pete before the wheels of his Ford Taurus reached the expressway. Fleshing out some background details, Father Pete was finished in fifteen minutes as Father Mike walked into his own office. After hanging up with Father Pete, Father Mike began to pour over maps of the Detroit suburbs, stopping only to punch the straying billionaire's name into his computer for as many biographical articles as could be printed out. After a half hour of research, his secretary informed him that Cardinal Fiat was calling. Father Mike picked up the phone.

"Your Eminence, how are you?"

"Always troubled, of late, how are you?"

"Ready to take one of your troubles on to my own shoulders today. Mr. Lexington is the very definition of self-made man, I see."

"Yes, Father, that he is. No college, straight into retail. He graduated with a Ph.D. from the school of hard knocks he'll tell you. But he's seventy-one now and feels as though the wealth and social recognition aren't enough anymore. He's looking for true love, and he's found a young lady that promises to give it to him."

"Pardon me, Your Eminence, but my thought is that she would be happy to truly love his money as well."

"Ahhh, there's the rub, Father. While it's true that the young lass used to entertain men with an inappropriate dance routine, she has since married a man of means and has some money of her own."

"So a second marriage is at stake as well?"

"Yes, sadly so. And the young lady's husband is supposedly a fine man as well. He treats her well, wouldn't dream of striking her, and adopted an illegitimate son of hers ten years ago for whom he has generously provided. From what I am able to gather, the lady wants for nothing."

"Perhaps, Your Eminence, a plot of sorts between the woman and her husband?"

"No, father, again my sources tell me that he is a family man, a church goer. He is more concerned about a fine reputation becoming tarnished than about making an illicit dollar."

"Why would the rich man choose her then? Is she that beautiful? Is she so enchanting and alluring that she cannot be turned down? What do they have in common?"

"They met during a tennis match. In spite of his age, he still plays quite well. I know that his wife of fifty years does not play. She is a fine woman and very fit, but does not participate in any sport nor does she show an inclination to."

"Speaking of sports, Your Eminence, how is your golf game?"

"Oh...I suppose with my bad knees I won't have many more years, although I still enjoy the game so..."

"After fifty years of marriage, they must have much in common."

"Well, he has worked hard for all that time. Much of that required being away from the home, and her life was about being a good mother to eight active children. She's still in contact with most of them on a daily basis. And there are twenty grandchildren too, most in the immediate area."

"How about the marital home? Do any children or even grandchildren still reside there?"

"Ahhh, no Father. The marital home is more of a monument. It was built six years ago as a tribute to the success of the man. Attempts have been made to give it a family atmosphere, but it was never meant to be so. It is more suited to large gatherings of society or to entertain substantial groups of friends. It is meant to impress more than house or embrace."

"Has the wealthy man forsaken his church as well?"

"No, I wouldn't say that. He still attends each Sunday. But there were times when five or six days a week were not uncommon. His most daunting battle is not with the devil, but with drink."

"Has he sought help?"

"I've heard no admission from him that he needs it. He is quite moderate with it in my presence. His family seems to think otherwise, and yet I've seen them do nothing to discourage it."

"Perhaps the man is easier to control when he is influenced by drink?"

"I am afraid that his relationship with all of them is a very complex one. In fact, the continued presence of all of them in the immediate community makes the entire situation more sensitive still."

"Just an observation, Your Eminence, but this one reminds me of that situation with the Texas oil man two years ago."

"Yes Father, it does. Only that man had far fewer offspring, as I recall. Incidentally, Bishop Winston tells me that the oil man has broken off all contact with that lady and is apparently back with his wife. How did you finally help him decide to change his course?"

"I found that the man rewarded loyalty above all among his employees. He thought it to be a most important quality. I merely suggested a simple test for his new lady friend. She did not perform well, and their relationship began to cool immediately."

"Bishop Winston was most pleased. You did well."

"Thank you, Your Eminence, please forgive me for asking. But is Mr. Lexington...ah...active...with his new companion?"

"This I cannot say. My sources don't seem to have the answer, or they are not willing to volunteer it. There is a man who drives him and performs other functions who may know, but my sources indicate that he probably wouldn't say."

"I see that my secretary has already been provided with contact numbers for Mr. Lexington."

"Yes, why don't you try his corporate offices first? His oldest daughter, Bertha, is entrusted with a major role there, and she will be most receptive to your call. She should be of great assistance in setting up an appointment for him to meet with you."

40

I ARRIVED AT the studio at 12:50 p.m. for my one o'clock with Summer. She arrived promptly at 1:45. My two o'clock arrived five minutes later. Summer beckoned me over to her treadmill.

"Sorry I'm late sweetie. I've been on the phone all morning. Guess what? I told Chuck that I need to get away from the winter weather this year. It's supposed to be a really cold one. Max gave me the name of a real estate agent down in Florida. She's in Boca, and if I fly down in two days she's going to show me some condos there! I want something near the water. Where is Max's penthouse? He said he can see the Atlantic on one side and the Intracoastal waterway on the other side."

"So, you're moving?" I said.

"Just until spring. Even Chuck agrees that I need to get away. I need to have time to myself to just think about what I want to do. I'll enroll in the community college down there, and take some classes. I just need…to get my head together about Chuck, about Max, about what direction I want to take!"

"If you'll excuse me a moment, I need to start my two o'clock's workout."

"Sweetie, do me a favor, ask one of your other trainers to start her. I'm going to need someone to move me down, and I'd like you to do it if you would. I'm going to move as many of my own things down as I can so that it won't feel so strange being down there by myself. So much of it is breakable. I don't want to trust it

301

to some idiots. The condos I'm looking at are furnished, but I'm still going to need a lot of my things."

"This all sounds like a big decision you're making," I said.

"Mark, it's just time that I did something for me. I sit every day waiting for Max to call. My son's away at college. Chuck's been flying down to Texas a lot lately working on some big deal. I need to get away, take some classes, join a little tennis club somewhere. It's twelve degrees outside today, and it's seventy-five in Boca. I thought about getting a hitch installed on my Mercedes and renting some kind of a trailer, but I've never even driven to Ohio by myself much less Florida! If I ask Max to cover your time and expenses, I know he will and I'd *really* appreciate it if you'd help me get my things down there. I checked into just shipping my car and it's only $800 but then I'd be without it until it got there. You know, if you could drive it and the trailer down with me I'd feel much better."

An Olympic caliber swimmer had vanquished every opponent that he had ever come across. One day, while taking a ferry across the English Channel, he decided that he had one opponent left. He would *swim* across the Channel. He trained for the feat for a year, and at the end of the year he was ready. With no fanfare or even a boat to follow him, he set off. He swam for hours in the choppy, cold waters. It had been many miles and he felt himself growing tired. When he was halfway across he decided that he couldn't make it, so he swam back!

Mrs. Lexington could barely speak to me. Her eight adult children and their spouses loathed me. Summer's husband would no doubt welcome an opportunity to run me over in his Mercedes. I was probably, however, more than halfway across the channel, and I wasn't going to quit. I wasn't going to be the one to swim back! I would drive Summer in her Mercedes to Florida. I would get Summer and her precious collectibles safely to Boca Raton. I'd make sure that she was moved in to her new condo. I would keep track of every penny spent and furnish a bill with all receipts to Mr. Lexington, who would graciously pay it. With Summer fifteen hundred miles away, my role with Mr. Lexington could return to normal. And soon, after he either cut back on the sauce or sought professional help, I could wean myself away. I could devote my full attention to my studio, my clients and Natasha. I could travel again. I could turn my cell phone off for days at a time and give my besieged eardrums a much deserved rest.

The Lexington household was tense at Christmas time. Very tense. Robert and the rest of the staff, looking for a less stressful job, considered applying to the Detroit Bomb Squad.

Summer found a condo, and Chuck gladly cut a check. The Pandora of Grosse Pointe Park began to mentally tag certain items around the house that she could simply not survive without.

41

O N JANUARY 6, the landing gear of Delta Airlines Flight 215 touched down on the runway at Detroit Metropolitan Airport. Father Mike rented a car at the airport and claimed his room at a modest hotel near Mr. Max Lexington's corporate headquarters. At six o'clock, Father Mike met Max alone for dinner at Andiamos, a local favorite of Max's. The two ate fine Italian cuisine and began a conversation that was to last long into the night. There were raised voices, there was table pounding, there were looks of disbelief, and that was just from the waiters. The two titans of persuasion, each convinced that his viewpoint was the only logical one, ranted and railed well past closing time.

The next day's afternoon meeting, in Max's exquisite corporate boardroom, was only a continuation of the night before. Father Mike talked about faith, about the time in this world being a very short one. He talked about the differences between temporary earthly happiness and eternal contentment. The eloquent padre compared and contrasted Max's future with a loving, supportive and appreciative family and a young lady whose motives were questionable at best.

"Who will take care of you in your old age?" Father Mike asked.

"I'll *pay* for the best care around the clock!" Max retorted.

"How do you *know* it's not about the money?" queried the priest.

"Who said I *ever* gave her any money?" snapped the billionaire.

"How about the wife you've been married to for fifty years?"

"She had fifty years to make me happy and I'm *not*!"

"Do you have any consideration for your children's feelings about this?"

"Last time I checked," Max fired back, "my youngest was thirty-one years old. This is *my* life, not theirs!"

"What about your place in the church?"

"I gave the church plenty of my money...they'd *better* save my place!"

"Aren't you concerned about what others in this community might think of you?"

"Half of *this* community is doing...or has done this. The other half wishes they could!" Max went on. "I worked sixty years, beginning with a paper route. I've set up my family for life. I've built churches and chapels. I employ four thousand people and that money feeds twelve thousand more. I've built boy's homes and hospital wings. The guy that sent you has cashed my checks, too! I'm paid up, Father. I don't owe any more!"

42

OUR FIRST STOP was in northern Ohio. A "Panera Bread" had caught Summer's eye. I drove the white Mercedes with Summer, and my two teenage helpers followed in a silver cargo van packed to the dome lights with every collectible and designer outfit imaginable. By Kentucky, I realized that I'd made a huge financial error. I should have quoted for my services by the word instead of by the hour. Summer chattered incessantly about every aspect of her relationship with Max. County by county, I was reminded that he was old in years but young and vibrant at heart. Declarations of love took place at every state line and at least once at mid-state. I was asked if there was any chance of the Grosse Pointe area accepting them. *Never,* I replied. I was asked how much I thought each family member hated her. *It goes you, Osama Bin Laden, Saddam Hussein, and then fourth is Adolph Hitler.*

Guilt set in on both of us whenever Chuck would call. He was amazed and proud of her that she was undertaking a trip like this by herself. He hoped that she was driving safely and intended to stop early for the night and get plenty of rest. The curiosity in his voice rose a bit when Summer was unable to tell him exactly where she was but dissipated whenever she changed the subject to him. The termination of each of these calls prompted a half-hour analysis of the marriage, and what was wrong with it. I had questions of my own. Did Summer have a plan that morning if Chuck came home unexpectedly to find me helping her pack cartons? Did he really believe that one of her socialite tennis partners was following alone in a cargo van? Was he convinced that his gregarious wife intended to spend months in Florida by herself, walking the beach and meditating?

The outside temperature rose gradually as we headed south, and my biggest challenge was no longer snow and ice. The Princess was a picky eater. Fast food was out of the question, and a restaurant's menu needed to be carefully examined before the establishment received our patronage.

Our scheduled 10 a.m. departure time had been bumped back considerably when I appeared in her driveway to find packing underway but far from over. We had left promptly at 1 p.m., and I felt fortunate to make Tennessee by the end of the day. Summer reserved three spacious rooms at "Hampton Inn" for us. With Neil and Jeff, my van drivers, settled in on one side of my room and Summer tucked away on the other, I dozed off for my nine hours. The Princess, however, didn't need nine hours, nor did she need eight. At 7:30 a.m., a rap on my door jolted me awake, and I opened it a crack to greet her, towel wrapped around her hair and cell phone in hand. She pulled the phone away from her mouth. "It's Max and he says hi. Are you ready to go sweetie?"

We found a restaurant that served oatmeal pancakes and latte and were back on the road by nine. Summer merrily juggled phone calls from her husband and her lover throughout northern Georgia. As we passed through Atlanta, she laid out the trip to Europe that she and Max intended to embark on. One of the highlights, she announced, would be the hot air balloon trip across southern France. Floating silently above the countryside while admiring castles and villages in sunlit, picturesque splendor, they would be pampered at night at different bed and breakfasts. Ballooning was the latest "in" way to tour Europe, and Summer couldn't wait. She scowled when I suggested that the only hot air she'd receive was if Max flew down for a visit.

A multitude of plans and scenarios were hatched in waves from across the Mercede's center console, each prefaced with "If we're together." We entered North Florida in the late afternoon, my right ear ringing with a twenty-five percent hearing loss. As we eased across the top of the state toward Jacksonville, the passenger compartment gradually grew quieter as Summer became more and more nauseated from motion sickness. I decided to let her drive for a time to see if the distraction would ease her discomfort and perhaps allow me a little nap. It proved to be a very bad idea. I sat bolt upright in the passenger's seat, with surges of adrenaline coursing through my veins every time she cut off a honking driver. Chattering animatedly once more, the Princess distractedly veered from one line of our lane to the other, changing when it suited her…and with no warning. She treated cars and trucks alike, cutting them off in a cachophany of beeps and obscene gestures from their drivers. At times, the blare of horns behind us sounded like we were in a wedding. She enraged every driver with the audacity to use *her* freeway. She got upset when I started clutching at my heart, but pulled off on a ramp after twenty minutes when I demanded a pit stop. Gassing up both vehicles, I was approached by the drivers in the chase van, and Neil said, "Uh, was everything all right up there? Is something wrong with the car? It looked like it was steering funny." I replied that the car was okay, but I would drive the rest of the way.

We snaked through the traffic of Jacksonville by 7 p.m. and worked our way down the East Coast toward Daytona.

The population of Florida is currently estimated at 16,700,000, making it the fourth most populous state. It is over three hundred miles long with hundreds upon hundreds of miles of coastline and beaches. Thousands of condo buildings, many spiking high into the air, house at least a million residents. Older residents pass on, leaving thousands of units for sale or rent weekly. "Snowbirds" coming down for the winter pick and choose from units that run up and down the length of the state as they jockey to be as near to the ocean as their budgets allow. Management companies dot each city, vying for the most reliable tenants for their units. Chuck had fronted a full three months rent at $3500 a month so that his wife may have the most desirable unit possible. As we eased down the coastal highway that night, Summer pointed out with a shout, "There's Max's condo building! I can see his penthouse from down here!"

Exactly one mile later, we turned into the driveway of her new residence. In spite of the late hour, the night manager gave us the keys to a demo unit, and I slept in a comatose state until a shaft of warm sunlight filtered through the window blinds and tickled me awake. A rejuvenated Princess directed the three of us as we unloaded the van and her car. She cackled like an irate hen whenever we brought up precious china and statuettes on the building's dolly cart. After two torturous hours, the vehicles were unloaded, and we all went out to lunch where Summer talked to her geriatric sweetheart until her food grew cold. When she put me on the phone to speak with him, he thanked me so profusely for her safe transport that for a moment I thought he had forgotten his promise to pay for it all.

On the return trip in the van with my crew, I used the off-time to calculate every hour and every expense of our mission. Each receipt had been carefully packed away in order of expenditure, and receiptless expenses were accounted for on a separate sheet. Any costs incurred by Summer were catalogued separately, if possible, and flagged if mixed in with other costs. Without ever mentioning names, it was an accurate and precise accounting of every dollar spent moving Max's mistress to Florida. I turned it all over to Max the day after my return. He promptly lost it.

I spent the week refiguring the bill, which totaled several thousand dollars, by contacting my credit card companies for current balances. I was able to estimate my cash expenditures and give him a verbal figure over the phone. I received an envelope full of cash by the end of the next week.

During my first week back, I received calls from Max every morning, some out of habit, and some to schedule workouts. I received calls from Summer also. She was frustrated that her confidant was fifteen hundred miles away but excited about an upcoming overnight visit from her mature lover. Mr. Lexington had two business trips scheduled back to back, and had slipped his pilots a secret itinerary without Bertha's knowledge. The jet would touch down in Boca Raton for twenty-four hours, enabling Max to touch base with his yacht captain as an alibi. That wasn't all that Max planned on touching, however, and Summer secured a suite at a local resort for the day. Their time together was too brief, but they savored every moment and promised each other more.

After a day of bliss, they decided to part company for a hour, he to check on his penthouse and she to pack and shower. She would be giving him a ride to the airport and his waiting jet, and she wanted his last look at her to be a memorable one.

That afternoon I received a panicked call from Summer.

"Mark!" she yelled, "Something's wrong with Max! I'm at his condo, he was supposed to meet me down here an hour ago! I've been calling and calling and he's not answering! You've got to do something!"

I grimaced at the ridiculous request. I was fifteen hundred miles away. If he was having a heart attack, was I supposed to give him CPR over the phone?

"Summer, go to the security desk. Tell the guard you work for Mr. Lexington. Tell him that it's not like him to be an hour late without calling, that he's seventy-one years old and takes medication, and you're worried. Then go up and pound on the door. On the way up ask the guard if management can get their hands on a passkey. Call me back."

A half hour later I got a call back.

"Oh, Mark, it was *so* funny! The guard let me go up by myself. I *pounded* on the door so hard I hurt my hand. I kept on dialing his phone too. *Finally*, he opened the door! Mark, he'd been taking a nap!"

"I guess you wore him out!"

"Yeah, but Mark, if you could have seen him standing there in just his underwear, with his hair sticking up all over! I just burst out laughing and he looked at me like I was crazy!"

I hung up with a feeling of relief. I don't fly and by the time I drove down to kick the door in, our friend would have been stiff for awhile. Max flew on to his next meeting still alive.

Two days later, I received another call from Summer. "Mark, the strangest thing happened to me today. I was walking into the dry cleaners and I saw this man in the parking lot standing next to a big Cadillac. He was leaning on it like he was waiting for someone and he looked just like a mobster like you see in a movie! He was staring straight at me and he watched me as I went in! I was inside maybe ten minutes and when I came out he was still there! And Mark, he was still staring at me. He never looked away or down but just kept staring. Then he started to open the driver door. When the door was open he started to take off his suit jacket. He can see that I'm looking back at him and he's being very deliberate. So he lays the jacket down first and Mark, he's got a strap thing around his torso and a holster with a gun! He's still looking right at me the whole time and then he gets into the car. Mark, he wanted me to see that gun, I know he did!"

"Summer, did you get the plate number?"

"No."

"Was it a Florida license plate?"

"I don't know, I don't remember."

I was going to tell her how to "clean" herself, or how to make sure she's not being followed, until I remembered the way she drove. She had trouble dealing with the traffic in front of her. The added task of checking behind her would have been a sure-fire formula for an accident.

43

M AX LEXINGTON HAS watched tennis matches with the President of the United States. He has had an audience with the Pope. He could pick up the phone anytime and confer with the Governor on an issue. He sits on corporate boards where his advice is carefully weighed and treated with respect and solemnity. He rubs elbows with CEOs, company presidents and other self-made millionaires. He belonged to many exclusive clubs and organizations, both local and national in scope. He has dined in the finest restaurants, in palaces, in mansions and on yachts.

Max Lexington could summon any one of a dozen of his own adoring vice-presidents or upper management people to jet or yacht with him. One of the last logical choices he would make as a vacation companion would be his part-time bodyguard. This suited me just fine because hurtling through the air at twenty-five thousand feet in an aluminum cylinder filled with jet fuel held no appeal to me whatsoever. I avoid planes the way albinos avoid sunlight. When I travel at any speed over ten miles per hour I like to have some input, and at six hundred miles per hour in a jet...I have none. I'm as likely to buy a plane ticket as Marlon Brando is to win the Boston Marathon.

Summer called my cell phone early that Wednesday. "Mark, guess what? He's flying down this Saturday and I need you to do me a favor, sweetie. If you would fly down with him I'm sure I could get him to stay for a week! We've never spent more than

313

twenty-four hours together at a time and I think our relationship needs more time than that!"

"Not just no, Summer, but hell no!" I said.

"Look, sweetie, I know we've put you through a lot and we appreciate it, we really do! But if you came down with him we'd be *much* more comfortable. We want to play tennis together at the Boca Club but people *know* him there and it would raise a lot of eyebrows if they see just us together. But if you're there with us they won't know if I'm with him or you!"

"I don't fly and I don't play tennis," I replied.

"I know, I know, but look, it's not a vacation. He'll pay you! You can take some Valium before the plane takes off! I always do! You can dine out every night with us, and we've got some *nice* places in mind. That way we won't get any weird looks when we go out, either! And he's got the yacht docked at the Boca Club! We'll spend at least two or three days boating, and Boomer will let you drive the yacht if you want!"

"I can't miss a week of workouts," I countered.

"Oh, but you can work out with us every day at the Boca Club! They have a gorgeous facility, and you can go as a guest. I need to workout with you again anyway. I think I've put on one or two!"

"I dunno Summer."

"Look, honey, if his family or whoever drives him sees you get on the plane with him they won't be so suspicious! I know you want to get back to your gym and cut back your hours with Max but he and I would be *very* grateful if you'd do this. It would be very wise to stay in his good graces even if you're not going to work for him anymore."

"They don't have baggage checkers at private airports, do they?"

"No, sweetie, so you can bring all the guns you want and nobody will say a thing! Mark, it's seventy-five degrees here today, what is it there? Ten?"

That Saturday morning, I finished my last workout with Terri Regis at eleven-thirty. I'd talked her into a ride to the airport, and we got there at eleven-fifty. I checked the pilot's eyes for redness and asked him it he'd had anything to drink within the last forty-eight hours. I wasn't smiling when I asked. His eyes were clear as he looked back at me with sincerity and said that no, he hadn't. The engines fired up again at eleven fifty-five and we were "wheels up" at exactly noon. Acceleration during takeoff was fast, but I'd driven motorcycles that took off faster. Max was across the narrow aisle from me, and I managed to refrain from sitting in his lap and clinging on to his neck. Too apprehensive to read at first, I busied myself by checking altitude, temperature and location readings on the screen in our cabin.

In the middle of the flight, Max began to tell me again how spoiled he was and then asked me, "So Maaark, what do you make of this? I mean this week that's coming up here?"

Feeling uncharacteristically blunt, I replied, "Well sir, you can't seem to forget about her, and *she's* still obsessed with you. I guess this week is about finding out if you enjoy each other's company for extended periods of time."

We examined my statement together for the next hour and a half until our wheels touched down on the runway at two forty-five. For the first time, though, the endless analysis was welcome, as it took my mind off the flight. In addition, the analyst was being paid for a change.

The captain of Max's yacht, Boomer, picked us up in the gold BMW that Max kept in the condo's parking garage. Boomer was a bit out of shape, but capable-looking and very affable. I guessed his age to be a weather-beaten thirty-five. The drive from Boca Executive to the condo was a short one at twelve minutes, and on the way the only two topics were the weather and Kaycee. Kaycee was tall, very thin, very blond and was Captain Boomer's live-in girlfriend. She was also the first mate on Max's yacht. Capable and classy, her skills ran the gamut from filling in as yacht pilot during sea borne engine checks to setting the main table. She could cook and serve with grace and ease and could play hostess quite convincingly to the ship's guests. As far as Max was concerned, Kaycee did have one flaw, however. Employed by the Lexington family for over two years, Kaycee adored Mrs. Lexington. Their fondness for each other was obvious whenever the lady was aboard, and their personalities meshed together like those of two old friends. Kaycee loved children too, and trips that included any of Elizabeth's favorite grandchildren were always made fun and relaxing by the first mate.

Max's concern was that Kaycee loathed the thought of his mistress even setting one manicured toe on board. She viewed Max's lover as a homewrecking witch from hell and had no trouble expressing her feelings to Boomer. The easygoing captain was visibly nervous at being caught in the crossfire but had managed to extract a promise from Kaycee. Kaycee would grit her teeth and stick out the week with the hope that it was a one-time occurrence and Summer would soon be gone. Boomer worded the agreement much more tactfully when he relayed it to his boss, but the general meaning came through like a tsunami.

We arrived at the condo building's underground garage, and Boomer found a valet cart. While he and I bundled the suitcases up the elevator to the penthouse, Max used my cell phone to call his beloved. It was decided that an elaborate snack that Summer had purchased would be brought over, and Max's visit would begin with shrimp, sushi and Bocelli. I was dispatched in the BMW to pick her up. She wasn't ready. After a half hour I began to receive impatient calls on my cell phone from the penthouse.

Their reunion was a tender one as I averted my eyes and tried to get the CD player to play more than one track at a time. The elaborate penthouse was a curious mix of late 1980s interiors and high-tech televisions that dropped out of the ceilings at the behest of remote controls. An even higher tech sound system required a box full of remotes to operate in conjunction with the surround-sound system speakers installed in the walls of every room. After the snack and several Crown Royals, Max guided Summer to the penthouse's giant master suite.

A half hour had passed, and I was still coaxing music out of the CD player when Summer came padding back down the hallway wearing only a dark robe. She held an empty wine glass and tumbler and was making a beeline to a small bar in the penthouse living room. She asked me to bring a few more ice cubes from the kitchen and I complied, meeting her at the bar as she poured. Her hair was long, dark, flowing and untied…and so was her robe. In fact, it didn't come equipped with any tie at all. As I stood a couple of feet back with ice in a glass watching her pour, her robe fell open. The right side had worked its way across and down her shoulder and could do its job no more, exposing her entire right side from neck to toe. It was readily apparent that she always wore a bikini when she tanned. She acted oblivious for a moment, finishing her task before setting down the bottle. With a demure sideways peek through her long tresses at my expressionless face, she reached over with her left hand and closed herself up. Picking up both glasses, she smiled and said, "Thanks, sweetie." She then passed through the living room's white, glass-walled, gold-mirrored décor and floated back down the hallway. After locking myself into my room, I found the stock channel on the television.

Dinner that night was at a restaurant not three miles from the condo. It was a decidedly upscale dining spot, and the service was above average. The portions were a bit on the small side for a professional glutton such as myself, but I made do with a couple pieces of normally verboten white bread. Max and Summer had insisted that I join them so that she wouldn't feel as age conscious in front of the other diners. Max seemed to flaunt the age difference as a badge of honor and pawed at Summer lightly on the way to the table.

Considering the atmosphere, dinner would have been quite reasonably priced if the three hundred dollar bottle of wine had not catapulted the final bill into the mid-four hundreds. As if embarrassed, the waiter never asked if we were ready for the check. We soon discovered that he was not embarrassed but busy, as he and the rest of the staff hovered near a computer terminal. It had broken down during their busiest night of the week, sending employees into a dither of figuring out who served what and what it cost. Half an hour after finishing, my sotted boss began to grow impatient between stories of who he knew in Florida and how he knew them. My second request to the waiter resulted in a handwritten bill, which I promptly returned with Mr. Lexington's platinum charge card. Ten minutes passed, then twenty. After half an hour, the three of us grew quite antsy. One hour and fifteen minutes after finishing dinner, I found our waiter amidst a cackle of employees at the useless terminal. Max's card was still tenth in a slow-moving line. Elbowing my way into their midst, I placed my first two fingers firmly on the card and said, "You've had Mr. Lexington's card long enough. Would you like an address to mail the bill to?" Three minutes later, after being moved to the head of the line and cashed out, I was headed back to the table with the card. I had had to forge the boss' signature but felt good about leaving the five-percent tip.

Our return to the penthouse after dinner was the beginning of another frenzied round of mating in the master suite while I hid in my room. My attempts to ignore them were interrupted periodically by plaintive wails for ice water by my penthouse mates. I obligingly played houseboy until their cries abated. As I drifted off at midnight, I was secure in the knowledge that I wouldn't be receiving an 8:30 a.m. wake-up call from either for a change.

At 7:30 a.m. I was awakened by what sounded like a clan of howling monkeys vandalizing a china shop. Max and Summer, luckily for me both early risers, were laughing and hooting in the kitchen as they made coffee together. Bleary eyed, I peeked in on them, and Summer looked up and said, "Oh hi, sweetie, come here a minute so I can show you how to do this for tomorrow." I looked at her as though she'd grown antlers and went back to my room, wondering if I could leave my luggage with the guard in the lobby and walk to a car rental. Before I could open up my cell phone, Summer came knocking on my doorway. "Hi, honey, sorry if we woke you. Say, we're scheduled to play tennis in one hour at the Boca Club. After that we're having brunch at the cathedral there! Could you be ready to go too?"

"I thought I may stay here this morning," I replied. "My tan needs work, and I might rent a car. My buddy Doc is down in Lauderdale with his boat."

"Oh, no, sweetie, we need you, we really do."

"Just try to make sure he doesn't drink and drive until I get back."

"That's not it. We're signed up at the courts at the Boca Club and if people there judge us before they get to know us we'll never be accepted! With you there for a while we'll be okay!"

When a homosexual man is openly gay, he doesn't care who knows it. Once he comes "out of the closet" it doesn't matter if others know because he has accepted it himself and isn't about to turn back. Sometimes, however, the gay man doesn't give any outward clues to his alternative persuasion. He might be afraid of his family shunning him. He may be afraid of losing lifelong friends once they discover the truth. At work, he may feel as though the social stigma attached to his homosexuality might be enough to prevent him from receiving well-deserved raises or promotions. Business opportunities bandied about in private when you are part of the "good ol' boys club" would be gone. But family get-togethers, weddings, birthday parties and company social functions are often expected to be attended with a "significant other." Showing up with a close friend, who is also male, fools no one anymore and just elicits a big "Aha, I *knew* it!"

Until they're ready to come out, many gay men feel the need for a "beard." A beard is a female friend willing to attend any potentially embarrassing social engagement while she functions as the man's date. The beard is usually privy to the gay man's secret although it's not an absolute necessity that she is. The beard must have an aura of plausibility. For example, perfectly groomed male model types do not typically date 450-pound women. I once had a male client whose beard was a lesbian woman who hadn't yet come out either. She would attend his functions as his date, and he would go to hers as her date.

During this week in Florida, it was Summer's intention to diffuse the obvious age difference between her and Max by inserting a beard into the equation. Any time that we were about to encounter a potentially uncomfortable social situation involving introductions, Summer would place herself equidistant between me and Max.

It was a fresh, clear Florida morning on the Gold Coast, and the tennis pros eyed Summer lasciviously as the three of us made our way to court number nineteen. The muscles in her firm, tanned legs flexed and shimmied as she walked next to her bow-legged partner. Their beard brought up the rear, with Max Lexington's racquet tucked under his arm. The brown, wiry, long-haired pros decided within two looks that I didn't play tennis and that I was the third wheel. It took the other players on our section of courts nearly twenty minutes to understand the same.

One of Max and Summer's female opponents wore a white tennis outfit that couldn't hide her 5 foot 10 inch height. Her bleached blond hair was arranged in a straight page boy haircut that ended an inch above her shoulders. She looked to be anywhere from 60 to 80 years of age despite a countenance drawn tight across her skull from a face-lift or two. Although a slim woman, her deeply tanned, leathery skin hung from her arms and legs in little foldlets that made her look like a two-legged alien Shar-Pei. She was quite athletic on the court, and she and her seventy-year-old male partner beat a slightly rusty Max and Summer several times. In between trips back to the clubhouse for water, I sat and stared at this woman. I was fascinated by this monied example of the worst skin elasticity I'd ever encountered in my life. After game two, she noticed my gawking, and began to smile at me after every time she scored. During between-game introductions, Shar-Pei woman was quick to drop clues to me that her partner was not her husband, who had in fact passed on. I started feeling a little cocky knowing that wherever I traveled, all the single chicks wanted me.

Brunch at "The Cathedral" was waiting for us after tennis. In spite of her fascination with the entire Boca Club, Summer was never able to clarify as to whether or not the immense dining room was an actual former cathedral. It was incorporated into the end of the quarter-mile long Boca Resort and Hotel complex and was staffed by a small army of foreign-accented waiters and waitresses. Fifteen tables, all draped in white cloths, were laid end to end down the room's center. Warming trays sat in a long silver row, burners lit, and held every brunch item known to mankind. At the end of the line was a huge semi-circular table where two waitresses and three omelet chefs custom-cooked for the finicky.

Ravenous enough by now to imagine mugging a nearby old lady for her danish, I sat down and waited for Max and Summer to order. As the waiter wrote, I excused myself and attacked the line of trays. After several plates, I placed my omelet orders with a French chef. Max and Summer were finished eating when I noticed that he, sitting directly across from me, was becoming obscured from view. My empty plates were starting to pile high in front of me to the concerned looks of my companions. I waddled away from the table as the busboy began the Herculean task of clearing it.

The yacht was docked not one hundred feet from the side of the complex. I shot the breeze with Boomer and was introduced to a tight-lipped but polite Kaycee while Max and Summer showered below. It was apparent that the appraisal process would begin immediately as Kaycee tried to determine whether I was friend or foe. I wanted to tell her that if she knew my true feelings, she would probably leap into my arms and begin nuzzling, my neck but instead I sighed and checked out my surroundings. About fifteen other yachts were docked in the little harbor off of the Intracoastal waterway. Some were larger than Max's and some were smaller, but none of them had the combination of power and ostentatiousness that the Azimut possessed. The crews on several of the others were cleaning and preparing for travel.

44

YACHTING UP AND down Florida Intracoastal waterways requires several key ingredients. The first is a sunny, or mostly sunny, day. A cloudy one will suffice if it's warm but, even if your aft deck is enclosed, a rainy day will spoil the entire see-and-be-seen appeal of the ride. The second ingredient is the yacht. I did not list the yacht first because the ride is often attempted in much smaller boats with varying degrees of success. The total effect, however, is best accomplished after starting with an actual yacht…in other words, a boat sixty-five feet in length or more. Yachts are built in all sizes, and no matter how big yours is there is always someone about to take delivery on a bigger one. Anything over 150 feet or so, though, begins to look like a wayward cruise ship. Worse yet, if it's too big, it begins to look like a chartered tour boat, and points are lost.

The third essential ingredient to successful yachting is the boat bimbo. In Michigan the common vernacular is "boat ho," but I don't believe that the phrase is popular in Florida yet. One may think that the owner is more important, but he's actually far down the list. As the yacht slides down the Intracostal Waterway past condo towers, waterfront mansions, marinas and waterfront restaurants packed with gawking patrons, at least one bimbo on back is required. Two is fine, three is okay, but four bimbos starts to smack of a party with "paid" entertainment. Bikini-clad bimbos are preferred, and blondes or brunettes are equally eye-catching with the ship as the backdrop. Thongs are, of course, allowed and encouraged. Too many thongs on board, however, has connotations of thirty-dollar-an-hour girls from an escort service and might make the owner seem needy.

The crew is number four because seldom does the man rich enough to afford a multi-million dollar playtoy have the desire or the practiced skills necessary to pilot his own boat. A uniformed, crisp-looking crew is much more impressive to both onlookers and passengers alike.

The fifth ingredient is the boss/owner. The owner should appear on the rear sundeck with at least one bimbo, and he should never be left alone. While younger yacht owners in South Florida are very common, for maximum credibility the owner should appear to be at least fifty years old. A shirt is not required, especially if the owner wants to show off his well-fed physique, but dark sunglasses are an absolute. I again suggest that the owner should never be left unattended on back. If he's an older man, the onlooker gets the impression that Grandpa is just going for a ride! A middle-aged owner alone on the back will garner a great deal of attention from gold-diggers on land, which could lead to a trip-threatening situation. In the worst case scenario, a desperate Florida gold-digger may endanger herself by leaping into the water in a frenzied attempt to swim to the yacht to meet the owner. Should she underestimate the speed of the yacht, entanglement in the ship's propellers could halt the trip until the Coast Guard completes the accident report.

A younger owner riding alone on the aft deck of his yacht should always carry a drink to distinguish himself from members of the crew. Barking orders at the crew and captain will also establish his authority and ownership of the vessel.

Max's whole presentation of the "really rich guy with the much younger girlfriend" was masterfully done. His eighty-two foot Italian yacht looked unique and impressive. It never failed to draw gapes and stares from shore as it slid powerfully by. Passengers of passing boats would nudge and point at the looming presence. The shape and hull's paint were reminiscent of a passive killer whale, poised and confident, but capable of forty miles an hour in an instant.

Max kept his gray-white mane carefully combed back with a bit of gel. His thick gold Rolex wasn't noticeable from more than two hundred feet away but his ruddy tan was, and it came bounding back after an hour in the hot Florida sun. His very manner of lounging on the back deck cushions was that of a man who had seen and done it all and was no longer easily impressed. The nonchalant way that he touched or caressed Summer made it clear that she was his, but others could look if they wanted. Summer's bikini fit her perfectly and lifted up her voluminous breasts appropriately. The bottoms were cut high enough to minimize her curvaceous hips, but not so high as to expose too much of her rump. She looked older when her dark hair was pulled back tight, but still looked thirty-five years his junior. With her tanned features partially covered by her dark Armanis and her white teeth flashing as she talked, Summer's presence next to Max said "expensive." Occasionally, we passed a point of interest, and it was pointed out to her. Summer had a pouty, bored way of checking it out that belied her actual elevated level of curiosity.

Initially, I lounged in the back also, opposite the pair. People-watching eventually became passe, however, and I began to gladly accept Boomer's gracious offers to pilot the yacht in his stead. Once the captain and Kaycee established what my role was, and understood that I often wished I were elsewhere, we developed an easy rapport.

Drawbridges crossing the waterway every few miles greatly impeded our progress. We sometimes idled for twenty minutes, waiting for pre-set openings from the bridgemaster. Many bridges were fixed and high enough to accommodate the Azimut, however, and we passed underneath unhindered as cars and trucks rumbled overhead.

Max's waterborne travel pattern in Florida, fifteen hundred miles from home, was exactly the same as in Michigan. His formula dictated boarding a big boat and cruising slowly along a scenic and preferably sun-drenched waterway while snacking and drinking. As we pulled up to a waterfront restaurant around dinnertime after listening to Bocelli over and over again, Boomer and Kaycee's southern drawls began to take on a slight Italian accent. Cruising back at night amidst streams of lights along the shore, I marveled as I peeked into the interior of one well-lit estate after another. My friend Doc once said that he used to think that he was old and rich. It wasn't until he began spending his winters in South Florida that he realized that he was young...and poor.

Boomer allowed me to log in hours at a time at the helm of the yacht and together the three of us watched its hull part the dark, shiny waters in front of us. Usually arriving back late, we slept onboard in sumptuous black-oak and gold staterooms. We drifted off to the sounds of wavelets lapping against the hull.

The boss' whiskey consumption finally began to taper off somewhat. Daily tennis matches on the courts and massages at the Boca Club spa seemed to distract the discontent billionaire. My fear of an accidental plunge by my charge into the salty Florida waters diminished as his sobriety returned. On Wednesday, I spoke to Summer quite frankly about the long-term effects of her lover's drinking. We were able to agree that she was more interested in his mind than his physique. At last, I saw the opening I needed to influence my client where family and friends up until now had failed. His relationship with Summer had become more than an obsession. It had evolved into a comfortable habit. He wasn't going to forget about her, and he would never give her up now. Perhaps it would be possible to wean him from one habit to a new one—especially if the new habit asked him to. Summer and I talked about the long-term effects of Max's alcohol abuse. We talked about the possibility of an early dementia beginning soon (if it hadn't already), and the inquisitive mind she loved so much being lost to her forever. Summer began to pale at the prospect of spending the next ten years with a man whose powerful intellect receded yearly until equal to that of a spoiled child. Goosebumps formed on her pampered skin as she considered spending her lover's final years as his nurse and nanny. She could do something about it now, I warned. She had a choke-hold on his attention and could put it to good use immediately! Summer listened intently and acted.

That night, after an intimate moment, she asked him to do something for her. She asked him to go for an entire day without drinking. It was the only thing she desired of him, and she would consider it a declaration of his love for her if he would try. Max thought about it for a brief moment…and then agreed. He would abstain all day and all night on Thursday, and thus prove his love for her. No announcements would be made, no hoopla would surround the gesture…just a quiet declaration of his adoration for her by this one act.

Thursday morning dawned warm, but cloudy. After tennis, we met for breakfast in the Cathedral again. With the boss sober and showing little inclination to venture out to anywhere dangerous, I plotted an escape. My quote to Max for a continuous week of service had not included round-the-clock servitude. I estimated that my forty hours were long over and resurrected my plan to drive to Doc's place in Lauderdale. Even if I missed Saturday's noon flight back, trading an extra week and a half of warm Florida breezes for a long solo drive back to Michigan seemed fair. My plans were delayed, however, when Max and Summer insisted that I work them out at the Boca Club's posh fitness facility…their first workout in weeks. Anxious to encourage the new leaf to remain turned over for as long as I could, I agreed. Total time spent in the little gym was less than an hour, and we were soon dropping Summer off at her condo for wardrobe replenishment and a shower.

Max and I arrived back at the penthouse by one in the afternoon, and I mentally rehearsed my explanation for my sudden withdrawal. Visions of normal restaurants and dinners that were over in less than three hours danced in my head. Workouts with my buddy at the sweatiest hardcore gym we could find beckoned to me even more.

Suddenly, the penthouse phones reverberated in unison throughout every room. Max answered the phone in the master suite just as the messageless answering machine in the kitchen picked up and began to record and transmit over its speaker. It was Elizabeth. After trying for two days to reach her missing husband, she was furious. Feeding her anger was the evidence she had discovered two days ago while preparing suits for a dry cleaning pick-up. From the pocket of a dark blue pair of pants, she had pulled out a folded sheet of paper. On it, in Mark Steel's neatest printing, was an expense report covering a five-day period in mid-January. In great detail it covered van and hotel rentals, fuel stops and daily labor expenses for two young men. While never mentioning her name, it summarized fuel costs for a second vehicle, and the identity of its other occupant was quickly and correctly deduced by Elizabeth and Bertha.

Elizabeth was livid and raged at Max with gusto. The argument escalated steadily as Max fired back, threatening divorce by yelling, "So that's it then!" and "Why don't we just call it quits?"

Elizabeth shot back, yelling, "I'm not giving you up!" and "She's not going to have you!"

On the little map of Florida imprinted in my head, the Fort Lauderdale circle was only about fifteen miles away. After the first ten minutes of their argument, it was fifty miles away…after twenty minutes, five hundred miles away. I considered a last heroic act, envisioning myself picking up an extension and saying in my best Rodney King voice, "Hey, people, can't we all just get along?" I hadn't yet billed Max for the week, though, and soon thought twice about any attempt at mediation.

The little spat erupted on and off for nearly two hours, with each party slamming the phone down only to have one or the other call back within minutes for another round. Unless I packed up and snuck out, the Lauderdale circle would continue to grow farther away in my head until it was located next to Beijing.

"Fine then, have it your way!" Max shouted, and slammed the receiver down for a fifth time. He stormed out of the master suite, down the long hallway, and paced and circled in the kitchen. Before I could say, "Off the wagon," I heard ice clinking into an empty glass. The glass didn't stay empty long after Max found the bottle in the living room. I came out of my room just as he finished pouring, visualizing myself slapping the glass dramatically out of his hand and yelling, "Distilled demon, be gone!" Before I could reach him, Max took a huge gulp and began walking over to a sofa. With a heavy sigh, he sat down. He looked at his glass.

"I think I've got a problem buddy."

No shit, Sherlock. I thought.

"Summer asked me to stop for just one day. I told her I would. But I can't. I think I'm going to need some help."

"That might be a good idea," I replied.

"Do me a favor, buddy. Please go over to our friend's place and pick her up, will you?"

"Of course," I responded.

"Tell her…tell her I tried but couldn't do it. Tell her I'm sorry. But tell her that I've absolutely made up my mind. I'm going to get in a program, I'll find the best. I've heard Sierra Tucson is the best. Celebrities, CEOs, everybody goes there. I'll do a month if I have to. They're very discreet. I'll start right away."

I drove to Summer's condo while he called her to talk. By the time I got up to her floor she was fuming.

"Dammit! *One* thing I asked him to do for me! Just one! And he couldn't! This is a sign, Mark! It's a sign that I can't *trust* him anymore!"

I sat on Summer's sofa while she primped in the bathroom and vented. Every fifteen minutes or so, my cell phone would ring. Max's pleas to put Summer on were faithfully relayed but went unheeded. Finally, after two hours, Summer agreed to accompany me back. We returned to find the sloshed CEO where I'd left him…guzzling Crown Royals and slamming down the phone every twenty minutes or so. The two banes of my existence met up in the master suite, and I had some peace until dinnertime. When the time to leave rolled around I drove, with Summer by now consoling Max in the back seat for his failure to keep his promise.

Bertha had weathered her father's calls repeatedly that afternoon while she checked on the availability of a place in the Sierra Tucson Program. Heavy drinking at dinner was followed by even more vigorous drinking back at the penthouse. Summer steadfastly refused to stay the night, and I dropped her back home by midnight. The calls from Michigan abated and eventually, all the creatures were sleeping all through the house.

45

Friday morning was clear and seventy-five degrees. A perfect day for yacht shopping. It was also a fine day to run errands with the boss, provided he didn't insist on driving. He did insist, however, and we found our first destination, a dry cleaners, after only passing it twice. Directionally, we fared better on our way to our second destination, which was Summer's condo. Executionally, however, we did not. Sitting in the front passenger seat during a right-hand turn, my right eyebrow arched involuntarily when our right front wheel rode up the curb. I tensed and hung on tight when the left rear wheel followed. My billion dollar chauffeur was still drunk! His mighty liver had finally failed to purge all of the previous night's fermented grain by-product from his bloodstream, and my life was about to end in a BMW! Opening one squinty eye, I checked for a passenger side airbag. If it was an option that the car didn't have, I would open my door at the next light, and get out. I automatically knew that a confrontation would ensue when I insisted on driving or walking. But it was too pretty a day to die. The car *was* dual-airbag-equipped, however, and I decided to let Max drive drunk for two more miles. We passed a Highland Beach police car coming the opposite way. We were doing fifty-five in a thirty-five, but the officer had his radar unit switched off as he talked on his cell phone, and Max's amazing luck continued to hold! We continued our morning weave, and in two more minutes careened into Summer's condo entranceway. The guard waved us through, and the BMW's side mirror missed scraping the gate by a layer of wax. Once up in her condo, I explained that I forgot my phone in the car and politely requested the keys, which Max absently turned over, and I went downstairs to wait in the car's driver seat.

Yacht shopping went well as I followed our broker from one mighty new ship to another. The crews bowed and fawned over us, but none of the floating palaces tickled my hungover boss' fancy enough for him to make an offer. In between peeks at new boats, Max called Elizabeth and received a pitch about joining her in two weeks at the Winter Olympics. He angrily reminded her that he'd be in rehab and snapped my phone shut hard enough to crack it.

Saturday morning was clear and hot. The weather channel warned that conditions back in Detroit were clear, but it was cold. I decided that another five days in the sun in Lauderdale wasn't worth the two-day drive and packed my suitcases for the jet. I kept a small bag out. It held items I'd need immediately after landing at Detroit City Airport like my keys and my wallet. Since we *were* landing in Detroit, it also held my gun with an extra magazine of regular rounds. Max and Summer played a last round of tennis together and we transferred everything into her Mercedes for the short trip. I drove while the cuddling couple occupied the back. The jet was supposed to be wheels up at noon. We arrived at eleven forty and our luggage was whisked on board by eleven forty-two. As Max said a long good-bye to his paramour, I said hello to the pilots. I checked their eyes for redness and their breath for Jack Daniels and climbed up the steps into the jet. I placed my small bag onto the seat that faced mine and sat down on the aisle. I was making my last cell phone call to Natasha when a German Shepherd dog, leashed and followed by an agent in a green uniform, appeared in the aisle! The dog sniffed into the cockpit, working his way to the luggage compartment.

"Don't mind if we do an explosives check, do you?" the agent said affably.

Mind? I thought. *Of course I friggin' mind!* The dog had just stuck his nose into the compartment where my suitcase lie, one end crammed with a box of .45 caliber rounds and my spare gun. *If that wasn't explosive,* I thought, *what the hell was?* Now that damn furry stool pigeon was coming down the aisle toward me! I glanced ever so subtly at the black vinyl bag in front of me. Well, what the hell, I thought, my permit was in my wallet in the same bag. If the dog alerted, I was going to grab the bag, if only because having my favorite gun confiscated for even a moment was out of the question. As I grabbed I'd explain that my Michigan permit was recognized in Florida and ask if Mr. Agent man would like a look. If he got agitated and started fingering the Glock .9mm on his belt, I would freeze and start screaming that this was a private plane, and I'd like to see his intercoursing search warrant!

The dog must have been dead last in his class at boom-boom detection school because he passed right by me and my bag. A brief check in the back, and the furry moron and his uniformed handler walked back down the aisle and off the plane! I breathed a little sigh until the dumb squad turned right around on the tarmac and tried again! Again the incompetent duo walked by my suitcase full of tiny explosives as I inwardly rolled my eyes, remembering that my spare gun hadn't even been cleaned since I last fired it. The dog was either on strike, brain dead or hadn't taken his allergy medication for days! *I can almost smell the gunpowder, for Chrissake*, I thought. The second check was even shorter and soon Dudley Do-Right and his special-needs dog left the plane.

It wouldn't be until the next week that one of my cop buddies explained that in all probability we had been boarded by a *drug*-sniffing dog. The word "explosives" came up because number one, no one wants a bomb on board their private jet. Number two, few will invite a drug-sniffing dog onto their jet without a warrant. And number three, the feds will say *anything* for the opportunity to check out a flight from South Florida, the drug import capital of the U.S.

We were wheels up at 12:02 p.m. The seventy-eight degree temperatures and the steady sun had been getting old anyway. I began to mentally brace for eighteen degrees and cloudy as Max and I began our ascent.

Preparing for next week's entry into rehab, half of the passengers on our plane began to suck down Crown Royals. Guzzling as if every sip were his last ever, Max was slurring by twenty-nine thousand feet. He was completely wasted by Tennessee, nudging and confiding in me about the usual "wife doesn't understand," and "no one will accept a former stripper as my girlfriend" crap. With such wisdom available on my right, I left my *Time* magazine on the seat. He was asleep by Kentucky. I tilted my seat back to enjoy the turbulence and tried to read.

We began our descent in Northern Ohio. The ground in Michigan was gray and white instead of green and blue. Old factories hove into view as we descended below the last layer of clouds. My cabin mate was awake now, but without any of the mumbling reflections on his love life. Every muscle in my body relaxed the moment we touched down and slowed to taxi speed. When the plane stopped Max rose out of his seat uncertainly and began to hunt around for his glasses.

Two sets of pilots had transported the billionaire safely and swiftly for a total of three thousand miles. Boomer, Kaycee and I had ensured Max's waterborne safety and comfort for at least three hundred miles. In spite of the close proximity of everything in Boca, I had driven Max dependably and cautiously for another two hundred miles. *When he steps off the plane,* I thought, *he's on his own, because I'm resigning.* Max stepped off the plane onto the runway. He made it twenty feet to the sidewalk when his right foot found a patch of ice. As he started to pitch backward, I lunged forward to grab his arm and braced myself. He banged against me hard, but somehow stayed upright! Robert had parked forty feet away in the Mercedes station wagon and together we followed our shaky shepherd to the passenger seat. *He's all yours, Robert,* I thought. Five minutes later the skycap had the car loaded with Max's bags…and they were gone.

46

I WENT BACK to my gym the following Monday with joy and relief. Michelle had a new project for me: a pretty lady of Lebanese descent who had worked out for months without losing a pound. Forty years old, intelligent and the mother of three, Sissy Lavolvo was married to a Grosse Pointe cardiologist who worked long hours and dated other women for even longer hours. Sissy spent her nights at home with her children, playing computer games and making pans of brownies. Knowing that her client was at least twenty pounds overweight, Michelle had tried her on every machine in our studio, to no avail. Upon taking over her workouts, I knew I needed a novel approach. I needed to peel twenty-five pounds off of my doe-eyed charge. To do it, I needed an approach that was both clever and psychologically persuasive. I began to weigh Sissy…every workout…sometimes twice. A half-pound down and my elation was obvious. A half-pound up, and I acted devastated, putting my hand on my head as though in severe pain. It worked. Together, we (I mean Sissy) lost a pound and a half a week. I was back! My clients still needed me. It felt great!

Max went into rehab on schedule, flying out in his jet and checking in with a mixture of relief and trepidation.

Summer, elated that her intended was kicking his jones with the help of some of the best, waited for him. He was allotted two calls a day from the clinic's pay phone, and both were always to her. As he dried out, they talked of many things, but the subject repeatedly turned to his appreciation of her. He was grateful for

335

her act of selflessness when she issued her "booze or me" ultimatum. He had a deep gratitude for her faithful, constant support when he called. It was a one-month program, and Summer looked forward to the end of it and a lucid lover returning to her more and more each day. While Elizabeth and some of the daughters flew to the Winter Olympics, Summer waited with her cell phone by her side. When Elizabeth, Bertha and a son visited on family day, Max couldn't wait to excuse himself to phone his beautiful Florida supporter. At Sierra Tucson, groups were formed, the past was dissected and issues were resolved with the help of experienced professionals. At the end of thirty days, Max attended "graduation" and flew back. His appointment at an AA meeting already scheduled for the next morning, Max's resolve to stay sober strengthened with every day that passed. Using the same pragmatic approach that he took to sating his craving for money and success, Max wrestled a fifty-year problem to a cease fire.

Mr. Lexington's return to Michigan was a short one. He checked in with his company president and met with as many management people as possible. A week later, his jet was wheels up as he flew to the East Coast to view his suppliers' latest offerings. With his senses returning daily, the legendary success story put his nose back to the grindstone and readied his empire for a worsening recession.

During rehab, I had received periodic calls from his mollified mistress as she awaited her lover's return to her. Now he'd been out of rehab for over two weeks, and she could bear it no more. She *must* be with him. He *must* hold her again and whisper that the future was theirs alone. She longed to see him...to touch him...to receive from him reassurances that only a mature man could give to her. His mind grew clearer and healthier every day, she said. Though his counselors forbade him to make any life decisions until a year of sobriety had passed, surely it would do no harm to test the waters a bit? The time would come soon enough when each would need to leave their respective situations, no matter how painful the process, to be together at last.

Her call to me came at ten on a Friday night. From her condo in Boca, it shot like a lightning bolt into the night, relayed from tower to tower in an unseen fury that burned its way north to me. Her tirade, full of pathos and anguish, took time to surrender bits and pieces of what had happened.

At first I heard only a wall of sound in my earpiece, but gradually I began to pick out curse words…and then intelligible phrases began to follow, with key words like "promised" and "forever" lending shape and meaning. After twenty minutes, the shrieking subsided into sobbing, and sometimes whole sentences were actually formed. After forty-five minutes, I possessed an encapsulation of the dialogue that had ended in tonight's dramatic phone call.

It was their age difference, he assured her. It was *not* the fact that she was reviled by his family. It had *nothing* to do with her increasingly sullied reputation and growing notoriety as former friends and family lined up to lob gossip grenades her way. Being cast out from his religion of seventy-two years had no bearing on his decision, either. The prospect of being forced to vacate the mansion, the "love it or hate it" most talked about house in the Pointes, did not influence his decision one bit, he claimed. Most of all, he paid no heed to the scuttlebutt that he was a fool…the same derisive taunts that claimed that he'd been taken in by a conniving gold-digger in his golden years.

She cursed him. She cursed his family. Howitzer shells of invective were hurled at his standing in the community. His business was cussed out. His reputation and ability to keep his word were belittled and sworn at. Finally, his physique was critiqued in a torrent of descriptive words as, from head to toe, every wrinkle was covered. In the last hour of vilifying her former lover, Summer prefaced everything with "you tell him for me" or "let that piece of (excrement) know." By midnight, I felt like a UPS man the week before Christmas; so great were the number of delivery requests.

The next morning I received a call from (canine excrement) himself. "Hey buddy, wanted to call about the possibility of starting up our workouts again. How's our friend doing?"

"She's very angry, Mr. Lexington."

"Yes, yes, I truly, truly feel bad about what I must have put her through…"

We began sporadic workouts again, but my newly sober client kept turning all conversations to his obsession. He spoke half-heartedly about other potential beaus for both himself and for her as the pain from biting my tongue formed tears in my eyes.

Summer's condo lease ended, and she flew back into town, moving back in with Chuck as though nothing had ever happened. She resisted returning Max's calls to her cell phone for a record six days, finally giving in to an especially urgent one. It was about Max procuring a job at the Yacht Club for her son as an instructor. The opportunity would be lost forever if she failed to act. She bit. She began taking his calls again, albeit coolly. Summer, however, absolutely refused to have any face-to-face contact with her former lover, electing instead to attend marriage counseling with Chuck. The calls became ever more insistent, however, as they alluded to a secret so vital and of such importance that it could only be talked about in person.

They met ten miles north of his mansion, near a public beach. Max wasted no time. He dramatically pulled off his sunglasses, allowing Summer to stare for the first time into his clear, sober eyes.

"Look at me," he said, "look at me!" She looked. "I love you, I can't fight it anymore. I…love…you! And if you're with me, you'll never want for anything! I cannot be without you. I don't care about anyone else. I just want to be with you…and I *will* take care of you!"

47

T HE CALL CAME through on his direct line. *It wouldn't have mattered which one rang,* he thought, *Marcy is out sick again anyway and I've had to put out every fire myself.* He answered it.

"It's me," the voice on the other end said, "I know it's been two months, but you said you only wanted to hear from me if I had proof dey were togedder."

"Yes, I remember. What do you have?"

"He didn't go to his office yesterday. He drove out to Metro Beach and she met him ten minutes after dat. She got into his car. I tried to set up the parabolic mike, but some kids were playing right behind them, and I didn't get anything."

"How long did they stay?"

"An hour, maybe an hour and ten."

"Did they kiss?"

"Just a quick one, near da end."

"All right, then," he sighed heavily, "we may have to do what we talked about during our last meeting. Let me see if I can get an okay for it. Call me back if anything further develops. Otherwise call me on this day, at this time next week."

"Will do. Uh, that retainer dat I got is gettin' a little low…"

"When we meet again to discuss further actions we must take, I will bring another envelope."

"Uh, thanks."

He hung up the phone. Enough had been said over the phone already. He had no concerns about a wiretap on his end. He didn't completely trust the man on the other end, however and had no way of knowing if a recording was being made.

48

On a chilly day in April, I was preparing to drive in to my studio. My cell phone shrieked for attention with a familiar number on the caller ID.

"Mark! Where are you?" It was Summer.

"I'm at home, but I'm just leaving to go in," I answered.

"Can you leave right now? I'm with our friend. We're in a church parking lot. We've got a problem. There's some thug in a maroon mini-van and he's taking pictures of us! We met here and I noticed him pulling up a minute later! Mark, he has dark hair and he needs a shave but he looks like an ex-cop or something! Are you there?"

"I'm in my car now, but I'm still twenty minutes away."

"Mark, this guy is scary looking and he's not trying to be subtle. He just got right out of his car with his camera and was looking right at us and then just started snapping away!"

"Do you see any sign of a gun?"

"No, no but he's wearing a coat and he could have it under there! We're locked in Max's car and we're going to drive away but if he follows us you have to tell us where we can meet you!"

"I'm eighteen minutes away from the gym. Go there. Maybe you should call the police?"

"No, Max doesn't want to. He doesn't want the gossip to get any worse! This guy hasn't tried to approach us yet. He's giving us kind of a funny smirk like he's daring us to say anything."

"Can you see his license plate number?"

"Max's getting it now, but the guy doesn't seem to care. We've.....yes, honey, we've got it now and we're pulling away. He's not following us yet. Where are you?"

"I'm sixteen minutes from the gym. If you're not going to the police I want you to keep moving for sixteen minutes, Don't stop. Stay on main roads. Make sure there are cars and people around."

Fifteen minutes later, I pulled into the gym parking lot. Max's Mercedes, with both him and her in it, was already there. I got into the back of the car where Summer informed me that she was sure she hadn't been followed that morning. I rolled my eyes. The woman could have been followed by a taxiing jumbo jet and not have noticed. *My* main concern was that someone was taking the time to wait for Max to leave his house every morning. Carefully and precisely, the three of us went over every detail of the incident. Max had never seen the man before. I suggested places directly outside of the mansion's front gates where an innocuous looking mini-van could be parked for a time without drawing attention. Max was adamant that he would have noticed *anybody* lying in wait for him. I didn't argue. Instead I encouraged him to contact a lieutenant he knew at the local department. With luck, his connection would tie a name to the plate. If the name rang a bell with the followed financier, he could plan his next move from there.

Meanwhile, almost one year after her dalliance with Max began, Summer filed for divorce. A pre-nup that she had unwisely signed ten years ago provided for a modest yearly stipend of 35,000 dollars when she first told me about it. Summer's attorney, her reputation unparalleled by years in the trenches in Wayne County's Divorce Courts, was prepared to do battle. Ten years was a goodly number to be married, and there was some question as to whether Summer should have been represented and advised before the wedding by an attorney who was hand-picked by Chuck. As the paperwork began to move back and forth between the attorneys, the stipend that Summer had originally boasted about mysteriously became smaller. It quickly dropped to $32,000, and the final number eventually became $28,000.

"Mark!" She exclaimed at one point. "Twenty-eight a year doesn't even cover my hair, nails and trainer!"

If ever Summer's high priced attorney had a "hands off" client, it was the preoccupied Princess. While Chuck and his loyal brothers steadily hid their private real-estate company's assets, Summer jetted off to Florida to shop for new yachts with her intended.

Indignant at the gold-digger moniker being affixed daily to her, Summer had once boasted that Chuck's net worth had surpassed twelve million. Max guffawed when he heard it, and after Summer filed, the figure steadily dropped in papers filed with the court. A forensic accountant's detective work turned up only a small fraction of the original figure, with the assets of each huge property neatly pledged in order to buy another. On paper at least, Chuck was rapidly becoming a pauper, soon to be vying for a place in line at the soup kitchen. Before long, his assets were buried deeper than the devil's basement floor. Summer, off with Max in the Bahamas on one getaway after another, was about as useful in locating the assets as a clown troupe at a funeral.

Max Lexington celebrated four months of sobriety on the first of May. His liver, according to his amazed physician, had survived the whiskey's toxic effects relatively intact. His mind grew sharper every week, with sections that hadn't functioned at full capacity for months gradually re-introducing themselves.

Max's motto on every business deal was to "lock the door but leave a window open." This meant that he was insistent that the party he negotiated with sign every contract, cross every "t" and dot every "i." For himself, however, a way out was always buried deep in the wording. It might be an unobtrusive little clause that had no meaning unless the waffling billionaire wanted out, at which point it could be quickly turned into the "deal breaker." He applied his motto repeatedly in the next several months.

Max had spent the spring going on sea trials with new yachts and driving one expectant broker after another crazy. The rich man would envision himself with Summer on one new boat after another, make an offer and withdraw it at the last possible moment. His own Azimut would be offered for sale and a deposit would be accepted, only to have the sale fall through for one reason or another. After months, one of the deals was consummated, and Max found himself yachtless in South Florida. He concentrated instead on his people skills, breaking up with more finesse with Summer and without the finality of his drinking days. He would wait a few days before re-declaring his love for her, leaving her in an emotional whirlpool as her divorce progressed, motion by motion.

During one of his increasingly rare workouts with me, Max excitedly produced piles of glossy brochures depicting a Sea Ray 580. It was brand new, he crowed, and would make the perfect boat for the Grosse Pointe Yacht Club. At just over a million dollars, it was affordable, too. I looked over at "Mr. Smart Shopper," watching him stare at the brochure page that featured the large aft cabin. Although perhaps a little smaller, it rivaled any four-star hotel's accommodations. I looked around the den for a "Vogue" magazine, or anything else that boasted photos of models or other pretty women. I wanted to cut out a dark-haired one and position her on the aft cabin bed. It might assist Max in visualizing where his paramour would look best. I checked the coffee table, but there were only books of poems and photo books filled with grand-children.

49

THE NIGHT WAS an unusually cold one as I pulled onto the street indicated on the map. The subdivision's thoroughfares took several twists and turns, with house after house and lining each side of the randomly designed neighborhood. Max had vowed to "leave no stone unturned" in discovering the identity of their stalker in the church parking lot. The police lieutenant had furnished Mr. Lexington with a name and address which Max turned over to me. The minivan was registered to a lady who lived about twenty miles from Max. My working theory was that the lady's husband/ boyfriend was either a P.I. or some goon doing a favor for one of Max's offspring. After a quarter mile, I turned right a second time, and the residences turned into blocks of two-story condos. When the addresses descended close to the one of interest, I stuffed my car in between some others at an apartment building. Walking casually on foot without *ever* looking around, I moved down the line of condos, making a beeline for the unit that I thought would be the one. The front door jumped into view. The address matched the one given to me. All of the condos had an attached one-car garage and half of these garages had windows in the overhead door. The condo ahead was one of those, and I altered my course slightly to arrive at the window. Never once turning my head to look around, I stood on tiptoe to peek into the garage. There *was* no minivan, but there was a small late model Cavalier. With the aid of my small flashlight I read the number off of the plate. It was ridiculously easy to remember. It said 123 LEX! Lingering for a brief instant more to see if it was some kind of a vanity plate (it wasn't), I switched off my light and headed for the front door. The lower level was totally dark and heavy drapes were closed tightly against prying eyes such as mine. A second floor light was on, and the mirror that was against the wall and visible through the window looked like the kind that would be attached to a large bureau found in a bedroom. There was no obvious activity, but I decided to lurk for awhile in case "stalking man" came home in wifey's van. On the off chance that he did and neglected to lock it, I would quickly toss it for an ID of some sort…and then leave. I memorized the address of a vacant-looking condo on the block and began circling the block on foot. If questioned, I would ask for the address of the vacant condo. A half hour of "walk bys" yielded nothing. On my sixth trip, a shirtless neighbor began peering at me from his brightly lit bedroom window. The man needed a bra, and he needed to begin working out immediately but I gave him a friendly wave instead of shouting out any suggestions. On my seventh round he was still there, his curiosity obviously piqued. I walked back to my car and left without ever encountering any mini van.

I knew I wasn't driving away empty-handed, however, because I had another license plate number for the lieutenant to run. I turned the number over to Summer, patiently explaining its importance. "If Mr. Goon is in the habit of swapping cars with wifey before he goes on a mission," I told her, "then there is a fifty-fifty chance that running 123 LEX will yield his name."

Summer exclaimed that she'd turn the new number over to Max immediately upon seeing him. I never heard anything about the matter again.

50

"C'MON, HONEY, YOU'VE got to do it!" Summer was urging me to play captain one more time. She had called just after ten to tell me about the new Sea Ray. It was being delivered in one week, and Max's excitement had rubbed off on her as though *her* name would appear on the title too.

"Summer," I replied, "it didn't really work out too well last time. Everything was too last-minute…too disorganized. I was expected to drop whatever I was doing to punch in for a few hours. There was…ah…some resistance to the first mate that I hired, and I couldn't really look for another one because I had no idea how many hours I could offer."

"Sweetie, this boat is brand new, it's beautiful. You'll love it. It sells for a million five but I think he's getting it for one-point-two."

"I have a boat already. I like it. It may not cost one-point-two but it runs fine."

"Mark, after all you've done for us we want you with us. We don't want some stranger on the boat with us. It would feel odd. We feel comfortable with you. I told him I wanted you as the captain this summer and he said 'Oh yes, by all means.' He just assumed you would do it. Please don't burn your bridges now!"

"Summer, there's a difference between burning my bridges and cutting my losses. I've paid employees thousands extra over the last year so that I could be at his beck and call. Since this whole thing with you started my cell phone bills have gone through the roof. I've paid thousands in extra charges from my phone company, no matter how often I upgraded my plan. I've spent *hundreds* of unpaid hours on the phone, so I lose both ways every time that phone rings. Between neglecting my business and spending my own money to keep up with you two, I'm maybe seventy-five grand in the hole overall. I want my life back."

"Mark, I've told him many, many times that we owe you a lot. He's said he knows, and that he'll take care you. You have nothing to worry about. But he does appreciate *loyalty* above everything else. I've already talked to him, if you ask he'll put you on salary. If you hire a first mate you can offer them a weekly salary too, just try to get somebody classy and experienced is all."

"All I've heard so far are promises. I can't put gas in my boat with promises. They don't accept them at the gas dock. Remember when I played detective a couple of months ago? I had a total of eight hours into that. I didn't even get a thank you…much less get paid for it. Do you know anyone else who goes to work for an eight-hour shift and tells the boss it's on the house? I don't think you do. Does Max have guys at Corporate who spend time on the phone when they're in his employ? I think so. Do they do it for free? I'm sure they don't. Summer, I'm probably going to live a long time. It was an interesting year at times, and right now I can chalk it up to experience and maybe a reference if I ever need one."

"Mark, all I'm asking is that you don't burn your bridge. I'll make sure he takes care of you. He said he would."

Summer must have worked Max day and night on my behalf. Every other phrase out of her mouth must have had the word "owe" or "care" or "Mark" in it until Max caved just to get some peace.

The meeting was at Beach Grill. Summer was invited, but she was late. Max was already in the parking lot, and together we found a booth and ordered. I received a short speech about his and Summer's appreciation, but it sounded forced; like somebody in the booth behind him was pointing a gun at his back.

A rumor in the Pointes held that somewhere in the area, in a bank vault that listed Max as the only signer, were stacks of bills stashed away. More than just mad money or funds for a rainy day, it reputedly totaled well into the millions. Supposedly amassed secretly in the 1970s, its origins were as mysterious as its existence.

After delivering my half-hearted "attaboy" speech, Max, wincing, reached into this briefcase and pulled out a thick envelope. As he slid it painfully across the table, it dawned on me why he had ripped the case back out of my hands when I tried to carry it inside for him. There was more in that case…a lot more. His gesture of trust back in the parking lot was touching, but I tried not to dwell on it. The envelope completed its slow, painful journey to my side of the table, and I scooped it up, acting surprised and grateful at the same time. Max watched wistfully, as if bidding an old friend good-bye as I placed it in the same small bag that held my gun on the seat next to me. I felt as though another round of profuse thanks was in order, and I delivered it with gusto.

Proud and pleased as punch, Summer showed up. As she slid into the booth, Max recapped parts of the attaboy speech. I recapped my thank-you speech for the benefit of the mistress as she glowed with her accomplishment. After a few more minutes of accolades, I excused myself and made the short trip back to the studio for an accounting session. As I suspected after first holding the envelope, the total was about half of what I thought would be fair. I *was* intrigued, though, by the wrappers around each stack….simple and plain, the words "Bank Vault" were printed on each. Stamped underneath was a date: 12-21-78. A further examination revealed that not one of the bills was printed after 1978! Even Natasha commented, "Day are awl liddle hedds!"

51

"MAAAARK, I'M SURE our friend told you, I'm taking delivery on the fifty-eight footer next week."

"Yes, sir, she did."

"Do you think you can handle her, buddy?"

"No doubt in my mind. There are a couple of details I'd like to discuss with you, if I may."

"Oh sure, sure, what's on your mind?" We were in the lower level workout room at the mansion. Summer had worked me for two days until I agreed to give it one last shot. The envelope of little heads, while not exactly providing enough for an early retirement, had at least covered the huge checks I'd written to Sprint PCS over the last year. I reasoned that several days a week on a one-and-a half-million-dollar boat might not be a bad way to spend the summer.

We were in the middle of a light workout, the occurrence of which was as unusual as it was strained. Since the onset of his newfound sobriety, Max never looked me in the eye for more than a half second. When alcoholic beverages had gripped his judgement in the past, he needed at least five, and often ten seconds to stare at me…gauging…assessing…and appraising. Now, however, it was a glance here, or a flicker of recognition there. It might have been that my permanent (and certainly not unwelcome) termination was fast approaching. I had been employed for three years in one capacity or another. Max wasn't exactly an exercise fiend (although

351

with a billion to spend and limited years left to do it, one would think that health would be his number one priority). For this reason, and the fact that Elizabeth now resented my very existence, my trips to the mansion had become quite infrequent. My driving services only placed me in close proximity to nasty, backseat skirmishes as Max and Elizabeth sniped at each other during the ride. During one ill-advised attempt at re-enlisting my driving services, my hands grew sweaty on the wheel as the battle raged in back, and Elizabeth bored holes in the back of my skull with her eyes during cease-fires.

Workouts with Elizabeth were out of the question. It is difficult to exercise with someone who would rather be dissecting you with a butcher knife. My role as Mr. Lexington's bodyguard in the past two years had seemed to primarily involve protecting him from himself more than anybody else. His drinking had now ceased. His more impulsive decisions were on the wane. Personal protection for the well-known billionaire was still a damn good idea, but no longer an immediate life or death necessity. It also occurred to me that Max's unwillingness to look at me directly may be some residual embarrassment from the trove of awkward moments endured in the past year. Although usually anesthetized when they happened, Max's memories of them might have been re-emerging...and they weren't all good ones.

"Well, sir," I began, "I could have operated your boat last year to your standards, and much more efficiently, if I'd had more of an edict from you."

"How do you mean, buddy?"

"My understanding is that the going rate for a yacht captain is a thousand dollars a year in salary per foot of length. Is that true, sir?"

"I've heard something like that."

"My proposal is quite simple. If you could see your way to giving me a weekly salary...or even monthly if it's easier that way, I would take care of all of the labor. I have a first mate lined up. She's been boating since she was six years old. She's very nice, she's pretty, and she can cook. I have a friend of mine on call as a back-up captain, in case you'd like to sail on short notice and I can't make it. His name is Cory. He's experienced, he's capable, and he's in his mid-thirties. He's also a gourmet chef on the side. Since I'm not exactly on your family's Christmas card list right now, Cory would be a perfect choice in my place when any of your family members want to take the boat out. You can trust him, and your family would feel at ease with him. I would pay both Cory and the first mate out of my own salary, as often as you required them. I've also lined up a college student with extensive boat cleaning experience who will do a first class job."

"Okay, my friend. We'll give it a try. Sounds like a done deal!"

I left soon after, quite satisfied for a change. If I had free reign to run Max's yacht like a small, efficient business, we would have a very enjoyable, safe, and organized boating season. I doubted the rest of the family would use the boat more than twice, and I would be able to make myself scarce if they did.

52

I̴T WAS AN exquisite Monday morning in June. While the rest of the world had gone to work, I was on my way to Colony Bay Marina. I felt great... I felt organized...I felt prepared. A shakedown cruise on Saturday revealed no mechanical defects on my gorgeous boat. The optional high-performance super-charged diesel engines were responsive and powerful. Sunday's stem to stern cleaning had left the boat immaculate both inside and out. During the boat's two-hour trial, I had time to familiarize myself with every switch and dial. Every feature's location and capability was emblazoned into my memory like a cerebral owner's manual. The refrigerator was already stocked with soft drinks and snacks were plentiful as I awaited Max and Summer's food orders. Max had assured me that no first mate would be necessary as he had one meeting us there. I didn't mind. It was a perfect day for yachting and I was okay with breaking in somebody new.

I was an hour early. As I was opening up the canvas and checking fuel, oil and water, an old Chevy Cavalier pulled up and a pot-bellied, red-headed man, his baseball cap pulled down tight, got out.

"Is this Mr. Lexington's boat?" Red asked.

Wow, I thought, *this first mate is older than I expected.*

"Yes it is. Can I help you?"

"Yeah, I'm Captain Lance." I stared at the new arrival as though he had just offered to have my baby.

355

"Oookay…," I hesitated. "What's up?"

"Oh, I'm the new captain on his boat, here. I was supposed to meet this boat at the gas dock next door along with a friend of his, but I asked George in the office where Mr. Lexington kept it. I figured it would be at one of these wells anyway until I move it over to the Yacht Club."

I glanced around. Any minute now Max and Summer were going to pop out from behind a car, big smiles on their faces, yelling, "Ha, ha, ha, boy, did we have you going!" This clown would break into a grin, too, and tell Max that the first mate was running late for one lame reason or another.

But all "Lance the Red" did was lift up the bill of his cap and run a palm back across his sweating, bald head. He looked to be in his mid-thirties. The freckles on his forehead faded to white, unpigmented skin where the sun had burned them off repeatedly over many summers. Lance, the skin cancer candidate, replaced his cap and asked, "So, you work for Mr. Lexington, too?"

"You might say that," I replied tersely.

"Yeah, I crewed on the Azimut with Boomer when his first mate couldn't show. Now I've got my hundred-ton license and this'll be my first command."

Red's last statement dispelled all doubt that I'd misheard the first time. Captain Lance turned as Max's Mercedes pulled into a parking slot and the owner got out. I waited for him to clear up the misunderstanding.

"Hey, Mr. Lexington," Lance shouted out. "I'm an hour early so I thought I'd meet you here!" I stared at Max…he didn't return my gaze.

"Oh, heh, Laaance," he said. "Uh yeah, that's fine." Still unable to look at me, Max looked at the boat and spoke to me.

"Uh, heh, buddy, I see you two have already met. I was going to tell you about Lance. He's real good. He'll be a big help to you. He's got his Captain's license and he worked with Boomer." Max got on board. "Our friend is meeting us at Miller Marine's gas dock. If we could cast off and meet her there that would be great."

I looked wistfully at my Corvette parked in the sun. In fifteen seconds I could be in it and gone. Max owed me about three hundred dollars. I could walk away from the money and him, without a backward glance, right now. Summer's words rang out one more time. I decided that before I burned the bridge, I'd force the issue first. Red was on the boat in the Captain's seat, checking gauges and recording numbers in a notebook. I stepped on board and approached the helm.

"The engines are warm," Lance the Red said, "Do you want to untie the lines?" I stared down at the mighty sailing man.

"You can," I said. Lance's eyes opened wider. He looked me up and down, as if seeing me for the first time. He glanced at the doorway leading down below. Max was nowhere to be found. Lance's shoulders dropped, and he reluctantly got out of the seat. Slowly, he worked his way to the bow. I slid into the Captain's chair and moved his little notebook to the side. In no time, he had four lines off and coiled, with just the two stern lines to go. Max was right. Lance was a big help.

When the stern lines were off, I eased the new yacht out of the well. It was an eighth of a mile to Miller Marina's gas docks. My cell phone rang. It was Summer, and *she* was actually waiting for *us*. If my day hadn't suddenly turned so sour, I could have enjoyed witnessing this—an actual miracle in my lifetime. We crept up to the gas docks, and Lance threw a bow line to the attendant. Only after he scrambled to the stern to toss another line did he ask me how we were doing on fuel. Slightly puzzled, I answered "About half full."

Summer walked up, smiling and carrying a day bag and a plastic grocery bag. As Lance popped up from the back and she spotted him, her smile froze on her face.

"Hello," she said while barely moving her smile, "I'm Summer."

"Hi, I'm Lance," my unwelcome crewmate said as he extended one hand for her bags and the other to help her aboard. I watched our newest passenger step on, her looks my way guarded, but worried.

Lance the Usurper had found the filler caps for the yacht's huge tanks. After a word with the attendant, he waited for the diesel hose to be dragged toward the boat. I cut both engines and watched with intense interest. Topping off the tanks would require at least three hundred gallons. With the attendant's tip, the bill would total about six hundred dollars. I had turned in Max's personal fuel charge card at the end of the last boating season. I wondered if Captain Lance had six hundred dollars on him. He didn't look like he did. I had about three thousand on me but wasn't about to admit to it until my position and salary became crystal clear.

As the tanks filled, Summer slunk by me, watching where she stepped much more cautiously than usual. When she got within five feet, I said, "I see you've met Captain Lance."

"Uh, yeah, I did, uh…is Max below?"

"Yes he is," I answered.

Summer went below. The fueling continued.

My curiosity hadn't been this aroused since my favorite buffet restaurant announced three new menu items. Yet Red didn't seem concerned. Other than a nervous peek or two in my direction, he seemed at ease with the attendant, chatting amiably. Max, for his part, could probably tell by the absence of engine vibrations that we were docked, yet was making no effort to come up to pay. Ten more minutes went by, and the nozzle clicked off. The attendant dragged the hose back and disappeared behind the pump. Two minutes later, he was back out.

"Six-twenty-five thirty three!" he sang out.

Captain Lance reached into his pant pocket and pulled out a charge card. A black charge card! It had the same gold embossment as last year's black charge card. Lance would have no trouble paying today. Max had given him the fuel card entrusted to his yacht's captain!

My vision began to tunnel until it felt like I was looking through a wrapping paper tube. My blood pressure climbed steadily. Every muscle in my upper body flexed and signaled my brain that they were ready for action in a cacophony of electrical impulses.

Snapping Lance's head off his neck like a Pez dispenser wasn't going to resolve anything, however. Quitting, as soon and as graciously as possible, would. I walked over to the salon's stairway and ducked as I stepped down. Max and Summer were standing in the galley in a partial embrace. As though they were stealing cliches from old movies, she was reaching over to a counter and feeding him grapes, one by one. In the dimmer light, I stared until first one and then the other noticed me. Their smiles and their arms dropped almost simultaneously. Max was the first to respond.

"Heeeeyy buddy, c'mon, c'mon dowwwn! What's happening?"

"Mr. Lexington, it looks like I'm kind of redundant around here today. With your permission I'd like to have Lance drop me back off at the well where my car's parked."

Sir Laurence Olivier himself would have applauded at the ensuing performance.

Max's jaw dropped. His eyes opened wide, and his massive head began to shake back and forth.

"Now Maaark! Whyyy would you *say* that?" He seemed dumbfounded! Summer just seemed guilty.

"I was born at night sir, but not *last* night. Captain Lance will do a fine job, I'm sure."

"Listen, my friend, the only reason he's here at all is because the family would never accept you as the Captain when they're using the boat. Lance has a captain's license and they'll be okay with him because they don't really know him or blame him for anything that's happened! When we're on board here it's just you buddy. You've still got the bat, the ball and the glove."

My vision began to tunnel again. Max began to look like Eddie Murphy, loudly proclaiming that it wasn't him! I didn't see what I think I saw! It wasn't him! One bald-faced lie after another flew out from Max's lips as I insisted over and over on quitting.

Finally, after ten minutes of wrangling, Max's bootprint on my back began to itch. Summer's eyes switched from Max to me and then back in guilty confusion. I stepped up top to get out of the stink. The sour taste in my mouth was so bad that I wondered if gargling with a little diesel fuel would be an improvement. Amid the lies and apologies below, Max had promised a higher hourly figure. I could be well paid to make Lance miserable today, or I could just step off onto the dock and walk back a mile by land. I had arranged my schedule at the studio, as usual, around Max. My staff would be paid whether I showed up or not. Captain Lance was back at the helm, had restarted the engines, and was writing once again in his little captain's log. He looked very comfortable. He looked too comfortable. I hopped up next to Max's new boy. I stared down at him like the head wolf deciding how he's going to kill a young rival. Red pretended not to notice me at first and then looked up. The wolf just continued staring.

"The engines sound good," I finally said. He began to squirm. "Time to go," I said, somewhat ambiguously.

Captain Lance sighed, put down his notebook, and moved out of the seat.

We were out on the open water in eight minutes. I throttled up slowly until the boat planed off. Captain Lance had run out of things to check and had resigned himself to sitting down and trying to enjoy the ride. I set our course for the usual destination, the River Crab restaurant. Feeling a tinge of remorse at my behavior toward my freckled little helper, I answered somewhat civilly when he tried to engage me in conversation. During the next forty minutes, I learned that he owned Dirt Be Gone, a boat cleaning service that worked the marinas in the area. Mildly surprised that my unwanted sidekick had some entrepreneurial instincts, I quizzed him a little further. He had filled in *once* for the first mate when Boomer had the eighty-two footer up at the Yacht Club. He'd had his captain's license for almost a year. His first actual command had been an old wooden paddleboat that he piloted down the nearby Clinton River with a small load of bored sightseers. He'd sailed in this area for several years in his own tiny sailboat and had crewed on larger ones.

Still cruising at an easygoing twenty miles an hour, we completed the first leg of our trip across Lake St. Clair. Oncoming boat traffic was practically nonexistent, and I neatly bisected the wide gap in the channel markers of the South Channel on either side of the yacht. My pudgy red chatterbox began to look concerned, first at me and then ahead. Eyes fixed on the expanse of channel ahead, I saw two boats in the distance. We had just passed an anchored fishing boat, but the sleepy men on board barely looked up as they bobbed in our wake. Our twenty-mile-an-hour pace was only half of what the boat was capable of. The speed seemed like the perfect mix of "don't scare the passengers, and Daddy are we there yet?"

Red had something to tell me…he was *antsy*. I'd only known my fearless crewmate for an hour and a half, but we'd developed a strong kinship during that time. That bond made it easy for me to read the little backstabber's body language, and that body language right now said "agitated." Twitching as if his bladder were about to burst, Captain Lance looked to and fro, pausing only to glance at the speed gauge. The spotted man had something to say but hesitated to say it, looking longingly at the hatchway where our revered boss had disappeared. He needed to say something. He had to get it off his chest but didn't want to tell *me*. He wanted to tell Max, but that wasn't possible right now without interrupting God knows what on Red's first day. He was going to *have* to tell me. I could see it welling up inside of him. *I may not want to*, he was thinking, *but dammit, lives are at stake here!*

"Hey, uh, Mark…the whole Middle Channel is a no wake zone."

He was right! No wonder he was so distraught…at twenty miles an hour the big Sea Ray was creating a huge wake. I knew there were three possible routes to our destination. The North Channel required a longer journey across a shallow part of the lake to where its markers began. There would be a lot of little fishing boats, both crowding the channel and in it on this fine day, presenting many potential collisions to hinder our progress. The North Channel was not without its own no wake zone either, a one-mile stretch past some gas docks. In this area, boats of all sizes were required to slow down to about three or four miles an hour. At that gentle speed, their wakes thus wouldn't swamp and rock small craft as they docked, fueled, and entered other narrow channels in the area.

The Middle Channel meandered past a number of waterfront residences. During times of high water, the wakes of boats over twenty-six feet were deemed erosive to the beaches, seawalls and marshes along the entire seven or so miles. The speed limit was strictly enforced by bored sheriffs in their white boats who were backed up by the occasional Coast Guard patrol. The Middle Channel was the perfect scenic route to explore and wander northward on during a hot day. It was not, however, a good choice if the boss was impatient to go eat or even to return home. Going twenty miles an hour in the Middle Channel in a sixty-foot boat was asking for trouble. Getting pulled over, safety inspected, ticketed and yelled at by a squad of self-important deputies would be embarrassing and time-consuming. This would be compounded by the incomplete paperwork aboard our new yacht and the bevy of new questions that this lacking would prompt. Red had a point. The Middle Channel was no place to be speeding in any boat over twenty-six feet!

I knew I had to address my co-pilot's concerns quickly, before his anxiety attack caused him to lose control of his bowels or worse. Even now, the two dots in the distance that we had observed upon entering our channel were looming larger, and they looked like patrol boats!

"You're absolutely right," I said. "The entire length of the Middle Channel is a no wake zone, but we're in the *South* Channel and the South Channel doesn't have a no wake zone. I think it would inhibit the *six-hundred-foot freighters* that use it every *twenty minutes*. They like to travel at about ten miles an hour, you know."

Lance the Lost looked at me as if I'd just drawn my sword and announced a mutiny. Frantically, he eyed the rapidly approaching sheriff's boats with such angst and trepidation that even I gave them a second glance. Even if they failed to spot our temporary registration and ordered us to heave to, I figured that my cohort and his new captain's license would actually come in handy as we explained. It would be interesting to see if we could resolve everything in a minute or two without disturbing our busy boss down below. I kept my speed at twenty and moved over fifteen feet to give the oncoming boats ample room to pass. One sheriff's crewmember looked over and gave us a lazy wave. I waved back as they passed but Captain Lance did not because *Lance* was nowhere to be found! I whipped my head around, checking our wake for his freckled carcass. Nothing! I looked back behind the seat, thinking that he might be playing "Crouching Tiger, Hidden Lance." Still no sign of the little scamp! Had my fearless navigator jumped ship? He would have hit the water hard at twenty and I hadn't *seen* him put on any water wings in the last sixty seconds. Surely one of the patrol boats would have spotted him if he flung himself off and sounded an alarm of some sort. I kept checking in back for anything bobbing in the water as the law enforcement boats began to shrink into toys.

Suddenly, out of the corner of my eye, a white baseball cap! It belonged to my mysterious first mate! He was peeking out of the hatchway at the retreating sheriff's boats. Not only had Lance been lost, he hadn't *believed* me when I re-oriented him to our actual location! He had gone below to either hide or rat me out to the boss. Unless the galley's microwave had grown into a 3000-pound diesel engine, there wasn't anything down there that needed checking and besides, he'd picked a *most* curious time to do it. Max and Summer were doubtlessly holed up in the aft cabin with the door shut (thank God), and would not have required anything other than dim lights and Andrea Bocelli.

There was only one conclusion. At the first hint of trouble my first mate had abandoned me. Captain Lance had stared adversity (at least it looked like adversity to him) in the eye, tucked his tail in and run! He had been a terrific choice, and would make a *fine* captain for Max this summer.

As we neared The River Crab Restaurant my growling stomach left me with only two choices. The first would be to order from the hostess and eat on board with Captain Courageous. I could ask him thought-provoking questions such as, "If you order the chicken for dinner, does that make you a cannibal?" I was concerned, however, that prolonged contact with Lance would make me nauseous, or worse, make me scared of the dark or of monsters that hide under my bed. Dinner inside with Max and Summer was almost equally distasteful, but Max looked guilty and sheepish. With a waitress assisting me, I could run up my tab to gargantuan proportions, challenging even *his* charge card's prodigious limit. I chose the latter and ate very well, reveling in the looks I received every time I ordered an expensive menu item. The yacht ride back—the last time I would ever pilot a boat with Maxwell Lexington aboard—was serenely uneventful.

53

Tʜᴇ ᴛʀɪᴘ ᴡᴀs not without its value, however, and neither were the last three years for that matter. From beginning to end, many questions that nagged at me had been answered. What was loyalty worth to this man? Had sobriety parted the clouds of distrust through which he viewed everyone that surrounded him? Could he now make promises and decisions and stick with them? The answers were: nothing, no and hell no! I looked forward to returning to my neglected little world with a renewed eagerness and resolve. Michelle and Natasha had kept the little business alive, waiting for the full-time return of the prodigal parent.

Would I ever venture out of my tiny but safe universe again? Would I ever feel the need to test the waters yet another time…to find out if I could let somebody else call the shots? For twenty-five years, every credit card application, every form, every agreement that I'd ever entered into had "self-employed" printed on the line labeled "employer." The last three years, however, had answered some personal questions as well. I *could* work for somebody else, if necessary. I *could* live by the rules of others. I *was* able to let someone else make all of the decisions. Just like any other employee, of course, I reserved the right to terminate the relationship if I felt as though the employer's decisions were unreasonable. Unlike some of those others, I had a world that I could retreat back into. It was a world that I could hide and take refuge in and yet affect the health and lives of hundreds of people for the better. I could come out again for a compelling enough reason, and even should this reason arise I could still elect to stay within. I could shape, reduce, sculpt and mold the residents of the Pointes from within the brick and glass safety of my little studio. Should any one person that entered my world upset it or make outlandish demands, I had many different ways of asking *them* to leave. With their distracting ways gone, I could then address the priorities of the other one hundred and ninety-nine people who had entered my domain.

For two glorious weeks, the sun seemed brighter...the air smelled fresher. I found myself going to bed earlier so that I could arise sooner the next morning to enjoy every moment of each hot July day.

In mid-July, Max called my cell, beseeching me to pick up Summer from the offices of a Grosse Pointe plastic surgeon. She was in the physician's recovery room...a couple of floors above a trendy little cafe called "Jumps." I didn't jump, but I agreed to do it not as an employee, but as a friend.

Summer had elected to have the puffy area above her eyes reduced, and had called Max while still groggy from the anesthetic. She had spoken of driving herself home after she felt as though any adverse effects had worn off, and Max was in a panic. I was there in a half hour, inspecting some beautiful stitchwork above Summer's eyelids, when Max phoned yet again.

"Yes, I'm at the doctor's office," I told him. *Unlike you, I keep my promises, you lying sack of excrement*, I thought. I spirited Summer almost directly home, stopping only to procure a complex mix of cappuccino at her favorite "shoppe."

I received a plethora of profuse thank yous from Max for my humanitarian transportation gesture. I did not receive any financial thank you's...nor did I bother to ask for any. I paid the trainer who covered for me that afternoon out of my own pocket and chalked it up as a favor to Summer and other drivers throughout Grosse Pointe. I had finally learned what other employees of Max's before me had known for quite some time; it was cheaper for even a billionaire to pay in thank yous rather than cash.

Not once during my tumultuous period of employment did I ever see Max and Summer play any type of games other than mind games. One *might* argue that I once witnessed Summer and the corporate titan play a game of "swallow the leader" in the back seat of the Mercedes. I would argue in return, however, that there didn't seem to be any rules. There was only one possible winner, and no true game should make the spectator (me) nauseous. By the same token, "monkey see, monkey do" wasn't a game per se. It was more of an adage. It was an adage that aptly fit that July, however. As the post surgical puffiness receded above Summer's eyes and she began to look even more beautiful than before, Max began consulting doctors. He began to get surgical opinions on a procedure that Summer had been urging him to get for months. She had sugarcoated its name with phrases like "enhancing his jawline" and "bringing out the strength of his neck," but the truth was that Max's face was falling. The facelift's primary goal would be to eliminate all of the loose skin and fat in Max's neck immediately below his jaw. The secondary goal would be to stretch out any wrinkles in the jowls and laser away years of sun damage from tennis, golf and yachting. Two weeks to the day after Summer's outpatient surgery, Max went in. It was a longer and much more involved procedure than Summer's and at one point, the surgeon and his assistant became very nervous. Max's blood pressure began to drop inexplicably; the trauma of the operation was taking its toll on the seventy-two-year-old patient's regulatory systems. It was touch and go for over an hour as the puzzled team tested for one possible cause of the drop after another, finally calling outside the O.R. (in a panic) for a solution. The solution worked, and Max's blood pressure stabilized enough to complete the surgery. In the end, only one extra day of hospitalization was required, and forty-eight hours post-op, a heavily bandaged billionaire was driven home.

For two days, Max wandered the halls of his mansion, looking exactly like a seventy-two year old man with a very recent facelift. After forty-eight hours at home together, Elizabeth bid Max good-bye as *she* left for the hospital this time. Extensive foot surgery for the diminutive grandmother had been planned months ago, and she had no intention of prolonging the pain-relieving operation to play nursemaid to her misbehaving mate. Max would be on his own (at least until the last of the help had left at six o'clock).

On the third day, an urge began to well up inside of the mansion's recuperating resident. The post-surgical pain was under control. Even the swelling was kept in check by appropriately prescribed pills from a concerned doctor who *also* visited twice daily to check on his famous patient.

Max's desire to see Summer, however, could not be controlled by medication.

At six-fifteen my cell phone rang. "Hi sweetie, how are you?" It was Summer's voice; unmistakable and cheery.

"Fine, I think. Are you done healing yet?"

"I still have a little bit of a black eye on the right side, but the doctor said I can wear make-up again and now you can't tell I had anything done! He said all of the swelling would be gone in four more weeks. He said they're healing perfectly. I am sooo glad now that I had this done! So, baby, where are you anyway?"

"I'm working," I answered cautiously.

"Working?"

"Yes, work. It's where you perform a service for someone and with any luck, they pay you for it." My answer might have been a little caustic.

She ignored it. "Yes, but are you at the gym or what?"

"Yes," I replied in a toned-down fashion. "I just finished with two clients, and I've got more coming in."

"Honey, I wouldn't ask you this if there were *any* other way, but Max's been calling me for the last two hours and *begging* me to come and see him. His doctors don't want him leaving the house yet and they *certainly* don't want him to drive! He says that all of the staff is gone by six and that Elizabeth won't be back until tomorrow. This could be our only chance to see each other and I'm *dying* to see my baby after his surgery! Will you *please, please*

take me over there? I'll duck down when we go in the gates in
case the daughters have got a watch going on!"

"I can't. I've got more clients coming in at seven."

"Okay, okay, so just *drive* me then. Drop me off, and then go
back. I'll *walk* back to your gym if I have to…or you can pick me
up after nine when you're finished. I've never been inside his house
and I may never get a chance to see the inside again. This is not
my idea you know. I mean, even with everybody gone I'll still feel
creepy being there. But he keeps calling my cell again and again
and saying that if I do this he will never, ever forget it! I'm two
minutes away but I can't just go there in my car. We could go in
yours and that wouldn't raise as many flags if somebody's watching
him. I know him and once he gets an idea in his head he won't
stop until it happens."

I heard a beep in my earpiece as somebody tried to dial in. A
brief glance showed a familiar number. It originated at the very
mansion that we were talking about.

"Summer," I sighed, "It's guess who on the other line."

"Okay, take it sweetie, I'll be there in two minutes!"

"Hello?"

"Maaark! How's it going buddy? Listen, I need to ask you a
very important question, and I would truly, *truly* appreciate it if
you could help in any way!"

"I've already heard from her, Mr. Lexington."

"Oh, you haaaave? Why that's excellent, it really is. Do you
think it might be possible then for you to get away for awhile? I'm
not sure where she's at right now. I would be so *very* grateful if
you could find her."

"She's pulling into my parking lot right now."

"Reeeaaally? Oh, that's fantaaastic! Well, Mark, I want you to
know how much I really, truly appreciate this!"

"You're welcome (another sigh), see you soon."

I shut my phone. *What an incredibly bad idea*! I thought. I
wondered how many of his children actually had a key to that
house? I was ready to bet that Bertha did. I tried to imagine what

her raspy smoker's voice sounded like when she brought it up to a full yell. The echo alone in the marble and frescoed hallways would probably be enough to raise the dead. In my head, I heard Bertha bellowing Summer's and my name as she ascended a spiral stone stairway—sounding like the very hounds of hell unleashed. What if they decided to make the final confrontation a family affair with each descendant and heir pulling up outside, blocking my car in where it hid? I knew that hustling Summer out to the street as I phoned for a trainer to pick us up would be my only option, or could I just leave alone until the ashes had settled to the inlaid tile floor? Also on my mind were the odds of one of the incensed daughters carrying pepper spray in her purse, and how best to avoid her when it was produced.

Summer, in spite of her lapse in workout activity, was still not a large woman by any measure. Regardless of her lack of size, there still wasn't much room to hide in my Corvette as we approached the gates. My pretty passenger slunk down in her seat as far as possible, her long legs nearly doubled up underneath the dash.

From all outward appearances, the mansion was unoccupied. No one toiled in the flowerbeds. Nobody pruned at the property's one hundred trees or squeegeed the huge windows that dotted the front. Draperies were partially or fully closed, the front fountain was off, and even the koy hovered motionless in their rock-ringed pool. I parked on the side and waited for a garage door to come up. As the middle one began its dignified ascent, Summer and I dashed from my car and were nearly in the garage before it arrived at the top. Its descent began almost immediately as Max pushed the button again from the house's dimly-lit garage-side entranceway.

After not much more than an arm-squeeze and an air kiss, Max began Summer's tour of the mansion. Each room was provided only a cursory sentence or two of explanation as our shiny-skinned, red-faced host eagerly led us through each room on the lower level. I could have given a far superior rendition of each area's highlights and features, but I didn't speak. During most of this brief guided tour of the lower level, I was unable to get a good clear look at the outcome of Max's recent hospital stay. It wasn't until we arrived in the exercise room and Max started dialing up the extra lighting enhancements that I received the full effect. The sagging, wrinkled, hanging skin under his chin in the front of his neck was gone. Although some fatty tissue and swelling still remained, I had seen forty-year-old men with saggier looking necks than Max. The skin on Max's entire face, however, was stretched so tight that I found it remarkable that he could move his jaw to talk. I watched in fascination every time he blinked, expecting to see his taut forehead split open in a line across the middle as his eyelids used the last remaining slack. The man in front of me somewhat resembled my former boss, but could not easily have been picked out if he wore a hat and stood in a lineup. Summer's shock was evident too as she carefully chose her words and tried to look without staring.

Our tour continued in the back "yard." It began with the outdoor swimming pool and the rock-faced waterfall that fed it. It quickly progressed to a rear-garden oasis replete with a footbridge over a pond. The footbridge ended at an enclosed gazebo large enough to double as most people's vacation home. Summer's paranoia at being in the open grew visibly, and she seemed relieved when we reentered the house through the back. We climbed the marble-stepped middle staircase to the ground level of the house and an impossibly long hallway that remained well lit from the setting sun in spite of partially lowered blinds. As I trailed behind Max and Summer, I glanced out of a front window when a flurry of motion on the driveway caught my eye. I stared and gave the object my full attention. It was a gray Jeep Grand Cherokee! It looked exactly like the one that Robert drove, and it was leaving rapidly! My impression that we were alone on the property was dashed as I squinted to try to catch the plate number. Although the house manager's apartment had formerly been above the detached garage, he had vacated it months ago to co-habit with his "friend" Jamie. Robert was normally off work by five o'clock and gone by five-o-five. My cell phone said seven o'clock. I caught up with Max and

Summer in an upstairs living room as the phone in his den began to ring. Before I could announce my sighting, Max traipsed past me and down the hallway. I whispered about my observation to Summer and her sutured eyelids opened wide and disappeared under her dark plucked eyebrows.

"Are you sure?" she asked. I nodded.

She followed me to the den where I had sat to either wait or give counsel so many times. Near the winding wooded staircase stood an easel with a glass-framed essay purportedly done by one of Max's grandchildren. The essay was from a class assignment by the eleven-year old girl's sixth grade teacher. In it, she wrote of her grandpa being the greatest man she had ever met. While the first paragraph merely talked about his humble beginnings and how hard he worked, the second began outlining his successes. Each ensuing paragraph spouted on about the famous people he'd met, the enormous amounts of money he gave away and the hundreds of people who looked up to him. It ended with a few sentences about how all twenty grandchildren loved him and their grandmother very much and spoke of the girl's awe of their fifty years of marriage. The girl's mention of her grandfather's prominence in the community was superceded only by the complete essay's prominent place in the den. The tearjerker had been framed and spirited over by one of Max's daughters, the girl's mother, and presented by the author herself. The rays of guilt that projected out from it stabbed at Max every time he entered the room. For reasons unclear, he had allowed it to stay out on display.

Summer began to read the essay, but we were both soon distracted by the steadily increasing volume of Max's phone conversation.

"Missy, I'm fiiiiine. There's no need to check on me. No, listen, no, I'm telling you, Robert left me with everything I need."

And Mark brought the rest, I thought.

"No, there's no neeeed for that, no, how…how's your mother? Have you checked on her? Yeah…uh-huh…well, is she awake now or still out of it?"

Another phone line rang—all three of us looked over at it in surprise.

"Just...just a minute Missy." Max pressed a hold button and punched the blinking one. "Hello?...Sharon? No, honey, I'm fine...I don't need you here...I just need to rest...really...no...that won't be necessary...because I'm *telling* you, that's why!"

I smiled and, backing out of the den, gave Summer a little wave as Max switched back and forth between the concerned daughters. Yet a third phone line began to ring. Max had been ratted out, quite possibly by a man in a gray Jeep. Max tried to hold me in the den by sticking a forefinger in the air. I wiggled my fingers in another little wave, smiled, and kept backing out. We were back in the hallway and Summer peered out a front window like a sniper.

"Sweetie, what should I do?"

"You can come with me if you like, but I'm leaving now."

"You *can't* go now. They think I'm *here*."

"You *are* here. Give everyone my love."

"Please, you *have* to stay."

"I have to get back to work. In three minutes I'll be fifteen minutes late. Call me at nine-o-five. I'll come back and get you."

"Okay, okay sweetie, but what should I do if he can't keep them away?"

"If they start coming in through the front gate, you'll have about a minute to walk to the gazebo. Go inside it, lock the door if it locks, and don't look out. Call my cell, and I'll be over in two minutes. Keep your phone on vibrate! Turn off the ringer. When I'm about to hit the driveway next door, I'll call you. Walk through the neighbor's yard to the driveway. Even if someone next door spots you we might be gone before the police get here...even if we're not, I know the lady and we might be okay without taking the whole night to explain. Bub-bye!"

I let myself out through a side door with Max still defending the fortress against a series of probing phone jabs from one daughter after another. Summer lingered on until well after dark, watching her septarian host field each incoming call so that he could rebuff every inquisitive or insistent relative before they breached the castle walls.

By the time I picked up Summer at ten, Max was wobbling on his feet from exhaustion and barely able to say good-bye to her. I was sure that someone watched from somewhere as the despised guest and her humble driver left the front gates, but no confrontation occurred.

The drive to work the following day was very serene as I relished the thought of having no dysfunctional families to deal with on that fine, hot day. No enraged heiresses in their Escalades or BMWs lurked in my lot to run me down, and I practically skipped into the building. A new client was ten minutes early and awaited my arrival. A welcoming blast of cool, dry air enveloped me as I entered my sanctuary. Grinning broadly, I extended my hand as I sat down and said, "Hi, Mark Steel. What kind of exercise have you done in the last year or two? Biking? Swimming? Walking?…"

54

THE MAN'S CELL phone rang. With more than a little pride at having gotten used to this new one so quickly, the man flicked it open and pressed "talk" before the second ring.

"Hello?"

"I didn't wanna bother ya this early, but I'm gettin' a lot of heat from da boss. They're both outta control and it don't look so good. She was at his house lass night when da wife was laid up in da hospital. Her divorce is almost final. We gotta do somethin' but we need your okay."

The man sighed heavily and rolled his eyes upward. If both of these bits of news were true, he was left with no choice but to act, and apparently little time to do so.

"All right then," he answered softly. "Call me back next week with a list of options. And try to be a little more creative this time. Try to come up with an idea that doesn't involve a gun. But under *no* circumstances does *any* scenario involve *him* or putting *him* in any kind of danger. And I want you to make sure that that guy that used to drive for him isn't anywhere around her. He could cause problems. Make sure she's alone."

"I'll send Ronnie to that lot across the street from his place to see if he's there."

"I said not to use names when we talk on the phone. Is that understood?"

"Yeah, I got it. I'll call ya."

The man clicked his phone off and sighed even more heavily than before. All he could do now was hope that any action did not create more problems than it resolved. He had waited too long already, though, and to wait any longer would be highly inadvisable.

Coming in Fall 2004

The captivating saga continues with…

GROSSE POINTE INFERNO

BOOK ORDER FORM

GROSSE POINTE PIMP

Name:_____

Address:_____

City: _____ State:_____ Zip:_____

Phone: (   )_____ Fax: (   )_____

E-mail:_____

Mail to Name:_____

Address:_____

City: _____ State: _____Zip:_____

U.S. Funds only

Book Price: $17.95

Shipping and Handling: $2.95

	Quantity	Cost/Book	Total
GROSSE POINTE PIMP		$17.95	
Shipping			
6% MI Tax			
Total			

Mail this form with check or money order to:

RIVETING PUBLISHING

23707 Jefferson

St. Clair Shores, MI 48080

(Make payable to: Riveting Publishing)

www.MarkSteelBooks.com